William R. King, Jr.

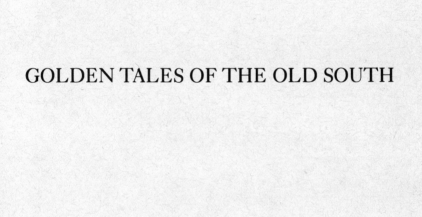

# GOLDEN TALES OF THE OLD SOUTH

# GOLDEN TALES OF
# THE OLD SOUTH

*Selected*

*With an Introduction*

*By*

MAY LAMBERTON BECKER

BONANZA BOOKS

NEW YORK

THE MILITIA COMPANY DRILL by Oliver Hillhouse Prince. From *Georgia Scenes, Characters, Incidents, etc., in the first Half Century of the Republic. By a Native Georgian*, 1835

TAKING THE CENSUS by Johnson Jones Hooper. From *Some Adventures of Captain Simon Suggs, Late of the Tallapoosa Volunteers*, 1845

"POSSON JONE'" by George W. Cable. From *Old Creole Days*, 1879. First published in *Appleton's Journal*, 1878 [This selection is used by permission of the publishers, Charles Scribner's Sons, New York.]

THE LEGEND OF L'ÎLE DERNIÈRE by Lafcadio Hearn. From *Chita*, 1889. [Copyrighted by Harper and Brothers. This selection is reprinted by permission of the publishers.]

A FAMILY FLIGHT IN THE FORTIES. THE LAST CHRISTMAS by Eliza Ripley. From *Social Life in Old New Orleans*, 1912. [This selection is used by permission of the publishers, D. Appleton and Company, New York.]

THE BALLOON HOAX by Edgar Allan Poe. First printed in the *New York Sun*, April 13, 1844

ON REVIEW by John Esten Cooke. From *Surry of Eagle's-Nest, or, the Memoirs of a Staff-Officer Serving in Virginia*, 1866

BILL ARP ADDRESSES ARTEMUS WARD by Charles Henry Smith (Bill Arp). From *Bill Arp—so-called*, 1873

A TRUE SOUTHERN LADY by Francis Hopkinson Smith. From *Colonel Carter of Cartersville*, 1902. [This selection is used by permission of, and by arrangement with, Houghton Mifflin Company, the authorized publishers.]

THE FATE OF MR. JACK SPARROW by Joel Chandler Harris. From *Uncle Remus, His Songs and Sayings*, 1880. [This selection is used by permission of the publishers, D. Appleton and Company, New York.]

ELECTIONEERIN' ON BIG INJUN MOUNTING by Mary Noailles Murfree (Charles Egbert Craddock). From *In the Tennessee Mountains*, 1884. [This selection is used by permission of, and by arrangement with, Houghton Mifflin Company, the authorized publishers.]

A CHRISTMAS GUEST by Ruth McEnery Stuart. From *Sonny*, 1897. [This selection is used by permission of the publishers, The Century Company, New York City.]

THE MOMENT OF VICTORY by William Sidney Porter (O. Henry). From *Options*, 1909. [This selection is used by permission of the publishers, Doubleday, Doran and Company, Inc., New York.]

THE LITTLE FADED FLAG by Edward Lucas White. From *The Atlantic Monthly*, 1908. [This selection is used by permission of the author and *The Atlantic Monthly*.]

THE BELLED BUZZARD by Irvin S. Cobb. From *The Escape of Mr. Trimm*, 1913. [This selection is used by permission of the author and the publishers, Doubleday, Doran and Company, Inc., New York.]

THE CREATION by James Weldon Johnson. From *God's Trombones*, 1927. [This selection is used by permission of the publishers, the Viking Press, New York.]

A MEAN JOKE by Don Marquis. From *A Variety of People*, 1928. [This selection is used by permission of the publishers, Doubleday, Doran and Company, Inc., New York.]

BUTTIN' BLOOD by Pernet Patterson. From *The Atlantic Monthly*, 1929. Reprinted in *Prize Stories of 1929, O. Henry Award*, 1929. [This selection is used by permission of the author, *The Atlantic Monthly*, and Doubleday, Doran and Company, Inc., New York.]

CROWDED by Maristan Chapman. From *The Atlantic Monthly*, 1928. [This selection is used by permission of the author and *The Atlantic Monthly*.]

THE HAZY HOUSEHOLD by Alice Hegan Rice. From *Lovey Mary*, 1902. [This selection is used by permission of the author and the publishers, The Century Company.]

This 1985 edition is published by Bonanza Books, distributed by Crown Publishers, Inc., by arrangement with Dodd, Mead & Company, Inc.
Manufactured in the United States of America
Library of Congress Cataloging in Publication Data
Main entry under title:
Golden tales of the Old South.
1. American literature—Southern States. 2. Short stories, American—Southern States. 3. Southern States—Literary collections. 4. Southern States—Fiction.
I. Becker, May Lamberton, 1873-1958.
PS551.G6    1985    813'.01'083275    84-23048
ISBN: 0-517-467925

h g f e d c b a

# ACKNOWLEDGMENT

The gratitude of the editor is due to the authors
  Alice Hegan Rice, Don Marquis, Pernet Patterson, Edward
  Lucas White, Irvin S. Cobb, James Weldon Johnson,
  Maristan Chapman, and to Elise Ripley Noyes, daughter of
  Eliza Ripley
and to the publishers
  D. Appleton and Company, New York; Century Company,
  New York; Harper and Brothers, New York; Charles
  Scribner's Sons, New York; Doubleday, Doran and Com-
  pany, New York; Houghton Mifflin Company, Boston; The
  Viking Press, New York, and to *The Atlantic Monthly,*
not only for permission to reprint (as set down in the table of
  contents) but for the advice and assistance in selection so
  kindly given,
and, as always in the work of the editor, to the staff of
  The New York Public Library, especially at the Forty-
  second Street Reading Room, and to the staff of the Reading
  Room of the British Museum,
who lightened the hours of research.

                              MAY LAMBERTON BECKER

# CONTENTS

# CONTENTS

# INTRODUCING THE STORIES

The favor accorded the first volume of GOLDEN TALES OF OUR AMERICA, and the belief of the editor and some of its readers that such a collection had its uses, not only as entertainment for the present but as documentation of the past, made a second volume a matter of course. The purpose in gathering these Golden Tales—a purpose lightly held but never forgotten—has been to present to Americans of today some aspects of life in an America that has ceased to be, and to do so not through historical narratives, but by those distillations of experience that make fiction and out of which literature may be made. Judge Longstreet, in the preface to his famous "Georgia Scenes," called them "nothing more than fanciful combinations of real incidents and characters." The stories here gathered are nothing less.

Each of those who wrote them had and used some unusual opportunity for getting the facts and the spirit, and the stories have been chosen quite as much for the spirit as for the facts. History may tell us what happened, but fiction can remind us what we thought about it or how we felt about it, and in the complex and delicate adventure of living, what we think and how we feel is as much a part of the facts of life as what we do.

It was quite as much a matter of course that the first section of the country to be thus separately represented should be the Old South. Life was lived richly there and then, and under conditions peculiar to the time and place. At first and for a long time they were conditions by no means favorable to the production of fiction. Life on these manorial estates, as Thomas Nelson Page has reminded us in "The Old South," was in the fields, or at least for a good part in the open air: an early interest in tobacco-growing, horse-racing, fox-hunting, gave a special turn to life in an agricultural state with a widely scattered people, lacking the interplay of opinions made possible by large cities. Add to this a social conservatism that considered a gentleman's business rather to appreciate literature than to produce it, and an increasingly uneasy preoccupation with problems of slavery—which blockaded so much of Southern thought by making so many subjects undebatable—and it will be seen how much worked against the writing of fiction before the Civil War. But with all this, the present anthology is not concerned; its program calls not so much for men of letters as for those "historians of the heart" who James Lane Allen declared were needed to set down the true story of the South.

There have been not a few of these in Southern literature, and sometimes their hearts have been more to their credit than their eyesight. The astute critic, George M. Bagby, of Virginia, complained that the eyes of his friend John Esten Cooke were in the back of his head and furthermore fitted with rose-colored goggles of enormous magnifying power. "The old times may have been mighty good," said he, "but there are some first-rate days and prime doings left." This was before the War; yet when, some years after it, Dr. Bagby himself wrote "The Old Virginia Gentleman"—surely the most beautiful of essays on the life of the old plantation—the very landscape is rosy with affection and a transfiguring light lies golden in the air. For in the interval everything had changed. An epoch had ended. "Not for a moment," said he, "could any Virginian say that there was nothing amiss in the old order. . . . But our Mother is dead, and much may be pardoned in a eulogy which would be inexcusable were the subject living."

This is the quality that distinguishes so much of the retrospective fiction of the Old South. These days were not only dead; they had met a violent death. Yesterday lingers in many

a remote corner of our country, but not the yesterdays on the
old plantation. They went down forever under the mortal
blow of the War. They have become a story forever.

Even to the North before the War, the Old South was a
country of romance. In "John Brown's Body," young Jack
Ellyat muses under a crisp Connecticut moon upon "that
languorous land . . ."

> The girls were always beautiful. The men
> Wore varnished boots, raced horses and played cards
> And drank mint-juleps till the time came round
> For fighting duels with their second-cousins . . .

> . . . The south . . . the honeysuckle . . . the hot sun . . .
> The taste of ripe persimmons and sugar-cane,
> The cloyed and waxy sweetness of magnolias,
> White cotton, blowing like a fallen cloud,
> And foxhounds belling the Virginia hills.

Oratory flourished in the older South, polemics and debate,
and poetry; fiction came later. It set off soon into rough
humor about rough times, reporting spiced with farce. Georgia
provided much of it, but a Virginian, Judge Baldwin, used his
experiences as a lawyer farther South in the vastly popular
"Flush Times in Alabama and Mississippi," published in the
*Southern Literary Messenger* and then in book form before he
moved on to California and the supreme court. Out of the
hurly-burly of the times he drew the character of Ovid Bolus,
"a natural liar, just as some horses are natural pacers, and some
dogs natural setters. What he did in that walk was from the
irresistible promptings of instinct and a disinterested love of
art." Ovid Bolus, it has been agreed, could no more be left
out of the literary history of the South than Falstaff out of the
biography of Prince Hal. Some of these picaresque heroes were

pure sharpers, like Hooper's Simon Suggs—as well known in his own time and place as Sam Weller in England, but of whom it could never be said that the history of his conduct was blameless with the single exception of one amiable indiscretion. Simon Suggs was a blithe and shameless blackleg whose motto was "It is good to be shifty in a new country," and through this country he made his rollicking, plundering way. Sometimes these heroes were countrymen come to judgment on the town, like Dr. Bagby's "Moziz Addums," who reported in letters from Washington on pitfalls in and around the Patent Office. Once at least, in C. H. Smith's "Bill Arp, so-called," an honest sharp-witted cracker spoke out the thoughts of a stunned and suffering people. For years these and other rude humorists held the balance of Southern fiction against rose-colored or blindfold sentimentality; they were good reporters and their tempers were good. The life that comes back from their forgotten pages is full of juice and zest. Some of their pages are not yet forgotten, and those of one at least of their descendants—for Joel Chandler Harris is in the line of Georgia humorists—are unforgettable.

A certain difference marks the stories of this collection: difference not only one from another but from anything written in its time at the North. It was a difference arising not only from outer conditions but from a frame of mind felt perhaps most strongly in Virginia and expressed by Judge Baldwin in "Flush Times":—

The Virginian is a magnanimous man. He never throws up to a Yankee the fact of his birthplace. He feels on the subject as a man of delicacy feels in alluding to a rope in the presence of a person, one of whose brothers "stood upon nothing and kicked at the United States . . ." So far do they carry this refinement, that I have known one of my countrymen, on occasion of a Bostonian owning where he was born, generously protest that he had never heard of it before.

It was in Virginia, early in the seventies, that fiction began over again in the South, in what was to amount to a renaissance; in the eighties and nineties it was in full flower. Already before the War the *Southern Literary Messenger* had sought for "the man who can paint with pen and ink the real life around him, this Southern life rich with every element of humor and pathos." By the eighties they had come, those long-awaited historians of the heart, and they are still coming, to the enrichment of our national literature. From the writings of some of them these stories have been chosen. If some noted names do not appear, it may be, for instance, because Mary Johnston could not be properly represented without a whole novel like "The Long Roll," or because Ellen Glasgow's "They Stooped to Folly" exists as a work of art quite indivisible, or because James Branch Cabell preferred Poictesme to Richmond as a place of literary residence. Enough remained, however, to make the task of final selection far more difficult than that of gathering.

For the Civil War and reconstruction periods this task was simplified by keeping to fiction as nearly a record of personal experience as fiction can be proved to be. Thomas Nelson Page's "Marse Chan" is generally admitted to be the best short story of the Civil War, but for this collection the first-hand emotions and devotions of "Surry of Eagle's Nest" seemed more appropriate, with its romantic figure of a soldier-hero taking shape out of a generous hero-worship, and with its sense, thrilling even in this brief chapter, of having reached the page while the image was still clear in the eye, the sound in the ear, the dream unsullied in the heart. As for the Reconstruction period, I believe no one has spoken more truthfully or more temperately about his own part in it than "Bill Arp, so-called."

There are still regions south of Mason and Dixon's line where pockets of yesterday may be found, and men and women of the South still write of them with fidelity and understanding.

Yesterday will soon be gone there, before railroad, telegraph and telephone, before the wireless, the mountain school, the mail-order house and the movies. But before it goes it will have left its record in our literature. The mountaineers have had a long line of interpreters from Charles Egbert Craddock to Maristan Chapman, and farther South some of the lingering fragrance of old France has been caught for us before it could fade.

All this is part, not only of the South, but of our America. If much of it is part of "the golden dream of an America that has not been," it is also, in the deeper sense in which dreams make us what we are, part of the spirit of the America that is to be.

MAY LAMBERTON BECKER

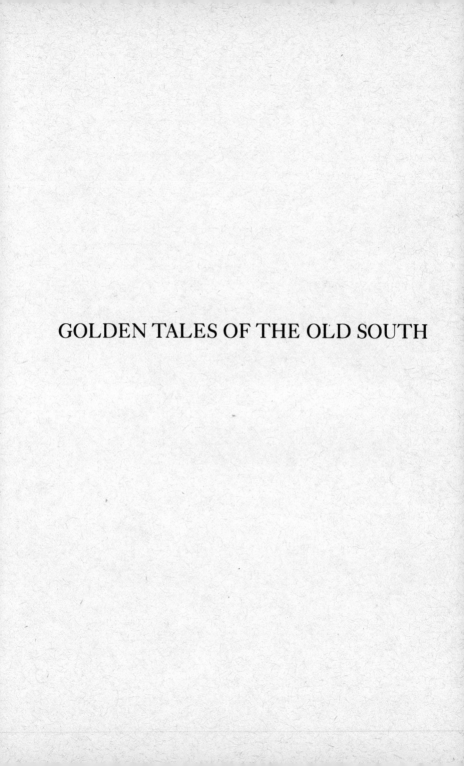

# GOLDEN TALES OF THE OLD SOUTH

# OLIVER HILLHOUSE PRINCE
## (1787–1837)

Augustus Baldwin Longstreet seems never to have thought much of "Georgia Scenes." When he was getting on in years he did his best to have it withdrawn from circulation, as beneath the dignity of a judge, a clergyman and a college professor—this being his triple glory in later life. Even when it first appeared, when he was young and comparatively frisky, he did not sign it. The title page of the first edition, printed in 1835 at the press of the *Sentinel*, Augusta, Georgia, to which the sketches had been contributed, set it down as "By a Native Georgian," and it was not until Harper brought out an edition in 1846 that the title page bore his name. Yet it is by this rich rough book that his name has been kept alive. Near a hundred years have not faded its fun.

One of these sketches, "The Turn Out," appeared in the first volume of "Golden Tales," and though it was not to be thought of that an anthology of the old South could be published without one, we may avoid duplication of names by choosing for this collection the only story in the volume to which report assigns another author. "One of the most humorous papers in 'Georgia Scenes,'" says Professor Trent, "is said to have been written by a friend of Judge Baldwin, Oliver Hillhouse Prince, who represented Georgia for a short time in the United States Senate." This story is the one about the militia company drill.

Whoever wrote it—and Thomas Hardy long after wrote something so much like it in "The Trumpet Major" that he must have found it to his taste—it is the work of a keen observer and a born writer, someone who can suffer fools gladly and chuckle over chuckleheadedness, someone economical with words, gifted in dialogue, and with a deft trick of pausing to let pictures take shape between the lines. From what the commanding officer is saying—and not saying—one gets a disconsertingly clear idea of what the company must be doing. This company, taking its own time and making its own shape; the officer with his helpful suggestion that the best way to avoid mistakes is to do it right the first time; the extraordinary range and nature of arms and equipment; the relation of officer and men, and the attitude of both to this military business that must be done with as soon as may be, all come back as fresh as on the day the shrewd observer set them down. We shall see something of this spirit lingering in O. Henry's story of a later military company and another state, "The Moment of Victory." It is a spirit that may not make things easier for a drillmaster in time of peace, but it does tend to lose as little time as possible in polishing off a war.

Fortunately for us, Judge Longstreet was never able to restrain "Georgia Scenes": year after year the book kept in print, and certain tales keep renewing their life in school books and collections even now. There is no striking central character like Sut Lovengood, Ovid Bolus or Major Jones; it is the scene that counts, crowded with living creatures of the time.

# THE MILITIA COMPANY DRILL

*By* "Oliver Hillhouse Prince" (Augustus Baldwin Longstreet)

I happened, not long since, to be present at the muster of a captain's company in a remote part of one of the counties; and as no general description could convey an accurate idea of the achievements of that day, I must be permitted to go a little into detail, as well as my recollection will serve me.

The men had been notified to meet at nine o'clock, "armed and equipped as the law directs"; that is to say, with a gun and cartridge box at least, but, as directed by the law of the United States, "with a good firelock, a sufficient bayonet and belt, and a pouch with a box to contain no less than twenty-four sufficient cartridges of powder and ball."

At twelve, about one third, perhaps one half, of the men had collected, and an inspector's return of the number present, and of their arms, would have stood nearly thus: 1 captain, 1 lieutenant; ensign, none; fifers, none; privates, present, 24; ditto, absent, 40; guns, 14; gunlocks, 12; ramrods, 10; rifle pouches, 3; bayonets, none; belts, none; spare flints, none; cartridges, none; horsewhips, walking canes, and umbrellas, 10. A little before one, the captain, whom I shall distinguish by the name

3

of Clodpole, gave directions for forming the line of parade. In obedience to this order, one of the sergeants, whose lungs had long supplied the place of a drum and fife, placed himself in front of the house, and began to bawl with great vehemence, "All Captain Clodpole's company parade here! Come, gentlemen, parade here!" says he; "all you that hasn't got guns fall into the lower *eend*." He might have bawled till this time, with as little success as the sirens sang to Ulysses, had he not changed his post to a neighboring shade. There he was immediately joined by all who were then at leisure; the others were at that time engaged as parties or spectators at a game of fives, and could not just then attend. However, in less than half an hour the game was finished and the captain enabled to form his company, and proceed to the duties of the day.

*"Look to the right and dress!"*

They were soon, by the help of the non-commissioned officers, placed in a straight line; but, as every man was anxious to see how the rest stood, those on the wings pressed forward for that purpose, till the whole line assumed nearly the form of a crescent.

"Why, look at 'em," says the captain; "why, gentlemen, you are all a-crooking in at both *eends*, so that you will get on to me by-and-by! Come, gentlemen, *dress, dress!*"

This was accordingly done, but, impelled by the same motives, as before, they soon resumed their former figure, and so they were permitted to remain.

"Now, gentlemen," says the captain, "I am going to carry you through the *revolutions* of the manual exercises; and I want you, gentlemen, if you please, to pay particular attention to the word of command, just exactly as I give it out to you. I hope you will have a little patience, gentlemen, if you please; and if I should be agoing wrong, I will be much obliged to any of you, gentlemen, to put me right again, for I mean all for the best, and I hope you will excuse me, if you please. And one thing, gentlemen, I caution you against, in particular, and that is this: not to make any *mistakes* if you can possibly help it; and the best way to do this will be to do all the motions right at first; and that will help us to get along so much the faster; and I will try to have it over as soon as possible. Come, boys, come to a shoulder.

"*Poise, foolk!* [1]

"*Cock, foolk!* Very handsomely done.

"*Take, aim!*

"*Ram down, catridge!* No! no! *Fire!* I recollect now that firing comes next after taking aim, according to Steuben; but, with your permission, gentlemen, I'll read the words of command just exactly as they are printed in the book, and then I shall be sure to be right."

"Oh, yes! read it, captain, read it!" exclaimed twenty voices at once; "that will save time."

"*'Tention the whole!* Please to observe, gentlemen, that at the word '*fire,*' you must fire; that is, if any of your guns are *loaden'd*, you must not shoot in *yearnest*,

---

[1] A contraction, and corruption, of "firelock." Thus "firelock," "f'lock," "foolk."—Author's note.

but only make pretence like; and you, gentlemen fellow-soldiers who's armed with nothing but sticks, riding-switches and corn-stalks, needn't go through the firings, but stand as you are, and keep yourselves to yourselves.

"*Half cock, foolk!* Very well done.

"*S-h-e-t* (spelling) *Shet, pan!* That too would have been handsomely done, if you hadn't handled catridge instead of shetting pan; but I suppose you wasn't notic-ing. Now, 'tention one and all, gentlemen, and do that motion again.

"*Shet, pan!* Very good, very well indeed; you did that motion equal to any old soldier; you improve aston-ishingly.

"*Handle, catridge!* Pretty well, considering you done it wrong end foremost, as if you took the catridge out of your mouth and bit off the twist with the catridge-box.

"*Draw, rammer!* Those who *have* no rammers to their guns need not draw, but only make the motion; it will do just as well, and save a great deal of time.

"*Return, rammer!* Very well again. But that would have been done, I think, with greater expertness if you had performed the motion with a little more dexterity.

"*S-h-o-u-l-Shoulder, foolk!* Very handsomely done indeed! Put your guns on the other shoulder, gentle-men.

"*Order, foolk!* Not quite so well, gentlemen; not quite altogether; but perhaps I did not speak loud enough for you to hear me all at once. Try once more, if you please. I hope you will be patient, gentlemen; we will soon be through.

"*Order, foolk!* Handsomely done, gentlemen! Very handsomely done! and all together too, except that one half of you were a *leetle* too soon, and the other half a *leetle* too late.

"In laying down your guns, gentlemen, take care to lay the locks up and the other side down.

" *'Tention the whole! Ground, foolk!* Very well.

"*Charge, bayonet!*"

(*Some of the men*)—"That can't be, captain: pray look again; for how can we charge bayonet without our guns?"

(*Captain*)—"I don't know as to that, but I know I'm right, for here 'tis printed in the book; c-h-a-r—yes, *charge, bayonet,* that's right, that's the word, if I know how to read. Come, gentlemen, do pray charge bayonet! Charge, I say! Why don't you charge! Do you think it aint so? Do you think I have lived to this time o' day, and don't know what charge bayonet is? Here, come here, you may see for yourselves; it's as plain as the nose on your fa—stop—stay—no—halt! no! Faith, I'm wrong! I turned over two leaves at once. I beg your pardon, we will not stay out long; and we'll have something to drink as soon as we have done. Come, boys, get off the stumps and logs, and take up your guns; we'll soon be done: excuse me if you please.

"*Fix, bayonet!*

"*Advance, arms!* Very well done: turn the stocks of your guns in front, gentlemen, and that will bring the barrels behind; hold them straight up and down, if you please; let go with your left, and take hold with your right hand below the guard. Steuben says the gun should be held p-e-r—*pertic'lar;* yes, you must always mind and hold your guns very pertic'lar. Now, boys, 'tention the whole!

"*Present, arms!* Very handsomely done! only hold your gun over t'other knee—t'other hand up—turn your hands round a little, and raise them up higher— draw t'other foot back—now you are nearly right—very well done.

"Gentlemen, we come now to the *revolutions.* Men, you have all got into a sort of snarl, as I may say; how did you all get into such a higglety pigglety?"

The fact was, the shade had moved considerably to the eastward, and had exposed the right wing of these hardy veterans to a galling fire of the sun. Being poorly provided with umbrellas at this end of the line, they found it convenient to follow the shade; and in huddling to the left for this purpose, they changed the figure of their line from that of a crescent to one which more nearly resembled a pair of pothooks.

"Come, gentlemen," says the captain, "spread yourselves out again into a straight line; and let us get into the wheelings and other matters as soon as possible."

But this was strenuously opposed by the soldiers. They objected to going into the *revolutions* at all, inasmuch as the weather was extremely hot, and they had already been kept in the field upward of three quarters of an hour. They reminded the captain of his repeated promise to be as short as he possibly could, and it was clear he could dispense with all this wheeling and flourishing if he chose. They were already very thirsty, and if he would not dismiss them, they declared they would go off without dismission, and get something to drink, and he might fine them if that would do him any good; they were able to pay their fine, but would not go without drink to please anybody; and they swore they would never vote for another captain who wished to be so unreasonably strict.

The captain behaved with great spirit upon the occasion, and a smart colloquy ensued; when at length becoming exasperated to the last degree, he roundly asserted that no soldier ought ever to *think hard* of the orders of his officer; and, finally, he went so far as to say, that he did not think any gentleman on that ground had any just cause to be offended with him. The dispute was finally settled by the captain sending for some grog for their present accommodation, and agreeing to omit reading the military law, and the performance of all the manœuvres, except two or three such easy and simple ones as could be performed within the compass of the shade. After they had drank their grog and had spread "themselves," they were divided into platoons.

"*'Tention the whole! To the right wheel!*"

Each man faced to the right about.

"Why, gentlemen, I did not mean for every man to stand still and turn himself *na*'trally right round; but when I told you to wheel to the right, I intended you to wheel round to the right, as it were. Please to try again, gentlemen; every right-hand man must stand fast, and only the others turn round."

In the previous part of the exercise, it had, for the purpose of sizing, been necessary to denominate every second person a "right-hand man." A very natural consequence was, that, on the present occasion, these right-hand men maintained their position, all the intermediate ones facing about as before.

"Why, look at 'em, now!" exclaimed the captain, in extreme vexation; "I'll be d—d if you understand a word I say. Excuse me, gentlemen, it *rayly* seems as if you could not come at it exactly. In wheeling to the right, the right-hand *eend* of the platoon stands fast, and the other *eend* comes round like a swingle-tree. Those on the outside must march faster than those on the inside. You certainly must understand me now, gentlemen; and please to try it once more."

In this they were a little more successful.

"*'Tention the whole! To the left—left, no—right —that is, the left—I mean the right—left wheel, march!*"

In this he was strictly obeyed; some wheeling to the

right, some to the left, and some to the right-left, or both ways.

"*Stop! halt!* Let us try it again! I could not just then tell my right hand from my left! You must excuse me, if you please; experience makes perfect, as the saying is. Long as I have served, I find something new to learn every day; but all's one for that. Now, gentlemen, do that motion once more."

By the help of a non-commissioned officer in front of each platoon, they wheeled this time with considerable regularity.

"Now, boys, you must try to wheel by divisions; and there is one thing in particular which I have to request of you, gentlemen, and that is, not to make any blunder in your wheeling. You must mind and keep at a wheeling distance, and not talk in the ranks, nor get out of fix again; for I want you to do this motion well, and not to make any blunder now.

" *'Tention the whole! By divisions, to the right wheel, march!*"

In doing this it seemed as if Bedlam had broke loose: every man took the command. Not so fast on the right! Slow now! Haul down those umbrellas! Faster on the left! Keep back a little there! Don't *scrouge* so! Hold up your gun, Sam! Go faster there! faster! Who trod on my—? D—n your huffs! Keep back! Stop us, captain, do stop us! Go faster there! I've lost my shoe! Get up again, Ned! Halt! halt! halt! Stop, gentlemen! stop! stop!

By this time they had got into utter and inextricable confusion, and so I left them.

> From *Georgia Scenes, Characters, Incidents, etc., in the first half century of the Republic.* By a native Georgian, (Augusta, Ga.; printed at the S. R. Sentinel Office, 1835).

# JOHNSON JONES HOOPER
## (1815–1863)

The retreat of the red man before advancing civilization has always been attended by incidents not altogether to civilization's credit. Where the Indian lands of Alabama were being thrown open to speculators, young Johnson Jones Hooper, a native of North Carolina, was first a lawyer, then a newspaper man in Lafayette, Alabama, looking at life with just the sort of light-hearted interest likely to get together material for impartial social history. If his feelings carried him away, it was in the direction of pure farce, and he clearly felt no call to lash the follies of his time. He must have met many an amusing rogue, either in court or as a news-gatherer, to have collected all the sharp practice in "Simon Suggs' Adventures and Travels," but Simon is no mere synthetic scamp; from the time he heatily leaves Georgia in the night—beating his father in a deal, and filling his mother's pipe with gunpowder as parting attentions—through his exploits in the Creek War as captain of the "Tallypoosy Volluntares" (otherwise know as the Forty Thieves) he is flamboyantly alive, living up to a philosophy that he puts into the simple sentence "it is good to be shifty in a new country." No wonder Thackeray enjoyed him; he is a sort of backwoods cousin of Barry Lyndon. His "Adventures and Travels," appearing first

13

in Hooper's paper, *The East Alabamian*, were in the form of a bogus political biography recommending Simon for the office of sheriff; with this was later bound up "Taking the Census," evidently the result of personal experience however heightened in the telling. The natural disposition of the countryside not to make things easier for the tax-gatherer of whom the census-man was popularly supposed to be a sort of advance-guard—the nature and extent of the information citizens were supposed to furnish the government, and the low opinion they had of this government as personified by Van Buren, are so many twinkling side-lights on the time. The practical joker of the period may have long since ceased to complicate the business of census-taking, but even in 1930 it was still sometimes enlivened by types who talked too little or too much and told nothing either way.

Hooper edited several newspapers, and with one of them, *The Montgomery Mail*, reached national reputation. He lived to see the War begin, and at his death was Secretary to the Senate of the Southern Confederacy.

# TAKING THE CENSUS

## By Johnson Jones Hooper

THE collection of statistical information concerning the resources and industry of the country, by the assistant marshals who were employed to take the last census, was a very difficult work. The popular impression, that a tremendous tax would follow the minute investigation of the private affairs of the people, caused the census-taker to be viewed in no better light than that of a tax-gatherer; and the consequence was, that the information sought by him was either withheld entirely, or given with great reluctance. . . . Bitter were the taunts, threats, and abuse which they received on all hands, but most particularly from the old women of the country. The dear old souls could not bear to be catechised about the product of their looms, poultry yards, and dairies; and when they did "come down" upon the unfortunate inquisitor, it was with a force and volubility that were sure to leave an impression. We speak from experience, and feelingly, on this subject; for it so happened, that the Marshal of the Southern District of Alabama, "reposing especial confidence" in our ability, invested us one day with all the powers of assistant Marshal; and arming us with the proper number of blanks, sent us forth to count the noses of all the men, women, children, and chickens resident upon those nine hundred square miles of rough country which constitute the county of Tallapoosa. Glorious sport, thought we; but it didn't turn out so. True, we escaped without any drubbings, although we came unpleasantly near catching a dozen . . . but then we were quizzed, laughed at, abused and nearly drowned. Children shouted "Yonder goes the chicken man!" Men said, "Yes, d—n him, he'll be after the *taxes* soon";—and the old women threatened, if he came to inquire about *their* chickens, "to set the dogs on him," while the young women observed "they didn't know what a man wanted to be so pertic'lar about gals' ages for, without he was agwine a-courtin'." . . .

We rode up one day to the residence of a widow rather past the prime of life—just that period at which nature supplies most abundantly the oil which lubricates the hinges of the female tongue—and hitching to the fence, walked into the house.

"Good morning, madam," said we, in our usual bland, and somewhat insinuating manner.

"Mornin'," said the widow gruffly.

Drawing our blanks from the case, we proceeded—"I am the man, madam, that takes the census, and—"

"The mischief you are!" said the old termagant. "Yes, I've hearn of you; Parson W. told me you was coming, and I told him jist what I tell you, that if you said 'cloth,' 'soap,' *ur* 'chickens' to *me*, I'd set the dogs on ye.—Here, Bull! here, Pomp!" Two wolfish curs responded to the call for Bull and Pomp, by coming to the door, smelling our feet with a slight growl, and then laid down on the steps. "Now," continued the old savage, "them's the severest dogs in the country. Last week Bill Stonecker's two-year-old steer jumped my yard fence, and Bull and Pomp tuk him by the throat, and they killed him afore my boys could break 'em loose, to save the world."

"Yes, ma'am," said we, meekly. "Bull and Pomp seem to be very fine dogs."

"You may well say that; what I tell them to do they do—and if I was to sick them on your old horse yonder, they'd eat him up afore you could say Jack Roberson. And it's jist what I shall do, if you try to pry into my consarns. They are none of your business, nor Mr. Van Buren's nuther, I reckon. Oh, old Van Buren! I wish I had you here, you old rascal. I'd show you what—I'd —I'd make Bull and Pomp show you how to be sendin' out men to take down what little stuff people's got, jist to tax it, when it's taxed enough a'ready!"

All this time we were perspiring through fear of the fierce guardians of the old widow's portal. At length, when the widow paused, we remarked that as she was determined not to answer questions about the produce of the farm, we would just set down the age, sex and complexion of each member of the family.

"No sich a thing—you'll do no sich a thing," said she; "I've got five in the family, and that's all you'll git from me. Old Van Buren must have a heap to do, the dratted old villyan, to send you to take down how old my children is. I've got five in family, and they are all between five and a hundred years old; they are all a plaguey sight whiter than you are, and whether they are *he* or *she*, is none of your consarns."

We told her we would report her to the Marshal, and she would be fined; but it only augmented her wrath.

"Yes! send your marshal, or your Mr. Van Buren here, if you're bad off to—let 'em come—let Mr. Van Buren come—" looking as savage as a Bengal tigress— "Oh, I wish he *would* come"—and her nostrils dilated, and her eyes gleamed—"I'd cut his head off!"

"That might kill him," we ventured to remark, by way of a joke.

"Kill him! kill him—oh—if I had him here by the *years* I reckon I *would* kill him. A pretty fellow to be eating his vittils out'n gold spoons that poor people's taxed for, and raisin' an army to get him made king of Ameriky—the oudacious, nasty, stinking old scamp!" She paused a moment, and then resumed, "And now, mister, just put down what I tell you on that paper, and don't be telling no lies to send to Washington City. Jest put down 'Judy Tompkins, ageable woman, and four children."

We objected to making any such entry, but the old hag vowed it should be done, to prevent any misrepresentation of her case. We, however, were pretty resolute, until she appealed to the couchant whelps, Bull and Pomp. At the first glimpse of their teeth, our courage gave way and we made the entry in a bold hand across a blank schedule—"Judy Tompkins, *ageable* woman and four children." . . .

Our next adventure was decidedly a dangerous one. Fording the Tallapoosa river, where its bed is extremely uneven, being formed of masses of rock full of fissures, and covered with slimy green moss, when about two thirds of the way across, we were hailed by Sol Todd from the bank we were approaching. We stopped to hear him more distinctly.

"Hellow! little squire, you a-chicken hunting today?"

Being answered affirmatively, he continued— "You better mind the holes in them ere rocks—if your horses's foot gits ketched in 'em you'll never git it out. You see that big black rock down to your right? Well, there's good bottom down below that. Strike down thar, outside that little riffle—and now cut right into that smooth water and come across!"

We followed Sol's directions to the letter, and plunging into the *smooth water*, we found it to be a basin surrounded with steep ledges of rock, and deep enough to swim the horse we rode. Round and round the poor old black toiled without finding any place where he could effect a landing, so precipitous were the sides. Sol occasionally asked us "if the bottom wasn't first rate," but did nothing to help us. At length we scrambled out, wet and chilled to the bone—for it was a sharp, September morning—and continued our journey, not a little annoyed by the boisterous, roaring laughter of the said Solomon, at our picturesque appearance.

We hadn't more than got out of hearing of Sol's cachinatory explosions, before we met one of his neighbors, who gave us to understand that the ducking we had just received, was but the fulfilment of a threat of Sol's, to make the "chicken-man" take a swim in the "Buck Hole." He had heard of our stopping on the opposite side of the river the night previous, and learning our intention to ford just where we did, fixed himself on the back to insure our finding the way into the "Buck Hole."

This information brought our nap right up, and requesting Bill Splawn to stay where he was till we returned, we galloped back to Sol's, and found that worthy, rod on shoulder, ready to leave on a fishing excursion.

"Sol, old fellow," said we, "that was a most unfortunate *lunge* I made into that hole in the river—I've lost twenty-five dollars in specie out of my coat pocket, and I'm certain it's in that hole, for I felt my pocket *get light* while I was scuffling about in there. The money was tied up tight in a buckskin pouch, and I must get you to help me get it."

This, of course, was a regular old-fashioned lie, as we had not seen the amount of cash mentioned as lost, in a "coon's age." It took, however, pretty well; and Sol concluded, as it was a pretty cold spell of weather for the season, and the water was almost like ice, that half the contents of the buckskin pouch would be just about fair for recovering it. After some chaffering, we agreed that Sol should dive for the money "on shares," and we

went down with him to the river, to point out the pre-
cise spot at which our pocket "grew light." We did so
with anxious exactness, and Sol soon denuded himself
and went under the water in the "Buck Hole" "like a
shuffler duck with his wing broke." Puff! puff! as he
rose to the surface. "Got it Sol?" "No dang it, here goes
again," and Sol disappeared a second time. Puff! puff!
and a considerable rattle of teeth as Sol once more rose
into "upper air." "What luck, old horse?" "By jings,
I felt it that time, but somehow it slid out of my fingers?" Down went Sol again, and up he came after the
lapse of a minute, still without the pouch. "Are you *right
sure* squire, that you lost it in this hole," said Sol, getting
out upon a large rock, while the chattering of his teeth
divided his words into rather more than their legitimate
number of syllables. "Oh perfectly certain Sol, perfectly certain. You know twenty-five dollars in hard
money weighs a pound or two. I didn't mention the circumstance when I first came out of the river, because I
was so scared and confused that I didn't remember
it. . . ."

Thus reassured, Sol took the water again, and, as we
were in a hurry, we requested him to bring the pouch
and half the money to Dadeville, if his diving should
prove successful. . . .

Our next encounter was with an old lady notorious in
her neighborhood for her garrulity and simple-minded-
ness. . . . She was interested in quite a large chancery
suit which had been "dragging its slow length along" for

several years, and furnished her with a conversational fund which she drew upon extensively. . . .

Striding into the house, and drawing our papers—

"Taking the census, ma'am!" quoth we.

"Ah! well! yes! bless your *soul*, honey, take a seat. Now do! Are you the gentleman that Mr. Van Buren has sent out to take the *sensis?* I wonder! well, good Lord look down, how *was* Mr. Van Buren and *family* when you seed him?"

We explained that we had never seen the president; didn't "know him from a side of sole leather"; and we had been written to, to take the census.

"Well, now, thar agin! Love your soul! Well, I s'pose Mr. Van Buren *writ* you a letter, did he? No? Well, I suppose some of his officers done it—bless my soul? Well, God be praised, there's mighty little *here* to take down—times is hard, God's will be done; but looks like people can't git their jest rights in this country; and the law is all for the rich and none for the poor, praise the Lord. Did you ever hear tell of that case my boys has got agin old Simpson? Looks like they never will git to the eend on it; glory to His name. . . . Did you ever see Judge B—? Yes? Well, the Lord preserve us! Did you ever hear him say what he was agwine to do in the boys' case agin Simpson? No! Good Lord! Well, squire, *will* you ax him the next time you see him, and write me word; and tell him what I say; I'm nothing but a poor widow, and my boys has got no larnin', and old Simpson tuk 'em in. . . ."

Here we interposed and told the old lady that our time was precious—that we wished to take down the number of her family, and the produce raised by her last year, and be off. After a good deal of trouble we got through with the descriptions of the members of her family, and the "statistical table" as far as the article "cloth."

"How many yards of cotton cloth did you weave in 1840, ma'am?"

"Well, now! The Lord have mercy!—less see! You know Sally Higgins used to live down in the Smith settlement? She was a powerful good hand to weave, and I *did* think she'd help me a power. . . . Well, arter she'd been here awhile, her baby hit took sick, and old Miss Stringer she undertuk to help it—she's a powerful good hand, old Miss Stringer, on roots, and yearbs, and sich like! . . . She made a sort of tea, as I was a-sayin', and she gin it to Sally's baby, but it got wuss—the poor creeter—and she gin it tea, and gin it tea, and looked like, the more she gin it tea, the more—"

"My dear madam, I am in a hurry—please tell me how many yards of cotton cloth you wove in 1840. I want to get through with you and go on."

"Well, well, the Lord-a-mercy! who'd a thought you'd 'a bin so snappish! Well, as I was a-sayin', Sal's child hit kept a gittin' wuss, and old Miss Stringer, she kept on a givin' it the yearb tea twell at last the child hit looked like hit *would* die anyhow. And 'bout the time the child was at its wust, old Daddy Sykes he come along, and he said if we'd get some night-shed berries, and stew 'em with a little cream and some hog's lard—now old Daddy Sykes is a might fine old man, and he gin the boys a heap of mighty good counsel about that case— boys, says he, I'll tell what you do; you go—"

"In God's name, old lady," said we, "tell about your cloth, and let the sick child and Miss Stringer, Daddy Sykes, the boys, and the law suit go to the devil. I'm in a hurry!"

"Gracious bless your dear soul! don't get aggrawated. I was jist a tellin' you how it come I didn't weave no cloth last year."

> From *Adventures of Captain Simon Suggs, late of the Tallapoosa Volunteers, together with "Taking the Census" and other Alabama Sketches* by the author of *Widow Rugby's Husband* (Philadelphia, 1858. Originally in book form 1845).

# GEORGE WASHINGTON CABLE
## (1844–1924)

"It would give me much pleasure," wrote George W. Cable to Fred Lewis Pattee, "to tell you just how I came to drop into the writing of romances, but I cannot. I just dropt. Money, fame, didactic or controversial impulse, I scarcely felt a throb of. I just wanted to do it because it seemed such a pity for the stuff to go so to waste."

It is easier to say why it was about New Orleans that these romances were written. He was born there, nineteen years before the War, in which he served in the Fourth Mississippi Cavalry; he played all about the old city, there he grew up, and there, earlier than most boys, he began conscientiously to work for a living. He worked for the most part as clerk in a cotton-factor's office; now and again he sent sketches to the *Picayune* or did a little reporting. "I was moved at last," said he, "to write some short sketches of old New Orleans. But I did not at the time seek a publisher; I laid them aside. In my reading I came to the old Black Code. In sheer indignation I wrote a story which years afterward became the foundation for the episode of *Bras Coupé* in 'The Grandissimes.'" The spark was kindled; he wrote on, story after story, from four o'clock in the morning until time for the counting house to open. In summer hours, when the counting house was idle, he went to the city archives and read hundreds of old newspapers. Here, he says, he found his inspiration for 'Tite Poulette, and here conceived the story of Posson Jone'.

It is seldom that a story without a date can be so accurately dated. Writing in 1878 to Scribner and Armstrong, Cable sends a list of his stories with the dates, which he says are "exactly correct," on which they take place; from "Jean-ah Poquelin" (1805) to "'Sieur George" (1850). On this list "Posson Jone'" is dated 1815. Those days lasted a long time in the old French city. When Joseph Pennell visited Cable he tells us, in "Adventures of an Illustrator," how

> We walked over to Canal street and turned down the Rue Royale, and right into old France. America stopped in the middle of Canal street. . . . The signs on one side were English, and on the other French, and newsboys yelled *The Picayune* on the left and *L'Abeille* on the right. As soon as we got into the Rue Royale, we stepped right into Cable's stories. . . .

These stories were to reach the North through the medium of Edward King, who visited New Orleans in search of material for a series of sketches, "The Great South," and took them away with him for magazine publication. Six of them appeared at intervals in *Scribner's Magazine;* "Posson Jone'," however, went the rounds till *Appleton's Journal* published it on April 1, 1876. When these stories were gathered into a book, if Cable had had his way it would have been called "Jadis . . ." the opening word of the French story-teller's magic phrase for "once upon a time." "Jadis reignait un prince . . ."—the sound brings back the fairy-tale. No doubt a certain doubtfulness about Northern fluency in French caused "Old Creole Days" to be used instead. The stories had been taken quietly as they came out one by one, but when the book brought them together, in 1879, it made one of those sensations in the North that were so often in the next few years to be made by first books by writers from the South. He had arrived, and for the rest of his life he was before the public.

He was deeply religious, of the Puritan type that, believing, cannot be moved; he believed in social betterment, and took his Christianity simply and seriously. After 1886 he lived in Massachusetts, and there, in 1924, he died. But the atmosphere of his fiction is the "tepid, orange-scented air" of the country of Madame Delphine and the debonair protector of Posson Jone'.

# "POSSON JONE'"

## By George Washington Cable

To Jules St.-Ange—elegant little heathen—there yet
remained at manhood a remembrance of having been
to school, and of having been taught by a stony-headed
Capuchin that the world is round—for example, like a
cheese. This round world is a cheese to be eaten through,
and Jules had nibbled quite into his cheese-world already
at twenty-two.

He realized this as he idled about one Sunday morning where the intersection of Royal and Conti Streets
some seventy years ago formed a central corner of New
Orleans. Yes, yes, the trouble was he had been waste-
ful and honest. He discussed the matter with that faithful friend and confidant, Baptiste, his yellow body-
servant. They concluded that, papa's patience and *tante's*
pin-money having been gnawed away quite to the rind,
there were left open only these few easily enumerated
resorts: to go to work—they shuddered; to join Major
Innerarity's filibustering expedition; or else—why not?
—to try some games of confidence. At twenty-two one
must begin to be something. Nothing else tempted; could
that avail? One could but try. It is noble to try; and, besides, they were hungry. If one could "make the friendship" of some person from the country, for instance,

with money, not expert at cards or dice, but, as one would say, willing to learn, one might find cause to say some "Hail Marys."

The sun broke through a clearing sky, and Baptiste pronounced it good for luck. There had been a hurricane in the night. The weed-grown tile-roofs were still dripping, and from lofty brick and low adobe walls a rising steam responded to the summer sunlight. Up-street, and across the Rue du Canal, one could get glimpses of the gardens in Faubourg Ste.-Marie standing in silent wretchedness, so many tearful Lucretias, tattered victims of the storm. Short remnants of the wind now and then came down the narrow street in erratic puffs heavily laden with odors of broken boughs and torn flowers, skimmed the little pools of rain-water in the deep ruts of the unpaved street, and suddenly went away to nothing, like a juggler's butterflies or a young man's money.

It was very picturesque, the Rue Royale. The rich and poor met together. The locksmith's swinging key creaked next door to the bank; across the way, crouching, and mendicant-like, in the shadow of a great importing-house, was the mud laboratory of the mender of broken combs. Light balconies overhung the rows of showy shops and stores open for trade this Sunday morning, and pretty Latin faces of the higher class glanced over their savagely-pronged railings upon the passers below. At some windows hung lace curtains, flannel duds at some, and at others only the scraping and sighing one-hinged shutter groaning toward Paris after its neglectful master.

M. St.-Ange stood looking up and down the street for nearly an hour. But few ladies, only the inveterate mass-goers, were out. About the entrance of the frequent *cafés* the masculine gentility stood leaning on canes, with which one and now another beckoned to Jules, some even adding pantomimic hints of the social cup.

M. St.-Ange remarked to his servant without turning his head that somehow he felt sure he should soon return those *bons* that the mulatto had lent him.

"What will you do with them?"

"Me!" said Baptiste, quickly; "I will go and see the bull-fight in the Place Congo."

"There is to be a bull-fight? But where is M. Caye-tano?"

"Ah, got all his affairs wet in the tornado. Instead of his circus, they are to have a bull-fight—not an ordi-nary bull-fight with sick horses, but a buffalo-and-tiger fight. I would not miss it."

Two or three persons ran to the opposite corner, and commenced striking at something with their canes. Oth-ers followed. Can M. St.-Ange and servant, who hasten forward—can the Creoles, Cubans, Spaniards, San Do-mingo refugees, and other loungers—can they hope it is a fight? They hurry forward. Is a man in a fit? The crowd pours in from the side-streets. Have they killed a so-long snake? Bare-headed shopmen leave their wives, who stand upon chairs. Those on the outside make little leaps into the air, trying to be tall.

"What is the matter?"

"Have they caught a real live rat?"

"Who is hurt?" asks some one in English.

"*Personne,*" replies a shopkeeper; "a man's hat blow' in the gutter; but he has it now. Jules pick' it. See, that is the man, head and shoulders on top the res'."

"He in the homespun?" asks a second shopkeeper. "Humph! an *Américain*—West-Floridian; bah!"

"But wait; 'st! he is speaking; listen!"

"To whom is he speak—?"

"Sh-sh-sh! to Jules."

"Jules who?"

"Silence, you! To Jules St.-Ange, what howe me a bill since long time. Sh-sh-sh!"

Then the voice was heard.

Its owner was a man of giant stature, with a slight stoop in his shoulders, as if he was making a constant, good-natured attempt to accommodate himself to ordinary doors and ceilings. His bones were those of an ox. His face was marked more by weather than age, and his narrow brow was bald and smooth. He had instantaneously formed an opinion of Jules St.-Ange, and the multitude of words, most of them lingual curiosities, with which he was rasping the wide-open ears of his listeners, signified, in short, that, as sure as his name was Parson Jones, the little Creole was a "plum gentleman."

M. St.-Ange bowed and smiled, and was about to call attention, by both gesture and speech, to a singular object on top of the still uncovered head, when the nervous motion of the *Américain* anticipated him, as, throwing up an immense hand, he drew down a large roll of bank-notes. The crowd laughed, the West-Floridian joining, and began to disperse.

"Why, that money belongs to Smyrny Church," said the giant.

"You are very dengerous to make your money expose like that, Misty Posson Jone', " said St.-Ange, counting it with his eyes.

The countryman gave a start and smile of surprise.

"How d'dyou know my name was Jones?" he asked; but, without pausing for the Creole's answer, furnished in his reckless way some further specimens of West-Floridian English; and the conciseness with which he presented full intelligence of his home, family, calling, lodging-house, and present and future plans, might have passed for consummate art, had it not been the most run-wild nature ."And I've done been to Mobile, you know, on bus*iness* for Bethesdy Church. It's the on'yest time I ever been from home; now you wouldn't of believed that, would you? But I admire to have saw you, that's so. You've got to come and eat with me. Me and my boy ain't been fed yit. What might one call yo' name? Jools? Come on, Jools. Come on, Colossus. That's my niggah— his name's Colossus of Rhodes. Is that yo' yallah boy, Jools? Fetch him along, Colossus. It seems like a special provid*ence*.—Jools, do you believe in a special provid*ence*?"

Jules said he did.

The new-made friends moved briskly off, followed by Baptiste and a short, square, old negro, very black and grotesque, who had introduced himself to the mulatto, with many glittering and cavernous smiles, as d'body-sarvant of d'Rev'n' Mr. Jones."

Both pairs enlivened their walk with conversation. Parson Jones descanted upon the doctrine he had mentioned, as illustrated in the perplexities of cotton-growing, and concluded that there would always be "a ·pecial provid*ence* again' cotton untell folks quits a-pressin' of it and haulin' of it on Sundays!"

"*Je dis*," said St.-Ange, in response, "I thing you is juz right. I believe, me, strong-strong in the improvidence, yes. You know my papa he hown a sugah-plantation, you know. 'Jules, me son,' he say one time to me, 'I goin' to make one baril sugah to fedge the moze high price in New Orleans.' Well, he take his bez baril sugah —I nevah see a so careful man like me papa always to make a so beautiful sugah *et sirop*. 'Jules, go at Father Pierre an' get this lill pitcher fill with holy-water, an' tell him sen' his tin bucket, and I will make it fill with *quitte*.' I ged the holy-water; me papa sprinkle it over the baril, an' make one cross on the 'ead of the baril."

"Why, Jools," said Parson Jones, "that didn't do no good."

"Din do no good? Id broughtd the so great value! You can strike me dead if thad baril sugah din fedge the more high cost than any other in the city. *Parce que*, the man what buy that baril sugah he make a mistake of one hundred pound"—falling back— "*Mais* certainlee!"

"And you think that was growin' out of the holy-water?" asked the parson.

"*Mais*, what could make it else? Id could not be the *quitte*, because my papa keep the bucket, an' forget to sen' the *quitte* to Father Pierre."

Parson Jones was disappointed.

"Well, now, Jools, you know, I don't think that was right. I reckon you must be a plum Catholic."

M. St.-Ange shrugged. He would not deny his faith.

"I am a *Catholique, mais*"—brightening as he hoped to recommend himself anew—"not a good one."

"Well, you know," said Jones—"where's Colossus? Oh! all right. Colossus strayed off a minute in Mobile, and I plum lost him for two days. Here's the place; come in. Colossus and this boy can go in the kitchen.—Now, Colossus, what *air* you a-beckonin' at me faw?"

He let his servant draw him aside and address him in a whisper.

"Oh, go 'way!" said the parson with a jerk. "Who's goin' to throw me? What? Speak louder. Why, Colossus, you shayn't talk so, saw. 'Pon my soul, you're the mightiest fool I ever taken up with. Jest you go down that alley-way with this yalla boy, and don't show yo' face untell yo' called!"

The negro begged; the master wrathily insisted.

"Colossus, will you do ez I tell you, or shell I hev to strike you, saw?"

"O Mahs Jimmy, I—I's gwine; but"—he ventured nearer—"don't on no account drink nothin', Mahs Jimmy."

Such was the negro's earnestness that he put one foot in the gutter, and fell heavily against his master. The parson threw him off angrily.

"Thar, now! Why, Colossus, you most of been dosted with sumthin'; yo' plum crazy.—Humph, come on, Jools, let's eat. Humph! to tell me that when I never taken a drop, exceptin' for chills, in my life—which he knows so as well as me!"

The two masters began to ascend a stair.

"*Mais*, he is a sassy; I would sell him, me," said the young Creole.

"No, I wouldn't do that," replied the parson; "though there is people in Bethesdy who says he is a rascal. He's a powerful smart fool. Why, that boy's got money, Jools; more money than religion, I reckon. I'm shore he fallen into mighty bad company"—they passed beyond earshot.

Baptiste and Colossus, instead of going to the tavern kitchen, passed to the next door and entered the dark rear corner of a low grocery, where, the law notwithstanding, liquor was covertly sold to slaves. There, in the quiet company of Baptiste and the grocer, the colloquial powers of Colossus, which were simply prodigious, began very soon to show themselves.

"For whilst," said he, "Mahs Jimmy has eddication, you know—whilst he has eddication, I has 'scretion. He has eddication and I has 'scretion, an' so we gits along."

He drew a black bottle down the counter, and, laying half his length upon the damp board, continued:

"As a p'inciple I discredits de imbimin' of awjus liquors. De imbimin' of awjus liquors, de wiolution of the Sabbaf, de playin' of de fiddle, and de usin' of by-words, dey is de fo' sins of de conscience; an' if any man sin de fo' sins of de conscience, de debble done sharp his fork fo' dat man.—Ain't that so, boss?"

The grocer was sure it was so.

"Neberdeless, mind you"—here the orator brimmed his glass from the bottle and swallowed the contents with a dry eye—"mind you, a roytious man, sech as ministers of de gospel and dere body-sarvants, can take a *leetle* for de weak stomach."

But the fascinations of Colossus's eloquence must not mislead us; this is the story of a true Christian; to wit, Parson Jones.

The parson and his new friend ate. But the coffee M. St.-Ange declared he could not touch; it was too wretchedly bad. At the French Market, near by, there was some noble coffee. This, however, would have to be bought, and Parson Jones had scruples.

"You see, Jools, every man has his conscience to guide him, which it does so in"—

"Oh, yes!" cried St.-Ange, "conscien'; thad is the bez, Posson Jone'. Certainlee! I am a *Catholique*, you is a *schismatique*; you thing it is wrong to dring some coffee—well, then, it *is* wrong; you thing it is wrong to make the sugah to ged the so large price—well, then it *is* wrong; I thing it is right—well, then, it *is* right; it is all 'abit; *c'est tout.* What a man thing is right, *is right;* 'tis all 'abit. A man muz nod go again' his conscien'. My faith! do you thing I would go again' my conscien'? *Mais allons,* led us go and ged some coffee."

"Jools."

"W'at?"

"Jools, it ain't the drinkin' of coffee, but the buyin' of it on a Sabbath. You must really excuse me, Jools, it's again' conscience, you know."

"Ah!" said St.-Ange, *"c'est* very true. For you it would be a sin, *mais* for me it is only 'abit. Rilligion is a very strange; I know a man one time, he thing it was wrong to go to cock-fight Sunday evening. I thing it is all 'abit. *Mais,* come, Posson Jone'; I have got one friend, Miguel; led us go at his house and ged some coffee. Come; Miguel have no familie; only him and Joe—always like to see friend; *allons,* led us come yonder."

"Why, Jools, my dear friend, you know," said the shamefaced parson, "I never visit on Sundays."

"Never w'at?" asked the astounded Creole.

"No," said Jones, smiling awkwardly.

"Never visite?"

"Exceptin' sometimes amongst church-members," said Parson Jones.

*"Mais,"* said the seductive St.-Ange, "Miguel and Joe is church-member'—certainlee! They love to talk about

rilligion. Come at Miguel and talk about some rilligion. I am nearly expire for me coffee."

Parson Jones took his hat from beneath his chair and rose up.

"Jools," said the weak giant, "I ought to be in church right now."

"*Mais*, the church is right yonder at Miguel', yes. Ah!" continued St.-Ange, as they descended the stairs, "I thing every man muz have the rilligion he like' the bez—me, I like the *Catholique* rilligion the bez—for me it *is* the bez. Every man will sure go to heaven if he like his rilligion the bez."

"Jools," said the West-Floridian, laying his great hand tenderly upon the Creole's shoulder, as they stepped out upon the *banquette*, "do you think you have any shore hopes of heaven?"

"Yass!" replied St.-Ange; "I am sure-sure. I thing everybody will go to heaven. I thing you will go, *et* I thing Miguel will go, *et* Joe—everybody, I thing— *mais*, hof course, not if they not have been christen'. Even I thing some niggers will go."

"Jools," said the parson, stopping in his walk—"Jools, I *don't* want to lose my niggah."

"You will not loose him. With Baptiste he *cannot* get loose."

But Colossus's master was not re-assured.

"Now," said he, still tarrying, "this is jest the way; had I of gone to church"—

"Posson Jone'," said Jules.

"What?"

"I tell you. We goin' to church!"

"Will you?" asked Jones, joyously.

"*Allons*, come along," said Jules, taking his elbow.

They walked down the Rue Chartres, passed several corners, and by and by turned into a cross street. The parson stopped an instant as they were turning and looked back up the street.

"W'at you lookin'?" asked his companion.

"I thought I saw Colossus," answered the parson, with an anxious face; "I reckon 'twa'nt him, though." And they went on.

The street they now entered was a very quiet one. The eye of any chance passer would have been at once drawn to a broad, heavy, white brick edifice on the lower side of the way, with a flag-pole standing out like a bowsprit from one of its great windows, and a pair of lamps hanging before a large closed entrance. It was a theatre, honey-combed with gambling-dens. At this morning hour all was still, and the only sign of life was a knot of little barefoot girls gathered within its narrow shade, and each carrying an infant relative. Into this place the parson and M. St.-Ange entered, the little nurses jumping up from the sills to let them pass in.

A half-hour may have passed. At the end of that time the whole juvenile company were laying alternate eyes and ears to the chinks, to gather what they could of an interesting quarrel going on within.

"I did not, saw! I given you no cause of offence, saw!

It's not so, saw! Mister Jools simply mistaken the house,
thinkin' it was a Sabbath-school! No such thing, saw; I
*ain't* bound to bet! Yes, I kin git out! Yes, without bet-
tin'! I hev a right to my opinion; I reckon I'm *a white
man,* saw! No saw! I on'y said I didn't think you could
get the game on them cards. 'Sno such thing, saw! I do
*not* know how to play! I wouldn't hev a rascal's money
ef I should win it! Shoot, ef you dare! You can kill me,
but you cayn't scare me! No, I shayn't bet! I'll die first!
Yes, saw; Mr. Jools can bet for me if he admires to; I
ain't his mostah."

Here the speaker seemed to direct his words to St.-
Ange.

"Saw, I don't understand you, saw. I never said I'd
loan you money to bet for me. I didn't suspicion this
from you, saw. No, I won't take any more lemonade;
it's the most notorious stuff I ever drank, saw!"

M. St.-Ange's replies were in *falsetto* and not without
effect; for presently the parson's indignation and anger
began to melt. "Don't ask me, Jools, I can't help you.
It's no use; it's a matter of conscience with me, Jools."

"*Mais oui!* 'tis a matt' of conscien' wid me, the same."

"But Jools, the money's none o' mine, nohow; it belongs to Smyrny, you know."

"If I could make jus' *one* bet," said the persuasive
St.-Ange, "I would leave this place, fas'—fas', yes. If I
had thing—*mais* I did not soupspicion this from you,
Posson Jone' "—

"Don't, Jools, don't!"

"No! Posson Jone'."

"You're bound to win?" said the parson, wavering.

"*Mais certainement!* But it is not to win that I want; 'tis me conscien'—me honor!"

"Well, Jools, I hope I'm not a-doin' no wrong. I'll loan you some of this money if you say you'll come right out 'thout takin' your winnin's."

All was still. The peeping children could see the parson as he lifted his hand to his breast-pocket. There it paused a moment in bewilderment, then plunged to the bottom. It came back empty, and fell lifelessly at his side. His head dropped upon his breast, his eyes were for a moment closed, his broad palms were lifted and pressed against his forehead, a tremor seized him, and he fell all in a lump to the floor. The children ran off with their infant-loads, leaving Jules St.-Ange swearing by all his deceased relatives, first to Miguel and Joe, and then to the lifted parson, that he did not know what had become of the money "except if" the black man had got it.

In the rear of ancient New Orleans, beyond the sites of the old rampart, a trio of Spanish forts, where the town has since sprung up and old, green with all the luxuriance of the wild Creole summer, lay the Congo Plains. Here stretched the canvas of the historic Cayetano, who Sunday after Sunday sowed the sawdust for his circus-ring.

But to-day the great showman had fallen short of

his printed promise. The hurricane had come by night, and with one fell swash had made an irretrievable sop of everything. The circus trailed away its bedraggled magnificence, and the ring was cleared for the bull.

Then the sun seemed to come out and work for the people. "See," said the Spaniards, looking up at the glorious sky with its great, white fleets drawn off upon the horizon—"see—heaven smiles upon the bull-fight!"

In the high upper seats of the rude amphitheatre sat the gayly decked wives and daughters of the Gascons, from the *métaries* along the Ridge, and the chattering Spanish women of the Market, their shining hair unbonneted to the sun. Next below were their husbands and lovers in Sunday blouses, milkmen, butchers, bakers, black-bearded fishermen, Sicilian fruiterers, swarthy Portuguese sailors, in little woollen caps, and strangers of the graver sort; mariners of England, Germany, and Holland. The lowest seats were full of trappers, smugglers, Canadian *voyageurs*, drinking and singing; *Américains*, too—more's the shame—from the upper rivers—who will not keep their seats—who ply the bottle, and who will get home by and by and tell how wicked Sodom is; broad-brimmed, silver-braided Mexicans, too, with their copper cheeks and bat's eyes and their tinkling spurred heels. Yonder, in that quieter section, are the quadroon women in their black lace shawls —and there is Baptiste; and below them are the turbaned black women, and there is—but he vanishes—Colossus.

The afternoon is advancing, yet the sport, though loudly demanded, does not begin. The *Américains* grow derisive and find pastime in gibes and raillery. They mock the various Latins with their national inflections, and answer their scowls with laughter. Some of the more aggressive shout pretty French greetings to the women of Gascony, and one bargeman, amid peals of applause, stands on a seat and hurls a kiss to the quadroons. The mariners of England, Germany, and Holland, as spectators, like the fun, while the Spaniards look black and cast defiant imprecations upon their persecutors. Some Gascons, with timely caution, pick their women out and depart, running a terrible fire of gallantries.

In hope of truce, a new call is raised for the bull: "The bull, the bull!—hush!"

In a tier near the ground a man is standing and calling —standing head and shoulders above the rest—calling in the *Américaine* tongue. Another man, big and red, named Joe, and a handsome little Creole in elegant dress and full of laughter, wish to stop him, but the flatboatmen, ha-ha-haing and cheering, will not suffer it. Ah, through some shameful knavery of the men, into whose hands he has fallen, he is drunk! Even the women can see that; and now he throws his arms wildly and raises his voice until the whole great circle hears it. He is preaching!

Ah! kind Lord, for a special providence now! The men of his own nation—men from the land of the open English Bible and temperance cup and song are cheering him on to mad disgrace. And now another call for the appointed sport is drowned by the flat-boatmen singing the ancient tune of Mear. You can hear the words—

"Old Grimes is dead, that good old soul"

—from ribald lips and throats turned brazen with laughter, from singers who toss their hats aloft and roll in their seats; the chorus swells to the accompaniment of a thousand brogans—

"He used to wear an old gray coat
All buttoned down before."

A ribboned man in the arena is trying to be heard, and the Latins raise one mighty cry for silence. The big red man gets a hand over the parson's mouth, and the ribboned man seizes his moment.

"They have been endeavoring for hours," he says, "to draw the terrible animals from their dens, but such is their strength and fierceness, that"—

His voice is drowned. Enough has been heard to warrant the inference that the beasts cannot be whipped out of the storm-drenched cages to which menagerie-life and long starvation have attached them, and from the roar of indignation the man of ribbons flies. The noise increases. Men are standing up by hundreds, and women are imploring to be let out of the turmoil. All at once, like the bursting of a dam, the whole mass pours down into the ring. They sweep across the arena and over the showman's barriers. Miguel gets a frightful tram-

pling. Who cares for gates or doors? They tear the
beasts' houses bar from bar, and, laying hold of the
gaunt buffalo, drag him forth by feet, ears and tail;
and in the midst of the *mêlée*, still head and shoulders
above all, wilder, with the cup of the wicked, than any
beast, is the man of God from the Florida parishes!

In his arms he bore—and all the people shouted at
once when they saw it—the tiger. He had lifted it high
up with its back to his breast, his arms clasped under its
shoulders; the wretched brute had curled up caterpillar-
wise, with its long tail curled against its belly, and
through its filed teeth grinned a fixed and impotent
wrath. And Parson Jones was shouting:

"The tiger and the buffler *shell* lay down together!
You dah to say they shayn't and I'll comb you with this
varmint from head to foot! The tiger and the buffler *shell*
lay down together. They *shell!* Now, you, Joe! Behold!
I am here to see it done! The lion and the buffler *shell*
lay down together!"

Mouthing these words again and again, the parson
forced his way through the surge in the wake of the buffalo. This creature the Latins had secured by a lariat
over his head, and were dragging across the old rampart
and into a street of the city.

The northern races were trying to prevent, and there
was pommelling and knocking down, cursing and knife-
drawing, until Jules St.-Ange was quite carried away
with the fun, laughed, clapped his hands, and swore
with delight, and ever kept close to the gallant parson.

Joe, contrariwise, counted all this child's-play an interruption. He had come to find Colossus and the money. In an unlucky moment he made bold to lay hold of the parson, but a piece of the broken barriers in the hands of a flat-boatman felled him to the sod, the terrible crowd swept over him, the lariat was cut and the giant parson hurled the tiger upon the buffalo's back. In another instant both brutes were dead at the hands of the mob; Jones was lifted from his feet, and prating of Scripture and the millennium, of Paul at Ephesus and Daniel in the "buffler's" den, was borne aloft upon the shoulders of the huzzaing *Américains*. Half an hour later he was sleeping heavily on the floor of a cell in the *calaboza*.

When Parson Jones awoke, a bell was somewhere tolling for midnight. Somebody was at the door of his cell with a key. The lock grated, the door swung, the turnkey looked in and stepped back, and a ray of moonlight fell upon M. Jules St.-Ange. The prisoner sat upon the empty shackles and ring-bolt in the centre of the floor.

"Misty Posson Jone'," said the visitor, softly.

"O Jools!"

"*Mais*, w'at de matter, Posson Jone'?"

"My sins, Jools, my sins!"

"Ah! Posson Jone', is that something to cry, because a man get sometime a litt' bit intoxicate? *Mais*, if a man keep *all the time* intoxicate, I thing that is again' the conscien'."

"Jools, Jools, your eyes is darkened—oh! Jools, where's my pore old niggah?"

"Posson Jone', never min'; he is wid Baptiste."

"Where?"

"I don' know w'ere—*mais* he is wid Baptiste. Baptiste is a beautiful to take care of somebody."

"Is he as good as you, Jools?" asked Parson Jones, sincerely.

Jules was slightly staggered.

"You know, Posson Jone,' you know, a nigger cannot be good as a w'ite man—*mais* Baptiste is a good nigger."

The parson moaned and dropped his chin into his hands.

"I was to of left for home to-morrow, sun-up, on the Isabella schooner. Pore Smyrny!" He deeply sighed.

"Posson Jone'," said Jules, leaning against the wall and smiling, "I swear you is the moz funny man I ever see. If I was you I would say, me, 'Ah! 'ow I am lucky! the money I los', it was not mine, anyhow!' My faith! shall a man make hisse'f to be the more sorry because the money he los' is not his? Me, I would say, 'it is a specious providence.'

"Ah, Misty Posson Jone'," he continued, "you make a so droll sermon ad the bull-ring. Ha! ha! I swear I thing you can make money to preach thad sermon many time ad the theatre St. Philippe. Hah! you is the moz brave dat I ever see, *mais* ad the same time the moz rilligious man. Where I'm goin' to fin' one priest to make like dat? *Mais*, why you can't cheer up an' be 'appy? Me, if I should be miserabl' like that I would kill meself."

The countryman only shook his head.

"*Bien*, Posson Jone', I have the so good news for you."

The prisoner looked up with eager inquiry.

"Las' evening when they lock' you, I come right off at M. De Blanc's house to get you let out of de cala-boose; M. de Blanc he is the judge. So soon I was entering— 'Ah, Jules, me boy, juz the one to make com-plete the game!' Posson Jone', it was a specious provi-dence! I win in t'ree hours more dan six hundred dollah! Look." He produced a mass of bank-notes, *bons*, and due-bills.

"And you got the pass?" asked the parson, regarding the money with a sadness incomprehensible to Jules.

"It is here; it takes the effect so soon the daylight."

"Jools, my friend, your kindness is in vain."

The Creole's face became a perfect blank.

"Because," said the parson, "for two reasons: firstly, I have broken the laws, and ought to stand the penalty; and secondly—you must really excuse me, Jools, you know, but the pass has been got onfairly, I'm afeerd. You told the judge I was innocent; and in neither case it don't become a Christian (which I hope I can still say I am one to 'do evil that good may come.' I muss stay."

M. St.-Ange stood up aghast, and for a moment speechless, at this exhibition of moral heroism; but an artifice was presently hit upon. "*Mais*, Posson Jone'!" —in his old *falsetto*—"de order—you cannot read it, it is in French—compel you to go hout, sir!"

"Is that so?" cried the parson, bounding up with radiant face—"is that so, Jools?"

The young man nodded, smiling; but, though he smiled, the fountain of his tenderness was opened. He made the sign of the cross as the parson knelt in prayer, and even whispered "Hail Mary," etc., quite through, twice over.

Morning broke in summer glory upon a cluster of villas behind the city, nestled under live-oaks and magnolias on the banks of a deep bayou, and known as Suburb St. Jean.

With the first beam came the West-Floridian and the Creole out upon the bank below the village. Upon the parson's arm hung a pair of antique saddle-bags. Baptiste limped wearily behind; both his eyes were encircled with broad, blue rings, and one cheek-bone bore the official impress of every knuckle of Colossus' left hand. The "beautiful to take care of somebody" had lost his charge. At mention of the negro he became wild, and, half in English, half in the "gumbo" dialect, said murderous things. Intimidated by Jules to calmness, he became able to speak confidently on one point; he could, would and did swear that Colossus had gone home to the Florida parishes; he was almost certain; in fact, he thought so.

There was clicking of pulleys as the three appeared upon the bayou's margin, and Baptiste pointed out, in the deep shadow of a great oak, the Isabella, moored among the bulrushes, and just spreading her sails for departure. Moving down to where she lay, the parson and his friend paused on the bank, loath to say farewell.

"O Jools!" said the parson, "supposin' Colossus ain't gone home! O Jools, if you'll look him out for me, I'll never forget you—I'll never forget **you**, nohow, Jools. No, Jools, I never will believe he taken that money. Yes, I know all niggahs will steal"—he set foot upon the gang-plank—"but Colossus wouldn't steal from me. Good-by."

"Misty Posson Jone'," said St.-Ange, putting his hand on the parson's arm with genuine affection, "hol' on. You see dis money—w'at I win las' night? Well, I win' it by a specious providence, ain't it?"

"There's no tellin'," said the humbled Jones. "Providence

'Moves in a mysterious way
His wonders to perform.'"

"Ah!" cried the Creole, "*c'est* very true. I ged this money in the mysterieuze way. *Mais,* if I keep dis money, you know where it goin' be to-night?"

"I really can't say," replied the parson.

"Goin' to de dev'," said the sweetly-smiling young man.

The schooner-captain, leaning against the shrouds, and even Baptiste, laughed outright.

"O Jools, you mustn't!"

"Well, den, w'at I shall do wid *it?*"

"Anything!" answered the parson; "better donate it away to some poor man"—

"Ah! Misty Posson Jone', dat is w'at I want. You los' five hondred dollar'—'twas me fault."

"No, it wa'n't, Jools."

"*Mais*, it was!"

"No!"

"It *was* me fault! I *swear* it was me fault! *Mais*, here is five hondred dollar'; I wish you shall take it. Here! I don't got no use for money.—Oh, my faith! Posson Jone', you must not begin to cry some more."

Parson Jones was choked with tears. When he found voice he said:

"O Jools, Jools, Jools! my pore, noble, dear, misguidened friend! ef you hed of hed a Christian raisin'! May the Lord show you your errors better'n I kin, and bless you for your good intentions—oh, no! I cayn't touch that money with a ten-foot pole; it wa'n't rightly got; you must really excuse me, my dear friend, but I cayn't touch it."

St.-Ange was petrified.

"Good-by, dear Jools," continued the parson. "I'm in the Lord's haynds, and he's very merciful, which I hope and trust you'll find it out. Good-by!"—the schooner swung slowly off before the breeze—"good-by!"

St.-Ange roused himself.

"Posson Jone'! make me hany'ow *dis* promise: you never, never, *never* will come back to New Orleans."

"Ah, Jools, the Lord willin', I'll never leave home again!"

"All right!" cried the Creole; "I thing he's willin'. Adieu, Posson Jone'. My faith'! you are the so fighting on' moz rilligious man as I never saw! Adieu! Adieu!"

Baptiste uttered a cry and presently ran by his master toward the schooner, his hands full of clods.

St.-Ange looked just in time to see the sable form of Colossus of Rhodes emerge from the vessel's hold, and the pastor of Smyrna and Bethesda seize him in his embrace.

"O Colossus! you outlandish old nigger! Thank the Lord! Thank the Lord!"

The little Creole almost wept. He ran down the towpath, laughing and swearing, and making confused allusion to the entire *personnel* and furniture of the lower regions.

By odd fortune, at the moment that St.-Ange further demonstrated his delight by tripping his mulatto into a bog, the schooner came brushing along the reedy bank with a graceful curve, the sails flapped, and the crew fell to poling her slowly along.

Parson Jones was on the deck, kneeling once more in prayer. His hat had fallen before him; behind him knelt his slave. In thundering tones he was confessing himself "a plum fool," from whom "the conceit had been jolted out," and who had been made to see that even his "nigger had the longest head of the two."

Colossus clasped his hands and groaned.

The parson prayed for a contrite heart.

"Oh, yes!" cried Colossus.

The master acknowledged countless mercies.

"Dat's so!" cried the slave.

The master prayed that they might still be "piled on."

"Glory!" cried the black man, clapping his hands; "pile on!"

"An' now," continued the parson, "bring this pore, backslidin' jackace of a parson and this pore ole fool nigger back to thar home in peace!"

"Pray fo' de money!" called Colossus.

But the parson prayed for Jules.

"Pray fo' de *money!*" repeated the negro.

"And oh, give thy servant back that there lost money!"

Colossus rose stealthily, and tiptoed by his still shouting master. St.-Ange, the captain, the crew, gazed in silent wonder at the strategist. Pausing but an instant over the master's hat to grin an acknowledgment of his beholders' speechless interest, he softly placed in it the faithfully-mourned and honestly-prayed-for Smyrna fund; then, saluted by the gesticulative, silent applause of St.-Ange and the schooner-men, he resumed his first attitude behind his roaring master.

"Amen!" cried Colossus, meaning to bring him to a close.

"Onworthy though I be"—cried Jones.

"*Amen!*" reiterated the negro.

"A-a-amen!" said Parson Jones.

He rose to his feet, and, stooping to take up his hat, beheld the well-known roll. As one stunned, he gazed for a moment upon his slave, who still knelt with clasped hands and rolling eyeballs; but when he became aware of the laughter and cheers that greeted him from both deck and shore, he lifted eyes and hands to heaven, and cried like the veriest babe. And when he looked at the roll again, and hugged and kissed it, St.-Ange tried to raise a second shout, but choked, and the crew fell to their poles.

And now up runs Baptiste, covered with slime, and prepares to cast his projectiles. The first one fell wide of the mark; the schooner swung round into a long reach of water, where the breeze was in her favor; another shout of laughter drowned the maledictions of the muddy man; the sails filled; Colossus of Rhodes, smiling and bowing as hero of the moment, ducked as the main boom swept round, and the schooner, leaning slightly to the pleasant influence, rustled a moment over the bulrushes, and then sped far away down the rippling bayou.

M. Jules St.-Ange stood long, gazing at the receding vessel as it now disappeared, now re-appeared beyond the tops of the high undergrowth; but, when an arm of the forest hid it finally from sight, he turned townward, followed by that fagged-out spaniel, his servant, saying, as he turned, "Baptiste."

"*Miché?*"

"You know w'at I goin' do wid dis money?"

"*Non, m'sieur.*"

"Well, you can strike me dead if I don't goin' to pay hall my debts! *Allons!*"

He began a merry little song to the effect that his

sweetheart was a wine-bottle, and master and man, leaving care behind, returned to the picturesque Rue Royale. The ways of Providence are indeed strange. In all Parson Jones's after-life, amid the many painful reminiscences of his visit to the City of the Plain, the sweet knowledge was withheld from him that by the light of the Christian virtue that shone from him even in his great fall, Jules St.-Ange arose, and went to his Father an honest man.

From *Old Creole Days*, by George W. Cable. (Charles Scribner's Sons, 1879. Edition 1929.)

# LAFCADIO HEARN

## (1850–1904)

The ten years Lafcadio Hearn spent in New Orleans were the first happy years of a life that had known much unhappiness, the first period of rest in a life's restless searching.

He was named for the Greek island of Lafcadia, on which he was born in 1850 of an Irish father and a Greek mother. Neither seemed to care much about him, and he was not cherished by the guardians to whom he was soon turned over; school in Ireland was hard and an accident there cost him the sight of an eye. He reached New York as an immigrant a little beyond the destitution point, worked at odd jobs, lived anyhow, became a reporter and worked at that here and there, hard pressed for a living and starved for beauty. Somehow he made his way to the *New Orleans Times-Democrat*. The lovely city filled his need for vivid coloring, sharp romantic contrasts, a present yet colorful and powerful, but above all, a resplendent past. Its culture was that of the Old World, but its colors, odors, and above all, its weather, were of the tropics. The French language, which he had spoken for two years of his unhappy boyhood at school in France, took on a barbarous exotic charm in "Ghombo," the patois of the negroes. "I see beauty all around me, tropical, intoxicating," he cried. To reach his rooms one passed through a huge and echoing archway into the inner court of an ancient mansion. He found friends, G. W. Cable among them; French society delighted him, and he read French authors, finding them of his own world. After a visit to Grande Isle in the Gulf of Mexico, he wrote a romance which was printed in the *Times-Democrat* as "Torn Letters," then in *Harper's Magazine*, April, 1888, under the name "Chita." It was at the moment when local color was highest in favor in American fiction, but no literary fashion determined the color of this story. It may be loosely put together, and it would be no wonder if the parts were greater than the whole, for one of the parts is the greatest hurricane in literature. No one will skip this storm as "description"; it is not the background but the leading character. The ship's captain sees truly when he sees it whirling with the sea in a last titanic waltz, and the hotel goes down as if beneath the directed blows of some vast unearthly arm.

The decade over, Hearn moved on, first to the Windward Islands, at length to Japan, where he came to anchor, became a college professor, married a Japanese wife and now lies buried in a Buddhist cemetery. There he found, for a long time at least, contentment and a measure of realization. In the list of his published works, by far the greater number of titles have to do with his adopted yet alien country. But it is in "Chita" that his genius rose untrammeled on the wings of the storm.

# THE LEGEND OF L'ÎLE DERNIÈRE

*By* LAFCADIO HEARN

THIRTY years ago, Last Island lay steeped in the enormous light of even such magical days. July was dying;—for weeks no fleck of cloud had broken the heaven's blue dream of eternity; winds held their breath; slow wavelets caressed the bland brown beach with a sound as of kisses and of whispers. To one who found himself alone, beyond the limits of the village and beyond the hearing of its voices,—the vast silence, the vast light, seemed full of weirdness. And these hushes, these transparencies, do not always inspire a causeless apprehension: they are omens sometimes—omens of coming tempest. Nature,—incomprehensible Sphinx!—before her mightiest bursts of rage, ever puts forth her divinest witchery makes more manifest her awful beauty. . . .

But in that forgotten summer the witchery lasted many long days,—days born in rose-light, buried in gold. It was the height of the season. The long myrtle-shadowed village was thronged with its summer population;—the big hotel could hardly accommodate all its guests;—the bathing-houses were too few for the crowds who flocked to them morning and evening. There were diversions for all,—hunting, and fishing parties, yachting excur-

sions, rides, music, games, promenades. Carriage wheels
whirled flickering along the beach, seaming its smoothness noiselessly, as if muffled. Love wrote its dreams
upon the sand. . . .

. . . Then one great noon, when the blue abyss of day
seemed to yawn over the world more deeply than ever
before, a sudden change touched the quicksilver smoothness of the waters—the swaying shadow of a vast motion. First the whole sea-circle appeared to rise up bodily
at the sky; the horizon-curve lifted to a straight line;
the line darkened and approached,—a monstrous wrinkle, an immeasurable fold of green water, moving swift
as a cloud—shadow pursued by sunlight. But it had
looked formidable only by startling contrast with the
previous placidity of the open: it was scarcely two feet
high;—it curled slowly as it neared the beach, and
combed itself out in sheets of woolly foam with a low,
rich roll of whispered thunder. Swift in pursuit another
followed—a third—a feebler fourth; then the sea only
swayed a little, and stilled again. Minutes passed, and
the immeasurable heavings recommenced—one, two,
three, four . . . seven long swells this time;—and the
Gulf smoothed itself once more. Irregularly the phenomenon continued to repeat itself, each time with heav-
ier billowing and briefer intervals of quiet—until at last
the whole sea grew restless and shifted color and flick-
ered green;—the swells became shorter and changed
form. Then from horizon to shore ran one uninterrupted
heaving—one vast green swarming of snaky shapes, roll-

ing in to hiss and flatten upon the sand. Yet no single cirrus-speck revealed itself through all the violet heights: there was no wind!—you might have fancied the sea had been upheaved from beneath. . . .

And indeed the fancy of a seismic origin for a windless surge would not appear in these latitudes to be utterly without foundation. On the fairest days a south-east breeze may bear you an odor singular enough to startle you from sleep,—a strong, sharp smell as of fish-oil; and gazing at the sea you might be still more startled at the sudden apparition of great oleaginous patches spreading over the water, sheeting over the swells. That is, if you had never heard of the mysterious submarine oil-wells, the volcanic fountains, unexplored, that well up with the eternal pulsing of the Gulf Stream. . . .

But the pleasure-seekers of Last Island knew there must have been a "great blow" somewhere that day. Still the surf swelled; and a splendid surf made the evening bath delightful. Then, just at sundown, a beautiful cloud-bridge grew up and arched the sky with a single span of cottony pink vapor, that changed and deepened color with the dying of the iridescent day. And the cloud-bridge approached, stretched, strained, and swung round at last to make way for the coming of the gale,—even as the light bridges that traverse the dreamy Têche swing open when luggermen sound through their conch-shells the long, bellowing signal of approach.

Then the wind began to blow, with the passing of July. It blew from the north east, clear, cool. It blew in enor-

mous sighs, dying away at regular intervals, as if pausing to draw breath. All night it blew; and in each pause
could be heard the answering moan of the rising surf,—
as if the rhythm of the sea moulded itself after the
rhythm of the air,—as if the waving of the water responded precisely to the waving of the wind,—a billow
for every puff, a surge for every sigh.

The August morning broke in a bright sky;—the
breeze still came cool and clear from the north east. The
waves were running now at a sharp angle to the shore;
they began to carry fleeces, an innumerable flock of
vague green shapes, wind-driven to be despoiled of their
ghostly wool. Far as the eye could follow the line of the
beach, all the slope was white with the great shearing
of them. Clouds came, flew as in a panic against the face
of the sun, and passed. All that day and through the
night and into the morning again the breeze continued
from the north east, blowing like an equinoctial
gale. . . .

Then day by day the vast breath freshened steadily,
and the waters heightened. A week later sea-bathing had
become perilous: colossal breakers were herding in, like
moving leviathan-backs, twice the height of a man. Still
the gale grew, and the billowing waxed mightier, and
faster and faster overhead flew the tatters of torn cloud.
The gray morning of the ninth wanly lighted a surf that
appalled the best swimmers! the sea was one wild agony
of foam, the gale was rending off the heads of the waves
and veiling the horizon with a fog of salt spray. Shad-

owless and gray the day remained: there were mad bursts of lashing rain. Evening brought with it a sinister apparition, looming through a cloud-rent in the west—a scarlet sun in a green sky. His sanguine disk, enormously magnified, seemed barred like the body of a belted planet. A moment, and the crimson spectre vanished: and the moonless night came.

Then the Wind grew weird. It ceased being a breath; it became a Voice moaning across the world,—hooting,—uttering nightmare sounds,—*Whoo!—whoo!—whoo!*—and with each stupendous owl-cry the moving of the waters seemed to deepen more and more abysmally, through all the hours of darkness. From the north west the breakers of the bay began to roll high over the sandy slope, into the salines;—the village bayou broadened to a bellowing flood. . . . So the tumult swelled and the turmoil heightened until morning, and a morning of gray gloom and whistling rain. Rain of bursting clouds and rain of wind-blown brine from the great spuming agony of the sea.

The steamer *Star* was due from St. Mary's that fearful morning. Could she come? No one really believed it,—no one. And nevertheless men struggled to the roaring beach to look for her, because hope is stronger than reason. . . .

Even to-day, in these Creole islands, the advent of the steamer is the great event of the week. There are no telegraph lines, no telephones: the mail-packet is the only trustworthy medium of communication with the

outer world, bringing friends, news, letters. The magic
of steam has placed New Orleans nearer to New York
than to the Timbaliers, nearer to Washington than to
Wind Island, nearer to Chicago than to Barataria Bay.
And even during the deepest sleep of waves and winds
there will come betimes to sojourners in this unfamiliar
archipelago a feeling of lonesomeness that is a fear, a
feeling of isolation from the world of men,—totally
unlike that sense of solitude which haunts one in the
silence of mountain-heights, or amid the eternal tumult
of lofty granitic coasts: a sense of helpless insecurity.
The land seems but an undulation of the sea-bed: its
highest ridges do not rise more than the height of a man
above the salines on either side; the salines themselves
lie almost level with the level of the flood-tides; the
tides are variable, treacherous, mysterious. But when all
around and above these ever-changing shores the twin
vastnesses of heaven and sea begin to utter the tremendous revelation of themselves as infinite forces in
contention, then indeed this sense of separation from
humanity appals. . . . Perhaps it was such a feeling
that forced men, on the tenth day of August, eighteen
hundred and fifty-six, to hope against hope for the coming of the *Star*, and to strain their eyes towards far-off
Terrebonne. "It was a wind you could lie down on," said
my friend the pilot.

. . ."Great God!" shrieked a voice above the shouting of the storm,—"*she is coming!*" . . . It was true.
Down the Atchefalaya, and thence through strange

mazes of bayou, lakelet and pass, by a rear route familiar only to the best of pilots, the frail river-craft
had toiled into Caillou Bay, running close to the main
shore; and now she was heading right for the island,
with the wind aft, over the monstrous sea. On she came,
swaying, rocking, plunging,—with a great whiteness
wrapping her about like a cloud, and moving with her
moving;—a tempest-whirl of spray;—ghost-white and
like a ghost she came, for her smoke-stacks exhaled no
visible smoke—the wind devoured it! The excitement
on shore became wild;—men shouted themselves
hoarse; women laughed and cried. Every telescope and
opera-glass was directed upon the coming apparition;
all wondered how the pilot kept his feet; all marvelled
at the madness of the captain.

But Captain Abraham Smith was not mad. A veteran American sailor, he had learned to know the great
Gulf as scholars know deep books by heart: he knew
the birthplace of its tempests, the mystery of its tides,
the omens of its hurricanes. While lying at Brashear
City he felt the storm had not yet reached its highest,
vaguely foresaw a mighty peril, and resolved to wait
no longer for a lull. "Boys," he said, "we've got to
take her out in spite of Hell!" And they "took her
out." Through all the peril, the men stayed by him and
obeyed him. By mid-morning the wind had deepened
to a roar,—lowering sometimes to a rumble, sometimes
bursting upon the ears like a measureless and deafening
crash. Then the captain knew the *Star* was running a

race with Death. "She'll win it," he muttered;—"she'll stand it. . . . Perhaps they'll have need of me to-night."

She won! With a sonorous steam-chant of triumph the brave little vessel rode at last into the bayou, and anchored hard by her accustomed resting-place, in full view of the hotel, though not near enough to shore to lower her gang-plank. . . . But she had sung her swan-song. Gathering in from the north east, the waters of the bay were already marbling over the salines and half across the island; and still the wind increased its paroxysmal power.

Cottages began to rock. Some slid away from the solid props upon which they rested. A chimney tumbled. Shutters were wrenched off: verandas demolished. Light roofs lifted, dropped again, and flapped into ruin. Trees bent their heads to the earth. And still the storm grew louder and blacker with every passing hour.

The *Star* rose with the rising of the waters, dragging her anchor. Two more anchors were put out, and still she dragged—dragged in with the flood,—twisting, shuddering, careening in her agony. Evening fell: the sand began to move with the wind, stinging faces like a continuous fire of fine shot; and frenzied blasts came to buffet the steamer foreward, sideward. Then one of her hog-chains parted with a clang like the boom of a big bell. Then another! . . . Then the captain bade his men to cut away all her upper works, clean to the deck. Overboard into the seething went her stacks, her pilot-house, her cabins,—and whirled away. And the naked hull of the *Star*, still dragging her three anchors, labored on through the darkness, nearer and nearer to the immense silhouette of the hotel, whose hundred windows were now all aflame. The vast timber building seemed to defy the storm. The wind, roaring round its broad verandas,—hissing through every crevice with the sound and force of steam,—appeared to waste its rage. And in the half-lull between two terrible gusts there came to the captain's ears a sound that seemed strange in that night of multitudinous terrors . . . a sound of music!

. . . Almost every evening throughout the season there had been dancing in the great hall; there was dancing that night also. The population of the hotel had been augmented by the advent of families from other parts of the island, who found their summer cottages insecure places of shelter: there were really four hundred guests assembled. Perhaps it was for this reason that the entertainment had been prepared upon a grander plan than usual, that it assumed the form of a fashionable ball. And all those pleasure-seekers,—representing the wealth and beauty of the Creole parishes,—whether from Ascension or Assumption, St. Mary's or St. Landry's, Iberville or Terrebonne, whether inhabitants of the multi-colored and many-balconied Creole quarter of the quaint metropolis, or dwellers in the dreamy paradises of the Têche,—

mingled joyously, knowing each other, feeling in some
sort akin—whether affiliated by blood, connaturalized
by caste, or simply associated by traditional sympathies
of class sentiment and class interest. Perhaps in the
more than ordinary merriment of that evening something of nervous exaltation might have been discerned,
—something like a feverish resolve to oppose apprehension with gayety, to combat uneasiness by diversion.
But the hours passed in mirthfulness; the first general
feeling of depression began to weigh less and less upon
the guests; they had found reason to confide in the
solidity of the massive building; there were no positive
terrors, no outspoken fears; and the new conviction
of all had found expression in the words of the host
himself,—*"Il n'y a rien de mieux à faire que de
s'amuser!"* Of what avail to lament the prospective
devastation of cane-fields,—to discuss the possible ruin
of crops? Better to seek solace in choreigraphic har-
monies, in the rhythm of gracious motion and of perfect melody, than hearken to the discords of the wild
orchestra of storms;—wiser to admire the grace of
Parisian toilets, the eddy of trailing robes with its
fairy foam of lace, the ivorine loveliness of glossy
shoulders and jewelled throats, the glimmering of
satin-slippered feet,—than to watch the raging of the
flood without, or the flying of the wreck. . . .

So the music and the mirth went on: they made joy
for themselves—those elegant guests;—they jested

and sipped rich wines;—they pledged, and hoped, and loved, and promised, with never a thought of the morrow, on the night of the tenth of August, eighteen hundred and fifty-six. Observant parents were there, planning for the future bliss of their nearest and dearest;—mothers and fathers of handsome lads, lithe and elegant as young pines, and fresh from the polish of foreign university training;—mothers and fathers of splendid girls whose simplest attitudes were witcheries. Young cheeks flushed, young hearts fluttered with an emotion more puissant than the excitement of the dance;—young eyes betrayed the happy secret discreeter lips would have preserved. Slave-servants circled through the aristocratic press, bearing dainties and wines, praying permission to pass in terms at once humble and officious, always in the excellent French which well-trained house-servants were taught to use on such occasions.

. . . Night wore on: still the shining floor palpitated to the feet of the dancers; still the piano-forte pealed, and still the violins sang,—and the sound of the singing shrilled through the darkness, in gasps of the gale, to the ears of Captain Smith, as he strove to keep his footing on the spray-drenched deck of the *Star*.

—"Christ!" he muttered,—"a dance! If that wind whips round south, there'll be another dance! . . . But I guess the *Star* will stay."

Half an hour might have passed; still the lights

flamed calmly, and the violins trilled, and the per-
fumed whirl went on. . . . And suddenly the wind
veered!

Again the *Star* reeled, and shuddered, and turned,
and began to drag all her anchors. But she now dragged
away from the great building and its lights,—away
from the voluptuous thunder of the grand piano,—
even at that moment out-pouring the great joy of
Weber's melody orchestrated by Berlioz: *l'Invitation
à la Valse*,—with its marvellous musical swing.

"Waltzing!" cried the captain. "God help them!—
God help us all now! . . . *The Wind waltzes to-
night, with the Sea for his partner!*"

O the stupendous Valse-Tourbillon! O the mighty
Dancer! One-two-three! From north east to east, from
east to south east, from south east to south: then from
the south he came, whirling the Sea in his arms. . . .

. . . Some one shrieked in the midst of the revels;
—some girl who found her pretty slippers wet. What
could it be? Thin streams of water were spreading over
the level planking,—curling about the feet of the
dancers. . . . What could it be? All the land had
begun to quake, even as, but a moment before, the
polished floor was trembling to the pressure of circling
steps;—all the building shook now; every beam uttered its groan. What could it be? . . .

There was a clamor, a panic, a rush to the windy
night. Infinite darkness above and beyond; but the
lantern-beams danced far out over an unbroken circle

of heaving and swirling black water. Stealthily, swiftly, the measureless sea-flood was rising.

—"*Messieurs—mesdames, ce n'est rien.* Nothing serious, ladies, I assure you. . . . *Mais nous en avons vu bien souvent, les inondations comme colle-ci; ça passe vite!* The water will go down in a few hours, ladies;—it never rises higher than this; *il n'y a pas le moindre danger, je vous dis!* . . . *Allons! il n'y a—* My God! what is that?" . . .

For a moment there was a ghastly hush of voices. And through that hush there burst upon the ears of all a fearful and unfamiliar sound, as of a colossal cannonade—rolling up from the south, with volleying lightnings. Vastly and swiftly, nearer and nearer it came,—a ponderous and unbroken thunder-roll, terrible as the long muttering of an earthquake.

The nearest mainland,—across mad Caillou Bay to the sea-marshes,—lay twelve miles north; west, by the Gulf, the nearest solid ground was twenty miles distant. There were boats, yes!—but the stoutest swimmer might never reach them now! . . .

Then rose a frightful cry,—the hoarse, hideous, indescribable cry of hopeless fear,—the despairing animal-cry man utters when suddenly brought face to face with Nothingness, without preparation, without consolation, without possibility of respite. . . . *Sauve qui peut!* Some wrenched down the doors; some clung to the heavy banquet-tables, to the sofas, to the billiard-tables; during one terrible instant,—against fruitless heroisms,

against futile generosities,—raged all the frenzy of self-
ishness, all the brutalities of panic. And then—then
came thundering through the blackness, the giant
swells, boom on boom! . . . One crash!—the huge
frame building rocks like a cradle, seesaws, crackles.
What are human shrieks now?—the tornado is shrieking! Another!—chandeliers splinter; lights are dashed
out; a sweeping cataract hurls in; the immense hall
rises,—oscillates,—twirls as upon a pivot,—crepitates,
—crumbles into ruin. Crash again!—the swirling
wreck dissolves into the wallowing of another monster
billow; and a hundred cottages overturn, spin in sudden eddies, quiver, disjoint, and melt into the seething.

. . . So the hurricane passed,—tearing off the heads
of the prodigious waves, to hurl them a hundred feet
in air,—heaping up the ocean against the land,—up-
turning the woods. Bays and passes were swollen to
abysses; rivers regorged; the sea-marshes were changed
to raging wastes of water. . . . Far-off river steamers
tugged wildly at their cables,—shivering like tethered
creatures that hear by night the approaching howl of
destroyers. . . .

And over roaring Kaimbuck Pass,—over the agony
of Caillou Bay,—the billowing tide rushed unresisted
from the Gulf,—tearing and swallowing the land in its
course,—ploughing out deep-sea channels where sleek
herds had been grazing but a few hours before,—rending islands in twain,—and ever bearing with it, through

the night, enormous vortex of wreck and vast wan drift of corpses.

But the *Star* remained. And Captain Abraham Smith, with a long, good rope about his waist, dashed again and again into that awful surging to snatch victims from death,—clutching at passing hands, heads, garments, in the cataract-sweep of the seas,—saving, aiding, cheering, though blinded by spray and battered by drifting wreck, until his strength failed in the unequal struggle at last, and his men drew him aboard senseless, with some beautiful half-drowned girl safe in his arms. But well-nigh twoscore souls had been rescued by him; and the *Star* stayed through it all.

Long years after, the weed-grown ribs of her graceful skeleton could still be seen, curving up from the sand-dunes of Last Island, in valiant witness of how well she stayed.

Day breaks through the flying wrack, over the infinite heaving of the sea, over the low land made vast with desolation. It is a spectral dawn: a wan light, like the light of a dying sun.

The wind has waned and veered; the flood sinks slowly back to its abysses—abandoning its plunder,—scattering its piteous waifs over bar and dune, over shoal and marsh, among the silences of the mango-swamps, over the long low reaches of sand-grasses and drowned weeds, for more than a hundred miles. From the shell-reefs of Pointe-au-Fer to the shallows of Pello Bay the dead lie mingled with the high-heaped drift;—

from their cypress groves the vultures rise to dispute a share of the feast with the shrieking frigate-birds and squeaking gulls. And as the tremendous tide withdraws its plunging waters, all the pirates of air follow the great white-gleaming retreat; a storm of billowing wings and screaming throats.

And swift in the wake of gull and frigate-bird the Wreckers come, the Spoilers of the dead,—savage skimmers of the sea,—hurricane-riders wont to spread their canvas-pinions in the face of storms; Sicilian and Corsican outlaws, Manila-men from the marshes, deserters from many navies, Lascars, marooners, refugees of a hundred nationalities,—fishers and shrimpers by name, smugglers by opportunity,—wild channel finders from obscure bayous and unfamiliar *chénières,* all skilled in the mysteries of these mysterious waters beyond the comprehension of the oldest licensed pilot. . . .

There is plunder for all—birds and men. There are drowned sheep in multitude, heaped carcasses of kine. There are casks of claret and kegs of brandy and legions of bottles bobbing in the surf. There are billiard-tables overturned upon the sand;—there are sofas, pianos, footstools and music-stools, luxurious chairs, lounges of bamboo. There are chests of cedar, and toilet-tables of rosewood, and trunks of fine stamped leather stored with precious apparel. There are *objets de luxe* innumerable. There are children's playthings: French dolls in marvellous toilets, and toy carts, and wooden horses,

and wooden spades, and brave little wooden ships that
rode out the gale in which the great *Nautilus* went
down. There is money in notes and in coin—in purses,
in pocket-books, and in pockets: plenty of it! There
are silks, satins, laces, and fine linen to be stripped from
the bodies of the drowned,—and necklaces, bracelets,
watches, finger-rings and fine chains, brooches and
trinkets. . . ."*Chi bidizza!—Oh! chi bedda mughieri!
Eccu, la bidizza!*" That ball-dress was made in
Paris by— But you never heard of him, Sicilian Vi-
cenzu. . . . "*Che bella sposina!*" Her bethrothal ring
will not come off, Giuseppe; but the delicate bone snaps
easily: your oyster-knife can sever the tendon. . . .
"*Guardate! chi bedda picciota!*" Over her heart you
will find it, Valentino—the locket held by that fine
Swiss chain of woven hair—"*Caya manan!*" And it is
not your quadroon bondswoman, sweet lady, who now
disrobes you so roughly; those Malay hands are less
deft than hers,—but she slumbers very far away from
you, and may not be aroused from her sleep. "*Na quita
mo! dalaga!—na quita maganda!*" . . . Juan, the
fastenings of those diamond ear-drops are much too
complicated for your peon fingers; tear them out!
"*Dispense, chulita!*" . . .

. . . Suddenly a long, mighty silver trilling fills the
ears of all: there is a wild hurrying and scurrying;
swiftly, one after another, the over-burdened luggers
spread wings and flutter away.

Thrice the great cry rings rippling through the gray

air, and over the green sea, and over the far-flooded shell-reefs, where the huge white flashes are,—sheet lightning of breakers,—and over the weird wash of corpses coming in.

It is the steam-call of the relief-boat, hastening to rescue the living, to gather in the dead.

The tremendous tragedy is over!

From *Chita: A Memory of Last Island* by Lafcadio Hearn. (Harper, 1889.)

# ELIZA RIPLEY

## (1832–1912)

Judge Richard Chinn, whose ancestor Raleigh Chinn married Mary Ball's sister Esther, moved his household—wife, twelve children and sundry slaves—from Lexington, Kentucky to New Orleans in 1835. Eliza, born in 1832, was the tenth child, and retained throughout her long life vivid memories of these early American communities, and of the great changes brought about by the Civil War.

She married in 1852, and spent the succeeding decade as mistress of a large plantation near Baton Rouge. During the war years she traveled constantly with her husband and little children, in an open wagon, across Texas and Mexico, convoying Confederate cotton. When Lee surrendered they went to Cuba and eventually operated a sugar plantation there for several years, until her husband's death.

In the leisure hours of her latter years, after a second marriage, she recorded some of her reminiscences in "From Flag to Flag" (1888), and "Social Life in Old New Orleans" (1912), both now out of print. From the latter the following chapters have been taken. They have just enough of the melody and rhythm of fiction to permit their inclusion in a collection like this, but they are, for all that, actual records of personal experience, all

77

the more reliable because her character, and her writings were marked by an honest unsentimentality which is rather rare among survivors and records of the "Lost Cause." The historic value of these memories of the last plantation Christmas is at once apparent; the importance of a trustworthy and detailed account of long-distance steamboat and stage-coach travel by a gentleman's family before the War will be manifest to anyone who bears in mind how largely our social history is a history of transportation. Mrs. Trollope tells, in "Domestic Manners of the Americans," (reprinted by Dodd, Mead and Co.) of her journey in the *Belvidere* in January, 1828, on the Mississippi from New Orleans, during which she "liked the boat better than the habits of the people"; but there is a splendid rashness about starting out with a family of this size, and the foreknowledge that food must be foraged for along the way, that commends itself to present-day travelers in search of the picturesque.

# A FAMILY FLIGHT IN THE FORTIES

## By Eliza Ripley

ABOUT the Fourth of July every year our family migrated [1] to the old Kentucky homestead. The Fourth was not chosen from any patriotic motive, but law courts were closed and legal business suspended, and my father's vacation at hand at that date.

There was the famed *Grey Eagle,* "a No. 1 floating palace" it was called. There was the *Belle of the West* and the *Fashion* and the *Henry Clay.* One time and another we churned up the muddy Mississippi water in every one of them. Naturally the boats catered in every way to the predilections of the plantation owners, who were their main source of profit. *Grey Eagle* was the finest and best, and therefore the most popular boat. I recall with amusement an eight or ten days' trip on that palace. The cabins were divided by curtains, drawn at night for privacy. The ladies' cabin, at the stern, was equipped with ten or twelve small staterooms. The gentlemen's cabin stretched on down to the officers' quarters, bar, barber shop, pantries, etc., ending in what was called Social Hall, where the men sat about, smoking and chewing (the latter as common a

[1] From New Orleans.

79

habit as cigarette smoking is now) and talking—in other words, making themselves sociable.

On that same *Grey Eagle* I was for the first time promoted to the upper berth, in a stateroom shared by an older sister. The berth was so narrow that in attempting to turn over I fell out and landed in the wash basin, on the opposite side of the room! My sister had to sit on the lower berth to braid my pigtail, then sent me forth so she could have room to braid her own. There were no valises, suitcases or steamer trunks in those days of little travel, and unless you are three-quarters of a century old you can't imagine a more unwieldy article than a carpet-bag of seventy years ago.

The cabin was lighted with swinging whale-oil lamps, and one could light his stateroom if one had thought to provide a candle. Every family travelled with a man servant, whose business it was to be constantly at beck and call. Of course, there was always a colored chambermaid, and, equally of course, she frisked around and seemed to have very little responsibility—no bells, no means of summoning her from her little nodding naps if she happened to be beyond the sound of one's voice. The man servant's duties, therefore, were almost incessant. . . . When the boat stopped "to wood" every man servant rushed to the woodman's cabin to get eggs, chickens, milk, and what not.

And those men had the privilege of the kitchen to prepare private dishes for their white folks. I wonder how long a boat or hotel would stand that kind of management today; but in the days where my rocking-chair is transporting me, steamboat fare was not up to the standard of any self-respecting *pater familias*. There was no ice chest, no cold storage; in a word, no way of preserving fresh foods for any length of time, so passengers resorted to such means as presented themselves for their own bodily comfort. Those who had not the necessary appendage—a man servant—foraged for themselves, but the experienced and trusted servant, to use a vulgarism, "was never left."

The table for meals extended the length of the gentlemen's cabin, stretched out and out to its utmost length, if need be, so that every passenger had a seat. There was no second table, no second-class passengers —anybody was the equal of anybody else. If you could not possibly be that, you could find accommodation on the lower deck and eat from a tin plate.

It was quite customary, as I have mentioned, for passengers to have private dishes, prepared by their own servants. I recall with a smile, on one occasion, a very respectable-looking stranger boarded our boat at Helena or some such place. At dinner he reached for a bottle of wine. Cuthbert Bullitt touched the bottle with a fork, saying, "Private wine." The man, with a bow, withdrew his hand. Presently he reached for a dish of eggs. My father said, "Excuse me, private." There was something else he reached for, I forgot what, and another fellow-passenger touched the dish and said "Private." Presently dessert was served, and a fine, large pie happened to be placed in front of the Helena man. He promptly stuck his fork into it. "By gracious! this is a private pie." There was a roar of laughter.

After dinner the others, finding him delightfully congenial and entertaining, fraternized with him to the extent of a few games at cards. He was wonderfully lucky. He left the boat at an obscure river town during the night, and the next day our captain said he was a notorious gambler. From his capers at table the captain saw he was planning a way of winning attention to himself, therefore under cover of darkness he had been put ashore. My father, who did not play, was vastly amused when he found the smart gambler had carried off all the spare cash of those who had enjoyed the innocent sport.

Cousin Eliza Patrick used to relate the trip her family made about 1820 on a flatboat from Kentucky to Louisiana. The widowed mother wished to rejoin a son practicing medicine in the latter state, so she sold her land, and loaded her family and every movable object she possessed—slaves, cattle, farm implements, household effects—upon a huge "flat" and they floated by day and tied up to the bank by night, carrying on, during the weeks consumed by the trip, an existence which must have been somewhat like that of Noah's family in the Ark.[1]

---

[1] Flatboats, which were only rafts without propelling power, were broken up on arrival and sold for lumber, the boatmen returning upstream in packets to repeat the process.

We used entirely, even for drinking, the muddy river water, which was hauled up in buckets on the barber side of the boat, while the steward was emptying refuse to the fishes on the pantry side. . . . There was no place to sit but the general cabin; there was no library, very little reading, but much fancy work, mostly on canvas, foot stools and bell-pulls. A bell-pull, you may want to know, was a long band about three inches wide; it was hung from the parlor cornice and connected with a bell in the servant's region; it was quite the style to embroider them in gay vines and flower designs. . . . Our trip necessarily embraced at least one Sunday. I remember my father had a dear old relative of the deepest dyed Presbyterian type, who always on his river trips landed wherever he happened to be on Saturday and on Monday boarded another boat (if one came along), his scruples forbidding Sunday travel.

Arrived at the end of our river journey, father chartered a whole stage to take his family a two days' trip into the heart of the blue grass region. Nine passengers filled the interior of the coach, and four or five, if need be, could ride on top. The rumble (we always called it boot) was filled with baggage. The vehicle had no springs, but was swung on braces, which gave it a kind of swaying motion that always made me sick. However, we managed to start off in fine style, but every time there was a stop to change horses all of us alighted, stiff and tired, to "stretch our legs," like Squeers in

Dickens' "Nicholas Nickleby." At noon we rejoiced to hear our coachman's horn, a grand, loud blast, followed by toot, toot!—one toot for each passenger, so that the tavern man would know how many plates to lay, and his wife how many biscuits and chicken legs to have ready.

Late afternoon the stage winds up a hill, and in a woods pasture and surrounded by blue grass meadows the gable end of a red brick house can be seen. My dear, tired mother puts her head out of the window, "Driver, blow your horn." A great blast sounds over the waving grass and blossoming fields, and we know that they know we are coming. Tired as the horses are after the long, hard pull; tired as the coachman must be, he cracks his whip, and we gallop up the shady lane to the door as briskly as if we were fresh from the stable. Long before we are fully there, and the steps of the nine-passenger coach can be lowered; long before the boys can jump off the top, a host of dear faces, both white and black, is assembled to greet us. As a little child I always wondered why it was, when the occasion was so joyful, and all of us tumbled from that stage so beaming and happy, that as my aunt folded my mother in her arms, they both wept such copious tears. Now I know.

From *Social Life in Old New Orleans: Being Recollections of My Girlhood,* by Eliza Ripley, (Appleton, New York and London, 1912).

# THE LAST CHRISTMAS

### By Eliza Ripley

CHRISTMAS before the war. There never will be another in any land, with any peoples, like the Christmas of 1859—on the old plantation. Days beforehand preparations were in progress for the wedding at the quarters, and the ball at the "big house." Children coming home for the holidays were both amused and delighted to learn that Nancy Brackenridge was to be the quarter bride. "Nancy a bride! Oh, la!" they exclaimed. "Why Nancy must be forty years old." And she was going to marry Aleck, who, if he would wait a year or two, might marry Nancy's daughter. While the young school-girls were busy "letting out" the white satin balldress that had descended from the parlor dance to the quarter bride, and were picking out and freshening up the wreath and corsage bouquet of lilies of the valley that had been the wedding flowers of the mistress of the big house, and while the boys were ransacking the distant woods for holly branches and magnolia boughs, enough for the ballroom as well as the wedding supper table, the family were busy with the multitudinous preparations for the annual dance, for which Arlington, with its ample parlors and halls, and its proverbial hospitality, was noted far and wide.

The children made molasses gingerbread and sweet potato pies, and one big bride's cake, with a real ring in it. They spread the table in the big quarters nursery, and the boys decorated it with greenery and a lot of cut paper fly catchers, laid on the roast mutton and pig, and hot biscuits from the big house kitchen, and the pies and cakes of the girls' own make. The girls proceeded to dress Nancy Brackenridge, pulling together that refractory satin waist which, though it had been "let out" to its fullest extent, still showed a sad gap, to be concealed by a dextrous arrangement of some discarded hair ribbons. Nancy was black as a crow and had rather a startling look in that dazzling white satin dress and the pure white flowers pinned to her kinks. At length the girls gave a finishing pat to the toilet, and their brothers pronounced her "bully," and called Marthy Ann to see how fine her mammy was.

As was the custom, the whole household went to the quarter to witness the wedding. Lewis, the plantation preacher, in a cast-off swallow-tail coat of Marse Jim's that was uncomfortably tight, especially about the waist line, performed the ceremony. Then my husband advanced and made some remarks, to the effect that this marriage was a solemn tie, and there must be no shirking of its duties; they must behave and be faithful to each other; he would have no foolishness. These remarks, though by no means elegant, fitted the occasion to a fraction. There were no high flights of eloquence which the darky mind could not reach, it was plain, unvarnished admonition.

The following morning, Christmas Day, the field negroes were summoned to the back porch of the big house, where Marse Jim, after a few preliminary remarks, distributed the presents—a head handkerchief, a pocketknife, a pipe, a dress for the baby, shoes for the growing boy (his first pair, maybe), etc., etc., down the list. Each gift was received with a "Thankee, sir," and, perhaps, also a remark anent its usefulness. Then after Charlotte brought forth the jug of whiskey and the tin cups, and everyone had a comfortable dram, they filed off to the quarters, with a week of holiday before them and a trip to town to do their little buying.

The very last Christmas on the old plantation we had a tree. None of us had ever seen a Christmas tree; there were no cedars or pines, so we finally settled upon a tall althea bush, hung presents on it, for all the house servants, as well as for the family and a few guests. The tree had to be lighted up, so it was postponed till evening. The idea of the house servants having such a celebration quite upset the little negroes. I heard one remark, "All us house niggers is going to be hung on a tree." Before the dawn of another Christmas the negroes had become discontented, demoralized and scattered, freer than the whites, for the blacks recognized no responsibilities whatsoever. The family had already abandoned the old plantation home. We could not stand the changed condition of things any longer, and the Federals had entered into possession and completed the ruin. Very likely some reminiscent darky told new-found friends, "All de house niggers was hung on a tree last Christmas." I have heard from Northern lips even more astonishing stories of maltreated slaves than a wholesale hanging.

Frequently before the holidays some of the negroes were questioned as to what they would like to have, and the planter would make notes and have the order filled in the city. That, I think, was the custom at Whitehall plantation. I was visiting there on one occasion when a woman told Judge Chinn she wanted a mourning veil. "A mourning veil!" he replied. "I thought you were going to marry Tom this Christmas?" "Yis, marster, but you know Jim died last grinding, and I ain't never mourned none for 'im. I want to mourn some 'fore I marries agin." I did not remain to see, but I do not doubt she got the mourning veil and had the melancholy satisfaction of wearing it around the quarter lot a few days before she married Tom.

After the departure of our happy negroes, whose voices and laughter could be heard long after the yard gate was closed and they had vanished out of sight, we rushed around like wild to complete the preparations for the coming ball guests. They began to arrive in the afternoon from down the coast and from the opposite side of the river. Miles and miles some of them drove in carriages, with champagne baskets, capital forerunners of the modern suit case, tied on behind, and, like as not, a dusky maid perched on top of it; poor thing, the carriage being full, she had to travel in this precarious way, holding on for dear life. Those old-time turtle-back vehicles had outside a single seat for the coachman only. Parties came also in skiffs, with their champagne baskets and maids. Long before time for the guests from town to appear, mammas and maids were busy in the bedrooms, dressing their young ladies for the occasion. Meanwhile the plantation musicians were assembling, two violins, a flute, a triangle, and a tambourine. A platform had been erected at one end of the room, with kitchen chairs and cuspidors, for their accommodation. Our own negroes furnished the dance music, but we borrowed Col. Hicky's Washington for the tambourine. He was more expert than any "end man" you ever saw. He kicked it and butted it and struck it with elbow and heel, and rattled it in perfect unison with the other instruments, making more noise, and being himself a more inspiring sight, than all the rest of the band put together. Col. Hicky always said it was the only thing Washington was fit for, and he kept the worthless negro simply because he was the image (in bronze) of Gen. Lafayette. Col. Hicky was an octogenarian, and had seen Gen. Lafayette, so he could not have been mistaken. When Washington flagged, a few drops of whiskey was all he needed to refresh his energies.

The whirl of the dance waxed as the night waned. The tired paterfamiliases sat around the rooms, too true to their mission to retire for a little snooze. They were restored to consciousness at intervals by liberal cups of strong coffee. Black William, our first violin, called out the figures, "Ladies to the right!" "Set to your partners?"—and the young people whirled and swung around in the giddy reel as though they would never have such another opportunity to dance—as, indeed, many of them never did. From the porch and lawn windows black faces gazed on the inspiring scene. They never saw the like again, either.

Laughing, wide-awake girls and tired fathers and mothers started homeward at the first blush of dawn, when they could plainly see their way over the roads. I started too early from a party the year before, and the buggy I was in ran over a dirt-colored cow lying asleep in the road. The nodding maid again perilously perched on top the champagne basket, and skiffs with similar freight plied across the broad river as soon as there was sufficient light to enable them to dodge a passing steamboat.

The last ball was a noble success. We danced on and on, never thinking this was to be our last dance in the big house. Clouds were hovering all about us the following Christmas. No one had the heart to dance then. The negroes had already become restless and discontented. After that the Deluge! The big house long ago slid into the voracious Mississippi. The quarters where the wedding feast was spread have fallen into ruins, the negroes scattered or dead. The children, so happy and so busy then, are now old people—the only ones left to look on this imperfectly drawn picture with any personal interest. We lived, indeed, a life never to be lived again.

From *Social Life in Old New Orleans: Being Recollections of My Girlhood*, by Eliza Mc-Hatton Ripley. (Appleton, New York and London, 1912.)

# EDGAR ALLAN POE

## (1809–1849)

The haunted life of Edgar Allan Poe had at least one brief
interval of cheerful everyday comfort. He had come away from
Baltimore with his young wife—for a while, at least, not cough-
ing—and set himself to storm the citadel of New York. Money
was pitifully scarce; there was not even enough to bring along
the invaluable Mrs. Clemm, waiting with the family cat till he
could earn the few poor dollars for her fare from the South.
But he found an honest boarding house down town, not beyond
his means, where the ham was excellent and the tea uncommon
strong; and that evening he wrote back to Mrs. Clemm a letter
often quoted. They have had a square solid meal, described
with the fervor of the ill-fed; he is not drinking at all, so that
trouble is done with forever; now they are upstairs in their room
and "Sis" is mending his pants, which he tore on a nail. In these
garments he set out next morning to the conquest of the city,
and if he did not bring it at once to his feet, he set it directly by
the ears. The first penny newspaper in the city, the *New York
Sun,* was beginning to treat the news in ways that forecast sen-
sational methods of a later day. On the Saturday after he came
to town, April 13, 1844, this paper carried a scare-head an-
nouncement, apparently inserted in haste, that a balloon had

just crossed the Atlantic and that an extra with full details of the flight would be issued at ten o'clock that day. In this extra appeared the story afterward included in his collected tales as "The Balloon Hoax."

If its effect was perhaps not quite so explosive as it seemed to the author, it certainly set the town to talking, and—till the truth could come by telegraph from Sullivan's Island—to believing, or at least hoping. Men had been hoping, ever since men crossed the ocean in ships, that some day it would be crossed through the air, and this reasonable report fell comfortably upon their expectations.

There was not, as there might have been at a later period, a sharp recoil of resentment when the truth became known, as it did almost at once. The hoax was the rich relation of the countrified practical joke, almost a national institution in the forties. This hoax indeed sent Poe into public notice with an admirable splash. He could take two rooms now and send for Mrs. Clemm and Cattarina. If not prosperity, it was at least something like plain everyday comfort—for a while. Then hack work began to creep up on him—and Virginia began once more to cough—and that trouble was not over. There was always Mrs. Clemm to stand by and to understand, and at last there was Cattarina warming with her wise body the chilled feet of the dying girl. But for a little there had been life like anybody's, in the boarding house on Greenwich street.

To this period, then, belongs one of the comparatively few stories of Poe with a distinctively Southern setting—at least for part of its time. "A Tale of the Rugged Mountains" has the scenery of the vicinity of Charlottesville, and in "The Oblong Box" a packet ship is wrecked on its way from Charleston to New York; the flying machine of the present story comes to land not far from the scene of "The Gold Bug" on an island he well remembered from the days of his military service. But as a teller of tales his genius was more at home in the cool air of dreams, and in such times and places as favor the grotesque and arabesque. Let his mind, however, get to work upon the world actually around him, whether of ideas or of geography, and he saw into and beyond it with clear keen eyes. If he could hoax his contemporaries more than once, it was because he could see not only what was there but what might well be. So when, eighty years after this story appeared, the first dirigible did cross the Atlantic, its actual time was almost the same as this, and not a few of the incidents of the trip were much the same. One must know something of aeronautics to appreciate the extraordinary understanding of its principles and possibilities here displayed.

Poe laughed heartily, they say, at the effect this story made upon the public. It is good to be able to leave him laughing.

# THE BALLOON HOAX

## By EDGAR ALLAN POE

(ASTOUNDING News by Express, via Norfolk!—the Atlantic crossed in Three Days! Signal Triumph of Mr. Monck Mason's Flying Machine!—

Arrival at Sullivan's Island, near Charleston, S. C., Mr. Mason, Mr. Robert Holland, Mr. ·Henson, Mr. Harrison Ainsworth, and four others, in the Steering Balloon "Victoria," after a passage of Seventy-five Hours from Land to Land! Full particulars of the Voyage!

The subjoined *jeu d'esprit*, with the preceding heading in magnificent capitals, well interspersed with notes of admiration, was originally published, as a matter of fact, in the "New York Sun," a daily newspaper, and therein fully subserved the purpose of creating indigestible aliment for the *quidnuncs* during the few hours intervening between a couple of the Charleston mails. The rush for the "sole paper which had the news" was something beyond even the prodigious; and, in fact, if (as some assert) the "Victoria" *did* not absolutely accomplish the voyage recorded, it will be difficult to assign a reason why she *should* not have accomplished it.)

The great problem is at length solved! The air, as

well as the earth and the ocean, has been subdued by science, and will become a common and convenient highway for mankind. *The Atlantic* has been actually *crossed in a Balloon!* and this too without difficulty—without any great apparent danger—with thorough control of the machine—and in the inconceivably brief period of seventy-five hours from shore to shore! By the energy of an agent at Charleston, S. C., we are enabled to be the first to furnish the public with a detailed account of this most extraordinary voyage, which was performed between Saturday, the 6th instant, at 11 A. M., and 2 P. M. on Tuesday, the 9th instant, by Sir Everard Bringhurst; Mr. Osborne, a nephew of Lord Bentinck's; Mr. Monck Mason and Mr. Robert Holland, the well-known aeronauts; Mr. Harrison Ainsworth, author of "Jack Sheppard," etc.; and Mr. Henson, the projector of the late unsuccessful flying-machine, with two seamen from Woolwich; in all, eight persons. The particulars furnished below may be relied on as authentic and accurate in every respect, as, with a slight exception, they are copied *verbatim* from the joint diaries of Mr. Monck Mason and Mr. Harrison Ainsworth, to whose politeness our agent is also indebted for much verbal information respecting the balloon itself, its construction, and other matters of interest. The only alteration in the MS. received, has been made for the purpose of throwing the hurried account of our agent, Mr. Forsyth, into a connected and intelligible form.

### THE BALLOON

Two very decided failures of late—those of Mr. Henson and Sir George Cayley—had much weakened the public interest in the subject of aerial navigation. Mr. Henson's scheme (which at first was considered very feasible even by men of science) was founded upon the principle of an inclined plane, started from an eminence by an extrinsic force, applied and continued by the revolution of impinging vanes, in form and number resembling the vanes of a windmill. But, in all the experiments made with models at the Adelaide Gallery, it was found that the operation of these fans not only did not propel the machine, but actually impeded its flight. The only propelling force it ever exhibited was the mere *impetus* acquired from the descent of the inclined plane; and this *impetus* carried the machine farther when the vanes were at rest than when they were in motion, a fact which sufficiently demonstrates their inutility; and in the absence of the propelling, which was also the *sustaining* power, the whole fabric would necessarily descend. This consideration led Sir George Cayley to think only of adapting a propeller to some machine having of itself an independent power of support—in a word, to a balloon; the idea, however, being novel, or original with Sir George, only so far as regards the mode of its application to practice. He exhibited a model of his invention at the Polytechnic Institution. The propelling principle or power was here also applied to interrupted surface or vanes put in revolution. These vanes were four in number, but were found entirely ineffectual in moving the balloon, or in aiding its ascending power. The whole project was thus a complete failure.

It was at this juncture that Mr. Monck Mason (whose voyage from Dover to Weilburg in the Balloon, "Nassau," occasioned so much excitement in 1837) conceived the idea of employing the principles of the Archimedean screw for the purpose of propulsion through the air—rightly attributing the failure of Mr. Henson's scheme, and of Sir George Cayley's, to the interruption of surface in the independent vanes. He made the first public experiment at Willis's Rooms, but afterwards removed his model to the Adelaide Gallery.

Like Sir George Cayley's balloon, his own was an ellipsoid. Its length was thirteen feet six inches—height six feet eight inches. It contained about three hundred and twenty cubic feet of gas, which, if pure hydrogen, would support twenty-one pounds upon its first inflation, before the gas has time to deteriorate or escape. The weight of the whole machine and apparatus was seventeen pounds—leaving about four pounds to spare. Beneath the centre of the balloon, was a frame of light wood about nine feet long, and rigged on to the balloon itself with a network in the customary manner. From this framework was suspended a wicker basket or car.

The screw consists of an axis of hollow brass tube,

eighteen inches in length, through which, upon a semi-spiral inclined at fifteen degrees, pass a series of a steel wire radii, two feet long, and thus projecting a foot on either side. These radii are connected at the outer extremities by two bands of flattened wire—the whole in this manner forming the framework of the screw, which is completed by a covering of oiled silk cut into gores, and tightened so as to present a tolerably uniform surface. At each end of its axis this screw is supported by pillars of hollow brass tube descending from the hoop. In the lower ends of these tubes are holes in which the pivots of the axis revolve. From the end of the axis which is next the car, proceeds a shaft of steel, connecting the screw with the pinion of a piece of spring machinery fixed in the car. By the operation of this spring, the screw is made to revolve with great rapidity, communicating a progressive motion to the whole. By means of the rudder, the machine was readily turned in any direction. The spring was of great power compared with its dimensions, being capable of raising forty-five pounds upon a barrel of four inches diameter after the first turn, and gradually increasing as it was wound up. It weighed altogether eight pounds six ounces. The rudder was a light frame of cane covered with silk, shaped somewhat like a battle-dore, and was about three feet long, and at the widest one foot. Its weight was about two ounces. It could be turned *flat*, and directly upwards or downwards, as well as to the right or left; and thus enabled the aeronaut to transfer the resistance of the air, which in an inclined position it must generate in its passage, to any side upon which he might desire to act, thus determining the balloon in the opposite direction.

This model (which, through want of time, we have necessarily described in an imperfect manner) was put in action at the Adelaide Gallery, where it accomplished a velocity of five miles per hour; although, strange to say, it excited very little interest in comparison with the previous complex machine of Mr. Henson—so resolute is the world to despise anything which carries with it an air of simplicity. To accomplish the great desideratum of aerial navigation, it was very generally supposed that some exceedingly complicated application must be made of some unusually profound principle in dynamics.

So well satisfied, however, was Mr. Mason of the ultimate success of his invention, that he determined to construct immediately, if possible, a balloon of sufficient capacity to test the question by a voyage of some extent —the original design being to cross the British Channel as before in the Nassau balloon. To carry out his views, he solicited and obtained the patronage of Sir Everard Bringhurst and Mr. Osborne, two gentlemen well known for scientific acquirement, and especially for the interest they have exhibited in the progress of aerostation. The project, at the desire of Mr. Osborne, was kept a profound secret from the public—the only persons entrusted with the design being those actually engaged in the construction of the machine, which was built (under the superintendence of Mr. Mason, Mr. Holland,

Sir Everard Bringhurst, and Mr. Osborne) at the seat of the latter gentleman near Penstruthal, in Wales. Mr. Henson, accompanied by his friend Mr. Ainsworth, was admitted to a private view of the balloon on Saturday last—when the two gentlemen made final arrangements to be included in the adventure. We are not informed for what reason the two seamen were also included in the party—but, in the course of a day or two, we shall put our readers in possession of the minutest particulars respecting this extraordinary voyage.

The balloon is composed of silk, varnished with the liquid gum caoutchouc. It is of vast dimensions, containing more than 40,000 cubic feet of gas; but as coal-gas was employed in place of the more expensive and inconvenient hydrogen, the supporting power of the machine when fully inflated, and immediately after inflation, is not more than about 2500 pounds. The coal-gas is not only much less costly, but is easily procured and managed.

For its introduction into common use for purposes of aerostation we are indebted to Mr. Charles Green. Up to his discovery, the process of inflation was not only exceedingly expensive, but uncertain. Two, and even three days, have frequently been wasted in futile attempts to procure a sufficiency of hydrogen to fill a balloon, from which it had great tendency to escape, owing to its extreme subtlety, and its affinity for the surrounding atmosphere. In a balloon sufficiently perfect to retain its contents of coal-gas unaltered in quality or amount for six months, an equal quantity of hydrogen could not be maintained in equal purity for six weeks.

The supporting power being estimated at 2500 pounds, and the united weights of the party amounting only to about 1200, there was left a surplus of 1300, of which again 1200 was exhausted by ballast, arranged in bags of different sizes, with their respective weights marked upon them; by cordage, barometers, telescopes, barrels containing provision for a fortnight, water-casks, cloaks, carpet-bags, and various other indispensable matters, including a coffee-warmer, contrived for warming coffee by means of slack-lime, so as to dispense altogether with fire, if it should be judged prudent to do so. All these articles, with the exception of the ballast and a few trifles, were suspended from the hoop overhead. The car is much smaller and lighter in proportion than the one appended to the model. It is formed of a light wicker, and is wonderfully strong for so frail-looking a machine. Its rim is about four feet deep. The rudder is also very much larger in proportion than that of the model; and the screw is considerably smaller. The balloon is furnished besides with a grapnel and a guide-rope; which latter is of the most indispensable importance. A few words in explanation will here be necessary for such of our readers as are not conversant with the details of aerostation.

(These, as they explain how any guide-rope is used in free ballooning, are here omitted.)

As the original design was to cross the British Channel, and alight as near Paris as possible, the voyagers had taken the precaution to prepare themselves with passports directed to all parts of the Continent, specifying the nature of the expedition, as in the case of the Nassau voyage, and entitling the adventurers to exemption from the usual formalities of office. Unexpected events, however, rendered these passports superfluous.

The inflation was commenced very quietly at daybreak, on Saturday morning, the 6th instant, in the courtyard of Wheal-Vor House, Mr. Osborne's seat, about a mile from Penstruthal, in North Wales; and at seven minutes past eleven, everything being ready for departure, the balloon was set free, rising gently but steadily in a direction nearly south, no use being made for the first half-hour of either the screw or the rudder. We proceed now with the journal as transcribed by Mr. Forsyth from the joint MSS. of Mr. Monck Mason and Mr. Ainsworth. The body of the journal, as given, is in the handwriting of Mr. Mason, and a P.S. is appended each day by Mr. Ainsworth, who has in preparation, and will shortly give the public, a more minute and, no doubt, a thrillingly interesting account of the voyage.

### THE JOURNAL

*Saturday, April the 6th.*—Every preparation likely to embarrass us having been made overnight, we commenced the inflation this morning at daybreak; but owing to a thick fog, which encumbered the folds of the silk and rendered it unmanageable, we did not get through before nearly eleven o'clock. Cut loose, then, in high spirits, and rose gently but steadily, with a light breeze at north, which bore us in the direction of the British Channel. Found the ascending force greater than we had expected; and as we arose higher and so got clear of the cliffs, and more in the sun's rays, our ascent became very rapid. I did not wish, however, to lose gas at so early a period of the adventure, and so concluded to ascend for the present. We soon ran out our guide-rope; but even when we had raised it clear of the earth, we still went up very rapidly. The balloon was unusually steady, and looked beautiful. In about ten minutes after starting the barometer indicated an altitude of 15,000 feet. The weather was remarkably fine, and the view of the subjacent country—a most romantic one when seen from any point—was now especially sublime. The numerous deep gorges presented the appearance of lakes, on account of the dense vapors with which they were filled, and the pinnacles and crags to the southeast, piled in inextricable confusion, resembled nothing so much as the giant cities of eastern fable. We were rapidly approaching the mountains in the south, but our elevation was more than sufficient to enable us to pass them in safety. In a few minutes we soared over them in fine style; and Mr. Ainsworth, with the seamen, was surprised at their apparent want of altitude when viewed from the car, the tendency of great elevation in a balloon being to reduce inequalities of the surface below to nearly a dead level. At half-past eleven, still proceeding nearly south, we obtained our first view of the Bristol Channel; and, in fifteen minutes afterwards, the line of breakers on the coast appeared immediately beneath us, and we were fairly out at sea. We now resolved to let off enough gas to bring our guide-rope, with the buoys affixed, into the water. This was immediately done, and we commenced a gradual descent. In about twenty minutes our first buoy dipped, and at the touch of the second soon afterwards we remained stationary as to elevation. We were all now anxious to test the efficiency of the rudder and screw, and we put them both into requisition forthwith, for the purpose of altering our direction more to the eastward, and in a line for Paris. By means of the rudder we instantly effected the necessary change of direction, and our course was brought nearly at right angles to that of the wind; when we set in motion the spring of the screw, and were rejoiced to find it propel us readily as desired. Upon this we gave nine hearty cheers, and dropped into the sea a bottle, enclosing a slip of parchment with a brief account of the principles of the invention. Hardly, however, had we done with our rejoicings, when an unforeseen accident occurred which discouraged us in no little degree. The steel rod connecting the spring with the propeller was suddenly jerked out of place at the car end (by a swaying of the car through some movement of one of the two seamen we had taken up) and in an instant hung dangling out of reach from the pivot of the axis of the screw.

While we were endeavoring to regain it, our attention being completely absorbed, we became involved in a strong current of wind from the east, which bore us with rapidly increasing force towards the Atlantic. We soon found ourselves driving out to sea at the rate of not less, certainly, than fifty or sixty miles an hour, so that we came up with Cape Clear, at some forty miles to our north, before we had secured the rod and had time to think what we were about. It was now that Mr. Ainsworth made an extraordinary, but, to my fancy, a by no means unreasonable or chimerical proposition, in which he was instantly seconded by Mr. Holland—viz., that we should take advantage of the strong gale which bore us on, and in place of beating back to Paris, make an attempt to reach the coast of North America. After slight reflection I gave a willing assent to this bold proposition, which (strange to say) met with objection from the two seamen only. As the stronger party, however, we overruled their fears, and kept resolutely upon our course. We steered due west; but as the trailing of the buoys materially impeded our progress, and we had the balloon abundantly at command, either for ascent or descent, we first threw out fifty pounds of ballast, and then wound up (by means of a windlass) so much of a rope as brought it quite clear of the sea. We perceived the effect of this manœuvre immediately in a vastly increased rate of progress; and, as the gale freshened, we flew with a velocity nearly inconceivable—the guide rope flying out behind the car like a streamer from a ves-

sel. It is needless to say that a very short time sufficed us
to lose sight of the coast. We passed over innumerable
vessels of all kinds, a few of which were endeavoring to
beat up, but the most of them lying to. We occasioned
the greatest excitement on board all—an excitement
greatly relished by ourselves, and especially by our two
men, who, now under the influence of a dram of Geneva,
seemed resolved to give all scruple or fear to the wind.
Many of the vessels fired signal guns; and in all we were
saluted with loud cheers (which we heard with surprising distinctness) and the waving of caps and handker-
chiefs. We kept on in this manner throughout the day
with no material incident, and as the shades of night
closed around us we made a rough estimate of the distance traversed. It could not have been less than five
hundred miles, and was probably much more. The propeller was kept in constant operation, and no doubt
aided our progress materially. As the sun went down,
the gale freshened into an absolute hurricane, and the
ocean beneath was clearly visible on account of its phos-
phorescence. The wind was from the east all night, and
gave us the brightest omen of success. We suffered no
little from cold, and the dampness of the atmosphere
was most unpleasant; but the ample space in the car
enabled us to lie down, and by means of cloaks and a
few blankets, we did sufficiently well.

P.S. (By Mr. Ainsworth.) The last nine hours have
been unquestionably the most exciting of my life. I can
conceive nothing more sublimating than the strange

peril and novelty of an adventure such as this. May God grant that we succeed! I ask not success for mere safety to my insignificant person, but for the sake of human knowledge, and for the vastness of the triumph. And yet the feat is only so evidently feasible that the sole wonder is why men have scrupled to attempt it before. One single gale such as now befriends us—let such a tempest whirl forward a balloon for four or five days (these gales often last longer) and the voyager will be easily borne in that period from coast to coast. In view of such a gale the broad Atlantic becomes a mere lake. I am more struck just now with the supreme silence which reigns in the sea beneath us, notwithstanding its agitation, than with any other phenomenon presenting itself. The waters give up no voice to the heavens. The immense flaming ocean writhes and is tortured uncomplainingly. The mountainous surges suggest the idea of innumerable dumb gigantic fiends struggling in impotent agony. In a night such as this to me, a man *lives*—lives a whole century of ordinary life—nor would I forego this rapturous delight for that of a whole century of ordinary existence.

*Sunday, the 7th.* (Mr. Mason's MS). This morning the gale, by 10, had subsided to an eight or nine knot breeze (for a vessel at sea) and bears us, perhaps, thirty miles per hour or more. It has veered, however, very considerably to the north; and now, at sundown, we are holding our course due west, principally by the screw and rudder, which answer their purposes to admiration.

I regard the project as thoroughly successful, and the easy navigation of the air in any direction (not exactly in the teeth of a gale) as no longer problematical. We could not have made head against the strong wind of yesterday; but, by ascending, we might have got out of its influence if requisite. Against a pretty stiff breeze, I feel convinced we can make our way with the propeller. At noon today ascended to an elevation of nearly 25,000 feet by discharging ballast. Did this to search for a more direct current, but found none so favorable as the one we are now in. We have an abundance of gas to take us across this small pond even should the voyage last three weeks. I have not the slightest fear for the result. The difficulty has been strangely exaggerated and misapprehended. I can choose my current, and should I find *all* currents against me, I can make very tolerable headway with the propeller. We have had no incidents worth recording. The night promises fair.

P.S. (By Mr. Ainsworth.) I have little to record, except the fact (to me quite a surprising one) that, at an elevation equal to that of Cotopaxi, I experienced neither very intense cold, nor headache, nor difficulty of breathing; neither, I find, did Mr. Mason, nor Mr. Holland, nor Sir Everard. Mr. Osborne complained of constriction of the chest—but this soon wore off. We have flown at a great rate during the day, and we must be more than half way across the Atlantic. We have passed over some twenty or thirty vessels of various kinds, and all seem to be delightfully astonished. Crossing the ocean in a balloon is not so difficult a feat after all. *Omne ignotum pro magnifico. Mem.*—At 25,000 feet elevation the sky appears nearly black, and the stars are distinctly visible; while the sea does not seem convex (as one might suppose) but absolutely and most unequivocally concave.[1]

*Monday the 8th.* (Mr. Mason's MS.) This morning we had again some little trouble with the rod of the propeller, which must be entirely remodelled for fear of serious accidents—I mean the steel rod, not the vanes. The latter could not be improved. The wind has been blowing steadily and strongly from the northeast all day; and so far fortune seems bent upon favoring us. Just before day we were all somewhat alarmed at some odd noises and concussions in the balloon, accompanied with the apparent rapid subsidence of the whole machine. These phenomena were occasioned by the expansion of the gas, through increase of heat in the atmosphere, and

---

[1] Mr. Ainsworth has not attempted to account for this phenomenon, which, however, is quite susceptible of explanation. A line dropped from an elevation of 25,000 feet perpendicularly to the surface of the earth (or sea) would form the perpendicular of a right-angle triangle, of which the base would extend from the right angle to the horizon, and the hypothenuse from the horizon to the balloon. But the 25,000 feet of altitude is little or nothing in comparison with the extent of the prospect. In other words, the base and hypothenuse of the supposed triangle would be so long when compared with the perpendicular, that the two former may be regarded as nearly parallel. In this manner the horizon of the aeronaut would appear to be *on a level* with the car. But as the point immediately beneath him seems, and is, at a great distance below him, it seems, of course, also at a great distance below the horizon. Hence the impression of *concavity;* and this impression must remain until the elevation shall bear so great a proportion to the extent of prospect, that the apparent parallelism of the base and hypothenuse disappears—when the earth's real convexity must become apparent.

the consequent disruption of the minute particles of ice, with which the net-work had become encrusted during the night. Threw down several bottles to the vessels below. Saw one of them picked up by a large ship—seemingly one of the New York line packets. Endeavored to make out her name, but could not be sure of it. Mr. Osborne's telescope made it out something like "Atalanta." It is now twelve at night, and we are still going nearly west at a rapid pace. The sea is peculiarly phosphorescent.

P.S. (By Mr. Ainsworth.) It is now two A. M., and nearly calm, as well as I can judge—but it is very difficult to determine this point, since we move *with* the air so completely. I have not slept since quitting Wheal-Vor, but can stand it no longer, and must take a nap. We cannot be far from the American coast.

*Tuesday the 9th.* (Mr. Ainsworth's MS.) One P. M. *We are in full view of the low coast of South Carolina.* The great problem is accomplished. We have crossed the Atlantic—fairly and *easily* crossed it in a balloon! God be praised! Who shall say that anything is impossible hereafter!

The journal here ceases. Some particulars of the descent were communicated, however, by Mr. Ainsworth to Mr. Forsyth. It was nearly dead calm when the voyagers first came in view of the coast, which was immediately recognized by both the seamen, and by Mr. Osborne. The latter gentleman, having acquaintances at Fort Moultrie, it was immediately resolved to descend in its vicinity. The balloon was brought over the beach (the tide being out and the sand hard, smooth, and admirably adapted for a descent) and the grapnel let go, which took firm hold at once. The inhabitants of the island and of the fort thronged out of course to see the balloon; but it was with the greatest difficulty that anyone could be made to credit the actual voyage—*the crossing of the Atlantic.* The grapnel caught at two P. M. precisely; and thus the whole voyage was completed in seventy-five hours, or rather less, counting from shore to shore. No serious accidents occurred. No real danger was at any time apprehended. The balloon was exhausted and secured without trouble; and when the MS. from which this narrative is compiled was despatched from Charleston the party was still at Fort Moultrie. Their further intentions were not ascertained, but we can safely promise our readers some additional information either on Monday or in the course of the next day at furthest.

This is unquestionably the most stupendous, the most interesting, and the most important undertaking ever accomplished or even attempted by man. What magnificent events may ensue it would be useless now to think of determining.

> Published in the New York Sun, April 13, 1844.

# JOHN ESTEN COOKE
## (1830–1886)

As a minnesinger dedicated his harp to his lady and sang always in her praise, so John Esten Cooke offered his pen to Virginia, his native state.

He was born in the Shenandoah Valley, at Winchester, and brought up in Richmond; one of his ancestors helped to settle Boston, and his grandfather, a physician in the Revolutionary War, was taken a prisoner to Bermuda and married the daughter of a government official who had been president of the Bermuda Assembly. After the War they came to Virginia, by way of the Bahamas, and brought up fourteen children, of whom two became nationally known writers; the third, born in Bermuda, helped draft the new constitution of Virginia and served in the War of 1812; he was the father of John Esten Cooke, his brilliant elder brother Philip Pendleton Cooke, and eleven other children.

It was a happy family, bound by deep affection that extended to the family retainers; John Esten Cooke's own nurse helped to bring up his children forty years later. He was reflective and romantic; would not go to Charlottesville; and read Carlyle, Tennyson, Irving, Emerson and Dumas, then somewhat to be explained away, as "light reading." At any rate he kept vowing to "improve his mind" and "throw general literature to the devil." In like manner he began to write rather in spite of himself, for his career was supposed to be in the law. But Harper paid him ten dollars for a story, and that seems always to confirm a beginner in the pursuit of literature. "This is not breaking my resolution," he explained, "I always excepted writing for pay." In 1852 came his first serious novel, "Leather Stocking and Silk," one of the group of romances of early Virginia of which the one likely longest to live is "The Virginia Comedians," a leisurely and somewhat involved narrative of colonial Williamsburg and the company that there began our theatrical history.

It was by "Surry of Eagle's Nest," however, that he most deeply moved the hearts of his generation. This was written in six weeks, with the money for it mortgaged in advance, in the midst of the crash that came upon his fortunes along with those of all Southern writers directly after the Civil War, and out of the fulness of recent personal experience. "It appears to me," says Surry, "that my memoirs are becoming a pure and simple history of the war in Virginia," and fortunately so they are, for all the romantic complications that keep dodging in and out of the main action. Cooke's uncle Philip was an officer in the Northern army; his daughter Flora married "Jeb" Stuart of Virginia, the greatest of Confederate cavalrymen, whose brilliant figure John Esten Cooke was to picture in the supposed "memoirs of a staff-officer serving in Virginia, edited from the mss. of Col. Surry." It was not necessary to change or even to furbish up the character of Stuart or the incidents in which it was displayed to use him as a hero of chivalry and a pattern of romance. Cooke made no effort to do so, and it is touching to see how often a footnote under some speech of Stuart's in the text carries the reverent assurance *His words. Beauregard, Mosby, McClellan (whom Surry meets when taken prisoner) and especially "Stonewall" Jackson, appear at full length; and the glimpses of Lee are singularly convincing, such as that at Fredericksburg:

General Lee's face filled with blood, and his eye flashed. Turning to one of his generals, who stood near, he said, as he drew his old riding-cape around his shoulders: "It is well this is so terrible—we would grow too fond of it!" These deep-toned words still ring in my ears.

The romance of the War was still ringing in his ears when he wrote this high-hearted memoir. Back at "Eagle's Nest" in 1865, Surry muses:

It was surely a dream—was it not?—that the South fought so stubbornly for these four long years? . . . but the dream was glorious—not even the *immedicabile vulnus* of surrender can efface its splendor. Still it moves me, and possesses me; and I live forever in that past.

He lived a long time after and wrote much; of all Southern writers he was one of the most voluminous. Another war romance, "Mohun," followed "Surry," and biographies of Jackson and of Lee; "Surry" parallels the life of Jackson (its action closes with his death and Surry declares "with the career of this man of destiny had waned the strength of the South") and "Mohun" that of Lee, having the same major events. He married the lady, Miss Mary Frances Page, whose portrait he had drawn in the heroine of "Surry," May Beverley. It is well for that novel's prospects of long life that it was so nearly, as he admitted, "a history of the war in Virginia," for it is the story of one of those to whom that war was no failure but a glorious adventure. It brings back with it a breath of grandeur.

# ON REVIEW

## By JOHN ESTEN COOKE

IN these memoirs, my dear reader, I intend to carefully avoid writing a history of the war. See the histories for that. I aim only at giving you a few pictures and relating some incidents.

Therefore, go to the grave and strictly reliable "official documents" for an account of the situation in May, 1861. I need only say, that at that moment the Federal Government threatened Virginia with three great columns—from Wheeling, Williamsport, and Alexandria; and that the second, commanded by Major-General Patterson, was about four or five times as great as the little "Army of Observation" at Harper's Ferry.

But that army was composed of excellent material. All classes were mingled fraternally in its ranks, by the hand of that great leveller called War. Here was the high-spirited boy, raised in his elegant home on the banks of the Shenandoah, and the hardy and athletic mountaineer from beyond the Alleghanies. The pale and slender student lay down side by side with the ruddy son of the poor farmer, who had dropped the handles of the plough to take up the musket. All were alike in one thing—their eager desire to meet the enemy.

On the day after my arrival, Colonel Jackon reviewed

the troops. As he rode along the line, above which rose the glittering hedge of bayonets, I heard many a smothered laugh at his singular appearance. In fact, the Colonel's odd costume and manners were enough to excite laughter. Fancy a sort of Don Quixote, reader—gaunt, bony, and angular—riding an old, stiff Rosinante, which he pushed into a trot with great difficulty. This figure was clad in a gray coat already growing rusty; a faded cap resting nearly upon the wearer's nose; top-boots, huge gauntlets, and a leather stock which propped up his chin and sawed his ears.

He rode leaning forward, with his knees drawn up, owing to the shortness of his stirrups; raised his chin in the air in order to look from beneath his cap-rim; and from time to time moved his head from side to side, above his stiff leather collar, with an air of profound abstraction. Add to this a curious fashion of slapping his right hand against his thigh, and the curt, abrupt "Good! —very good!" which was jerked from his lips when any report was made to him: and there is Colonel T. J. Jackson, of the Virginia forces.

The young volunteers evidently expected to see a gallant and imposing figure, richly clad, and superbly mounted. When this scarecrow appeared, they with difficulty restrained their laughter. When the review was over, and the young men were marched back to their quarters, I learned, afterward, that they made themselves exceedingly merry on the subject of their commander's appearance—not a few, who had been to the

Lexington Institute, repeating his former nickname of "Fool Tom Jackson."

What was the opinion, it may be asked, of his aide-de-camp, who saw him every hour, and had ample opportunity of observing the man? He did not impress me greatly: and I am obliged to disclaim the deep penetration of that mighty multitude who—long afterward—"always knew what was in Jackson from the first." I thought him matter-of-fact in character, rather dull in conversation, and possessed of only average abilities. He seemed a plodding, eccentric, commonplace martinet. That was the light in which I regarded this immortal.

If I did not admire his intellect, I, however, very greatly respected his moral character. His life was perfectly blameless, and he had not a single bad habit. Spirit never passed his lips, and I should as soon have expected the Potomac to flow backward as to have heard him utter an oath. He regularly said grace at his simple meals, spread on the lid of a camp-chest, and spent hours daily in religious reading and prayer. He was habitually charitable in his estimates of men, and seldom yielded to any sort of irritability. "Eccentric" he was, in the highest degree—but it was the eccentricity of a man whose thoughts were half the time in heaven.

Three days after my arrival, he called me into his tent, and began to talk to me about the war. He listened with an air of great modesty and attention to my crude views, and, when I expressed an opinion that Harper's Ferry would not be attacked, replied briefly:

"I think so too; it will be flanked."

He remained thoughtful for some moments, and then said:

"I wish you to carry a message for me to Colonel Stuart, Captain; you will find him near Martinsburg. Desire him to picket heavily the whole front toward Williamsport, and to establish relays of couriers to give me intelligence. I should like to hear what his scouts report. Before Patterson crosses I must be out of this place, ready to fight him on the"—

Suddenly the speaker paused, and looked keenly at me.

"Captain," he said, abruptly, "never remember any thing but the message I send. My intentions must be known to no one but myself. If my coat knew my plans, I would take it off and burn it.[1]

I saluted, ordered my horse, and in half an hour was on the road to Martinsburg.

Passing rapidly through the beautiful country skirting the banks of the Potomac, I approached the Opequon.

When in sight of that picturesque stream, with its grassy banks, studded with huge white-armed sycamores, I met a cavalryman, who informed me that Colonel Stuart, with a squadron from his regiment, was at that moment passing through the woods beyond. I hastened to come up with him, and, fording the stream, galloped on beneath the boughs of the gay spring forest, which was ringing with the songs of birds.

[1] His words.

Ere long I heard the tramp of hoofs, and a sonorous voice singing one of my favorite songs, "The dew is on the blossom." Five minutes afterward there appeared at a turn of the road, clearly relieved against the green background of the leafy covert, the head of a column of horsemen, in front of whom rode the singer.

Let me draw his outline. He was a man of twenty-five or thirty, of low stature, athletic figure, and with the air of a born cavalryman. There was no mistaking his arm of the service. He was the cavalier all over. His boot-tops covered the knee; his brass spurs were models of neatness; his sabre was light, flexible, and "handy"; his gauntlets reached to the elbows. The young cavalier was evidently at home in the saddle, and asked nothing better than "a fight or a frolic." He wore the blue undress uniform coat of the United States Army, gathered at the waist by his sword-belt; an old brown pair of velveteen pantaloons, rusty from long use, and his bold face was surmounted by a Zouave cap, from which depended a white "havelock," giving him the appearance of a mediæval knight with a chain-helmet. Upon that proud head, indeed, a helmet, with its flowing plume, seemed the fittest covering.

But I have not finished. I am drawing the portrait of one of the immortals, reader, and you can afford to listen to every detail. His saddle was a plain "McClellan tree" strapped over a red blanket for saddle-cloth; behind the cantel was his oil-cloth, containing a single blanket, and on the pommel was a light india-rubber overcoat for stormy days. The chest of his sorrel was decorated with a brilliant yellow breast-cap, a blazing heart in the centre, and the spirited animal champed a strong curb bit, to which was attached a single rein.[1]

I did not notice these details when I first saw Stuart that day. I was looking at his face. It was the picture of martial gayety and enjoyment. A lofty and massive forehead, blue eyes as brilliant and piercing as the eagle's, a prominent nose, a huge brown beard, and heavy mustache, whose long ends curled upward—there was Stuart's countenance. In that face and form, immense health and physical strength shone. This man, it was plain, could remain whole days and nights in the saddle, never growing weary; could march all night, fight all day, and then ride a dozen miles and dance until sunrise.

Such was the splendid war-machine which I saw before me; such the man who now paused in his song, looked at me keenly out of his clear blue eyes, and gave me the frank military salute with his gauntleted hand.

I introduced myself, delivered my message, and rode on with Stuart, who had cordially shaken hands and said:

"Glad to make your acquaintance, Captain. Come, and ride back to camp with me."

So we rode on, side by side, Stuart talking carelessly,

[1] Colonel Surry laughed, and said, when I read this passage: "Don't you think that long description will bore the reader fifty years hence?" My reply was: "The result will be just the contrary, Stuart will then rank with Harry of Navarre and Prince Rupert." Do you doubt that, reader?

with the ease and unreserve of the *bon compagnon,* instead of the stiffness of the West-Pointer.

"Jackson is right," he said, musing, with an absent air; and as he spoke he took off his cap, made a salute, apparently to some imaginary personage, and then replaced his cap. This curious habit I frequently observed in him afterward.

"The enemy will cross near Williamsport," he added; "I am convinced of that. The pickets are already doubled, Captain, and the relays established. I intend to inspect my pickets along the whole front to-morrow. Will you ride with me? You can then make an exact report of every thing."

I accepted this invitation, and Stuart then seemed to banish all "official" affairs from his mind. He turned his head, called out "Sweeny!" and there rode forward from his escort a tall, mild-looking man, of deferential bearing, who carried under his arm an old-fashioned Virginia banjo.

"Come! strike up, Sweeny," Stuart exclaimed, in a jovial voice. "Here is Captain Surry—give him a specimen of your music."

Sweeny saluted me with sad and deferential courtesy, and I expected him to play something like a dead march upon his instrument. Never was any one more mistaken. He struck up that popular song—"O Lord, ladies! don't you mind Stephen!" and if ever the spirit of wild and uproarious mirth spoke from any instrument, it was heard in the notes of Sweeny's banjo. After finishing this gay air, with its burden, "Come back, Stephen!—Stephen, come back!" he played a medley, with wonderful skill—a comic *vis* that was irresistible; and then Stuart, lying back on his horse for laughter, cried:

"Now give us the 'Old Gray Hoss,' Sweeny!"

And Sweeny commenced that most celebrated of recitations, which I heard and laughed at a hundred times afterward, but never without thinking of that gay spring scene—the long line of cavalry winding through the May forest, with Stuart at their head, shouting with laughter as he rode, and joining in the chorus, like an uproarious boy.

Sweeny played then, in succession, "O Johnny Booker, help this nigger!" "Sweet Evelina," and "Faded Flowers"—for this great musician could pass from gay to sad, and charm you more with his sentimental songs than he amused you with his comic *repertoire*. In the choruses Stuart joined—singing in a sonorous voice, with a perfectly correct ear—and thus the cavalcade passed over mile after mile, until, at sunset, we reached Stuart's quarters, near Martinsburg. That individual appeared to me more like some gay knight-errant of the elder-time than a commonplace cavalry officer of the year 1861; and I never afterward, through all his arduous career, could rid myself of this idea. I saw him everywhere during his long, hard work, as commander of the cavalry of General Lee's army, and as that great chief's "right hand"—but I could never think of him except as an ideal personage. He was not so much a soldier of the nineteenth century as a chevalier "from out the old romances."

Are you weary, my dear reader, of this long description? I should be sorry to think so; and I have still some words to add. In these pages Stuart will speak often, and perform many things. Here I wish, "once for all," to give you his outline. Then you will know what manner of man it was that spoke the words and struck the great blows. So I linger still in those old days, spent in the Shenandoah Valley, recalling every incident of my brief visit to the afterward celebrated "Jeb. Stuart."

> From *Surry of Eagle's-Nest*, by John Esten Cooke.

# CHARLES HENRY SMITH
## (BILL ARP)
### (1826–1903)

It has always seemed to me fortunate for one who would like to keep a clear and open mind to her country's history that, living in the North, I should have received my first notions of the Reconstruction period from "Bill Arp: *so called*." My father had brought it home after the War, a little red book with rough jolly woodcuts, and when years after I came upon it he told me it would give me a good idea of how things had been.

It would give anyone a good idea how people took these things in and around Rome, Georgia, to read over these undaunted reports of "runagees" and the fortunes of war, these irrepressible protests from the conditions of peace. The letter here given was called by the Louisville *Courier Journal* "the first chirp of any bird after the surrender," and there can be no doubt that it did give "relief and hope to thousands of drooping hearts." It was addressed, as an open letter, to one whose patriotism was everywhere as unquestioned as his good humor—"Artemus Ward," then on the tour of England, from which he was never to return. Artemus had written letters to the newspapers in time of war; he was now to receive one as from one humorist to another. We have never realized—or at least we have never fully recognized—the responsibility of our humorist in hard and trying times, nor the fashion in which the best of them have been faithful to it. "Bill Arp" helped to clear the air and in so far relieve the situation.

This situation was sufficiently strained. "I ain't got no twenty thousand dollars," says Bill, referring to the Amnesty Proclamation of 1865, by which any man possessed of property worth $20,000 was not permitted to take the oath of allegiance and so was denied the right to vote—a right denied to all commanding officers of the Confederacy and to everyone who had held under it a civil position higher than Justice of the Peace. Georgia had sent to the field 120,000 soldiers and in the War had lost three-quarters of her wealth; two thousand square miles of her territory lay waste, and the public debt was twenty-five million dollars. It was hard times for Bill and Mrs. Arp, for Big John the melishy man, Happy George and his wife Jenny Ann, and the rest of the folks in the little red book.

Charles Henry Smith, though his father came from Massachusetts, was born in Gwinnett County, Georgia, attended the State University and gave up the practice of law in this state to enter the Army of Northern Virginia, where he was a staff officer. His health withdrew him from active service, and he presided at a military court. Early in the War he began to send letters to *The Southern Confederacy*, a paper published at Rome, and he was reading out the first of these—an open letter to President Lincoln—to a group of friends on a street corner, when someone asked with what name it was to be signed. "I haven't thought of that yet," said he. "Take mine, then," cried an honest cracker, Bill Arp the town wag, "for them's my sentiments." At first Smith took his spelling too, for this was a day when phonetic spelling was supposed to be intrinsically funny, but in the edition of 1872 he wisely brought it back to approximately normal, and it is from this version that the selection has been taken.

After the War he went into the State Senate, then took up his law practice once more; toward the end of his life he retired to his plantation. He went on writing letters for the *Atlanta Constitution* for more than thirty years, cheerful homely stories of old times, country dances and frolics, simple home happiness, and such memories as cling to old treasures in old garrets. One may learn much about how we lived in the country long ago from "The Farm and the Fireside," published by the *Atlanta Constitution* press in 1892, and from his "Scrap Book" of 1884, but it will be by Bill Arp's peace papers and letters in time of war that he will be, and should be, longest remembered.

# BILL ARP ADDRESSES ARTEMUS WARD

*From Bill Arp, so-called: a Side Show of the Southern
Side of the War.*

*By* CHARLES H. SMITH

Rome, Ga., September 1, 1865.

MR. ARTEMUS WARD, *Showman*—

Sir: The reason why I write to you in perticler, is becaus you are about the only man I know in all "God's
country" *so-called*. For some several weeks I hav been
wantin' to say sumthin. For some several years we rebs,
*so-called*, but now late of said county deceased, have
been tryin mighty hard to do somethin. We didn't quite
do it, and now it's very painful, I assure you, to dry up
all of a sudden, and make out like we wasn't there.

My friend, I want to say somethin. I suppose there
is no law agin thinkin, but thinkin don't help me. It
don't let down my thermometer. I must explode myself generally so as to feel better. You see I'm tryin
to harmonize. I'm tryin to soften down my feelin's.
I'm endeavoring to subjugate myself to the level of
surroundin circumstances, *so-called*. But I can't do it
until I am allowed to say somethin. I want to quarrel
with sumbody and then make friends. I ain't no giant-
killer. I ain't no Norwegian bar. I ain't no boarconstrik-

130

ter, but I'll be hornswaggled if the talkin and the writin
and the slanderin has got to be all done on one side any
longer. Sum of your folks have got to dry up or turn
our folks loose. It's a blamed outrage, *so-called*. Ain't
your editors got nothin else to do but to peck at us, and
squib at us, and crow over us? Is every man what kan
write a paragraph to consider us as bars in a cage, and be
always a-jabbin at us to hear us growl? Now you see,
my friend, that's what's disharmonious, and do you jest
tell 'em, one and all, e pluribus unum, *so-called*, that
if they don't stop it at once or turn us loose to say what
we please, why we rebs, *so-called*, have unanimously and
jointly and severally resolved to—to—to—think very
hard of it—if not harder.

That's the way to talk it. I ain't agoin to commit myself. I know when to put on the breaks. I ain't agoin to
say *all* I think, like Mr. Etheridge, or *Mr. Adderrig, so-
called*. Nary time. No, sir. But I'll jest tell you, Artemus,
and you may tell it to your show: If we ain't allowd to
express our sentiments, we can take it out in *hatin;* and
hatin runs heavy in my family, shure. I hated a man so
bad once that all the hair cum off my head, and the
man drowned himself in a hog-waller that night. I could
do it agin, but you see I'm tryin to harmonize, to acqui-
esce, to becum calm and sereen.

Now I suppose that, poetically speakin'

"In Dixie's fall,
We sinned all."

But talkin the way I see it, a big feller and a little feller, *so-called*, got into a fite, and they fout and fout and fout a long time, and everybody all round kep hollerin hands off, but kep helpin the big feller, until finally the little feller caved in and hollered enuf. He made a bully fite I tell you, Selah. Well, what did the big feller do? Take him by the hand and help him up, and brush the dirt off his clothes? Nary time! No, sur! But he kicked him arter he was down, and throwd mud on him, and drug him about and rubbed sand in his eyes, and now he's gwine about huntin up his poor little property. Wants to confiscate it, *so-called*. Blame my jacket if it ain't enuf to make your head swim.

But *I'm* a good Union man, *so-called*. *I* ain't agwine to fight no more. *I* shan't vote for the next war. *I* ain't no gurilla. I've done tuk the oath, and I'm gwine to keep it, but as for my being subjugated, and humilyated, and amalgamated, and enervated, as Mr. Chase says, it ain't so—nary time. I ain't ashamed of nuthin neither —ain't repentin—ain't axin for no one-horse, short-winded pardon. Nobody needn't be playin priest around me. I ain't got no twenty thousand dollars. Wish I had; I'd give it these poor widders and orfins. I'd fatten my own numerous and interestin offspring in about two minits and a half. They shouldn't eat roots and drink branch-water no longer. Poor, unfortunate things! There's four or five of 'em that never saw a sirkis nor a monkey-show—never had a pocket-knife, nor a piece of cheese, nor a reesin. There's Bull Run Arp, and

Harper's Ferry Arp, and Chikahominy Arp, that never saw the pikters in a spellin book. I tell you, my friend, we are the poorest people on the face of the earth— but we are poor and proud. We made a bully fite, Selah, and the whole American nation ought to feel proud of it. It shows what Americans can do when they think they are imposed on—*"so-called."* Didn't our four fathers fight, bleed, and die about a little tax on tea, when not one in a thousand drunk it? Becaus they succeeded, wasn't it glory? But if they hadn't, I suppose it would have been treason, and they would have been bowin and scrapin round King George for pardon. So it goes, Artemus, and to my mind, if the whole thing was stewed down it would make about a helf pint of humbug. We had good men, great men, Christian men, who thought we was right, and many of 'em have gone to the undiscovered country, and have got a pardon as is a pardon. When I die I am mighty willin to risk myself under the shadow of their wings, whether the climate be hot or cold. So mote it be. Selah!

Well, maybe I've said enough. But I don't feel easy yet. I'm a good Union man, certain and sure. I've had my breeches died blue, and I've bot a *blue* bucket, and I very often feel *blue,* and about twice in a while I go to the doggery and git *blue,* and then I look up at the *blue* serulean heavens and sing the melancholy chorus of the *Blue*-tailed Fly. I'm doin my durndest to harmonize, and think I could succeed if it wasn't for sum things. When I see a black-guard goin around the streets with a gun on his shoulder, why right then, for a few minutes, I hate the whole Yanky nation. Jerusalem! how my blood biles! The institution what was handed down to us by the heavenly kingdom of Massachusetts, now put over us with powder and ball! Harmonize the devil! Ain't we human beins? Ain't we got eyes and ears and feelin and thinkin? Why, the whole of Africa has come to town, women and children and babies and baboons and all. A man can tell how fur it is to the city by the smell better than the mile-post. They won't work fir us and they won't work for themselves, and they'll per- ish to death this winter as shure as the devil is a hog, *so-called*. They are now baskin in the summer's sun, livin on roastin ears and freedom, with nary idee that the winter will come agin, or that castor-oil and salts costs money. Sum of 'em, a hundred years old, are whinin around about goin to kawlidge. The truth is, my friend, sumbody's badly fooled about this bizness. Sumbody has drawd the elefant in the lottery, and don't know what to do with him. He's jest throwin his snout loose, and by and by he'll hurt sumbody. Thes niggers will have to go back to the plantations and work. I ain't agoin to support nary on of 'em, and when you hear anybody say so, you tell 'em "it's a lie," *so-called*. I golly, I ain't got nuthin to support myself on. We fought ourselves out of every thing exceptin children and land, and I suppose the land are to be turned over to the niggers for graveyards.

Well, my friend, I don't want much. I ain't ambitious,

as I used to was. You all have got your shows and monkeys and sircusses and brass band and orgins, and can play on the petrolyum and the harp of a thousand strings, and so on, but I've only got one favor to ax of you. I want enough powder to kill a big yaller stump-tail dog that prowls round my premises at night. Pon honor, I won't shoot at any thing blue or black or mullater. Will you send it? Are you and your folks so skeered of me and my folks that you won't let us have any amunition? Are the squirrels and crows and black racoons to eat up our poor little corn-patches? Are the wild turkeys to gobble all around us with impunity? If a mad dog takes the hiderphoby, is the whole community to run itself to death to get out of the way? I golly! It looks like your people had all took the rebelphoby for good, and was never gwine to get over it. See here, my friend, you must send me a little powder and a ticket to your show, and me and you will harmonize sertin.

With these few remarks I think I feel better, and hope I hain't made nobody fitin mad, for I'm not on that line at this time.

I am truly your friend, all present or accounted for,

BILL ARP, *so-called*.

P. S.—Old man Harris wanted to buy my fiddle the other day with Confederit money. *He* sed it would be good agin. *He* says that Jim Funderbuk told him that Warren's Jack seen a man who had jest come from Virginny, and *he* said a man had told his cousin Mandy that Lee had whipped 'em *agin.* Old Harris says that a feller by the name of Mack C. Million is comin over with a million of men. But nevertheless, notwithstandin, somehow or somehow else, I'm dubus about the money. If you was me, Artemus, would you make the fiddle trade?

B. A.

From *Bill Arp, so-called,* a side show of the Southern side of the War. Motto: "I'm a good Union man, so-called; but I'll bet on Dixie as long as I've got a dollar."

New York: Metropolitan Record Office. 1866.

# GEORGE WILLIAM BAGBY
## (1828–1883)

Anyone who can remember the days when the elocutionist was a feature of the program at church sociables and parlor entertainments may recall a piece usually set down as "How Ruby Played," to which it is more than likely that he has listened. No doubt he listened to it more than once; it was a good old war-horse and local talent rode it freely, while visiting artists were quite likely to use it for galloping in. He will be somewhat astonished, however, to learn that it was written by an editor of the *Southern Literary Messenger* who was in later years the State Librarian of Virginia. He may even be a trifle taken aback to find that it was really written at all, it has been for so long one of those compositions that slip away from authorship and indeed altogether from print, to live on the lips and in the ears a disembodied existence.

This composition slipped away from its author so soon and so completely that he was not even the first to know that it had come into print at all. Everything about "Jud Brownin'" depends largely upon family tradition; this has it that when Dr. George William Bagby returned, some time after the War, from a lecture trip to New York that was not financially successful, he sought recuperation for his spirits and perhaps his purse by writing a humorous sketch of a countryman at a concert and sending it to a newspaper—whose name seems to have been politely forgotten—with a view to publication. The tale goes on that the editor sent back word that the sketch was unsuitable, but kept the manuscript. Some little time after, a friend of Dr. Bagby's read in print an unsigned story about a countryman at a concert so completely in this author's vein that he could not see why he had not set his name to it. Another friend in another place came upon the composition and declared that no one but Dr. Bagby could have produced it. Upon this they brought it to the author for an explanation, and in this manner he received his first intimation that it had been published.

He was never paid for it, then or thereafter, and, as it kept on with an anonymous career, even its fame was not set down to his credit—but he certainly reached through it more other Americans than by any other means at his command. He reached other countries as well; it was soon translated into German and published in a German musical magazine, where, the story goes, Rubinstein himself read and enjoyed it. Henry Watterson admitted it to his anthology of Southern humor, Edward S. Gregory declared that it reminded him "in structure—though the themes are wide enough apart," of the "Dream Fugue" attached to DeQuincey's "Vision of Sudden Death." It went into most of our readers and all of our speakers, and into not a few of those in England, and now, among compositions less humble, it takes its place here to represent one whose name is woven into the very fabric of literary life in the South for the three decades before 1880. Wherever one turns in the records of those times, one is likely to come upon the honest work, the sound criticism, the appreciation and the encouragement of Dr. Bagby.

Lynchburg is even now so lovely that it must have been beautiful in the early fifties, when it was a typical market town of the Old Dominion, not too busy for comfort, not too large for everyone to know everyone else. Patti gave a concert there, and the local musical society brought many excellent artists to play and to sing; besides, there was local talent and above all, a love of making music at home. At "Avenel," some five miles out, at Liberty, there was always music; young George Bagby's own baritone, his best friend's tenor, and the clear voices of the Burwell girls, daughters of the house. Long after, this plantation was to take its place in our literature: it was the original of the home in "The Old Virginia Gentleman," Dr. Bagby's idyl of the Old South brought back by Thomas Nelson Page into print in 1911. Young Bagby studied medicine and practiced for a while, but his popularity as a newspaper correspondent and the success of the letters of "Moziz Addums" to his friend "Billy Ivvins" showed that his field was journalism, and in one form or another he was a journalist for the greater part of his life. These Moziz Addums letters are supposed to come from a backwoodsman of Buckingham county, visiting Washington (where the author was a newspaper correspondent) and describing to a friend back home the pleasures and perils of getting a patent on a perpetual-motion machine. In the course of these proceedings he gets into various difficulties and is helped by a kind Irish servant-girl whom he marries. A good deal of the fun is supposed to come from the furiously bad spelling, but enough was left to make selections popular as public readings.

When the War broke out, he served on General Beauregard's staff; when it was over, he was broken in health, ruined in fortunes, and threatened with total blindness. It was lecture or starve, and he set to work not only to keep alive but to keep up the spirits of Richmond after the War. Some of these lectures have been preserved—"The Old Virginia Gentleman" was one of them—and their literary quality and the general tone of his writings makes it clear why he was known in his time as the "Elia of Virginia." Later on he became custodian of the State Library of Virginia and held that position as long as he lived.

As editor of the *Southern Literary Messenger* he showed a fortunate blend of good-will and critical judgment in his attitude to Southern writers. As a writer himself, his sense of the ludicrous so combined with realistic treatment that one of his sketches appearing in *Harper's*, "The Virginia Editor," though meant as a caricature, was taken so seriously that a duel was averted at the last possible moment, and only by the intervention of a Member of Congress. Dr. Bagby's life, as recorded by Joseph Leonard in "Dr. George William Bagby: a study of Virginia literature, 1850–1880" (Columbia University Press), is so bound up in that of his time that in following the work of this hard-working man one learns more about others than about the man himself.

# JUD BROWNING'S ACCOUNT OF RUBIN-
# STEIN'S PLAYING

*By* GEORGE WILLIAM BAGBY

"JUD, they say you heard Rubinstein play when you were in New York."

"I did, in the cool."

"Well, tell us about it."

"What? me? I might's well tell you about the creation of the world."

"Come, now; no mock modesty. Go ahead."

"Well, sir, he had the blamedest, biggest, cattycornedest pianner you ever laid eyes on; somethin' like a distractid billiard table on three legs. The lid was heisted, and mighty well it was. If it hadn't been, he'd tore the intire insides clean out, and scattered 'em to the four winds of heaven."

"Played well, did he?"

"You bet he did; but don't interrup' me. When he first set down he 'peared to keer mighty little 'bout playin', and wished he hadn't come. He tweedle-leedled a little on the trible; and twoodle-oodle-oodled some on the bass—just foolin' and boxin' the thing's jaws for bein' in his way. And I says to a man settin' next to me, s'I, 'What sort of fool playin' is that?' And he says, 'Heish!' But presently his hands commenced chasin' one

141

'nother up and down the keys, like a passel of rats scamperin' through a garret very swift. Parts of it was sweet, though, and reminded me of a sugar squirrel turnin' the wheel of a candy cage. 'Now,' I says to my neighbor, 'he's showin' off. He thinks he's a-doin' of it; but he ain't got no idee, no plan of nuthin'. If he'd play me up a tune of some kind or other, I'd—'

"But my neighbor says, 'Heish!' very impatient.

"I was just about to git up and go home, bein' tired of that foolishness, when I heard a little bird wakin' up way off in the woods, and callin' sleepy-like to his mate, and I looked up and I see that Ruben was beginnin' to take interest in his business, and I set down agin. It was the peep of day. The light come faint from the east, the breeze blowed gentle and fresh, some more birds waked up in the orchard, then some more in the trees near the house, and all begun singin', together. People begun to stir, and the gal opened the shutters. Just then the first beam of the sun fell upon the blossoms; a leetle more and it techt the roses on the bushes, and the next thing it was broad day; the sun fairly blazed; the birds sang like they'd split their little throats; all the leaves was movin', and flashin' diamonds of dew, and the whole wide world was bright and happy as a king. Seemed to me like there was a good breakfast in every house in the land, and not a sick child or woman anywhere. It was a fine mornin'.

"And I says to my neighbor, 'That's music, that is.'

"But he glared at me like he'd like to cut my throat.

"Presently the wind turned; it begun to thicken up, and a kind of gray mist come over things; I got low-spirited d'rectly. Then a silver rain begun to fall; I could see the drops touch the ground; some flashed up like long pearl earrings; and the rest rolled away like round rubies. It was pretty, but melancholy. Then the pearls gathered themselves into long strands and neck-laces, and then they melted into thin silver streams run-ning between golden gravels, and then the streams joined each other at the bottom of the hill, and made a brook that flowed silent except that you could kinder see the music specially when the bushes on the banks moved as the music went along down the valley. I could smell the flowers in the meadows. But the sun didn't shine, nor the birds sing; it was a foggy day, but not cold. Then the sun went down, it got dark, the wind moaned and wept like a lost child for its dead mother, and I could a-got up then and there and preached a better sermon than any I ever listened to. There wasn't a thing in the world left to live for, not a blame thing, and yet I didn't want the music to stop one bit. It was happier to be miserable than to be happy without being miserable. I couldn't understand it. . . . Then, all of a sudden, old Ruben changed his tune. He ripped and he rar'd, he tipped and he tar'd, he pranced and he charged like the grand entry at a circus. 'Peared to me like all the gas in the house was turned on at once, things got so bright, and I hilt up my head, ready to look any man in the face, and not afeard of nothin'. It was a circus, and

a brass band, and a big ball, all goin' on at the same
time. He lit into them keys like a thousand of brick, he
gave 'em no rest, day nor night; he set every livin'
joint in me agoin', and not bein' able to stand it no
longer, I jumpt spang onto my seat, and jest hollered:
'*Go it, my Rube!*'

"Every blamed man, woman, and child in the house
riz on me, and shouted, 'Put him out! Put him out!'

"With that some several p'licemen run up, and I had
to simmer down. But I would a-fit any fool that laid
hands on me, for I was bound to hear Ruby out or die.

"He had changed his tune agin. He hopt-light ladies
and tiptoed fine from eend to eend of the keyboard. He
played soft, and low, and solemn. I heard the church
bells over the hills. The candles in heaven was lit, one
by one. I saw the stars rise. The great organ of eternity
began to play from the world's end to the world's end,
and all the angels went to prayers. Then the music
changed to water, full of feeling that couldn't be thought,
and began to drop—drip, drop, drip, drop—clear and
sweet, like tears of joy fallin' into a lake of glory.

"He stopt a minute or two, to fetch breath. Then he
got mad. He run his fingers through his hair, he shoved
up his sleeves, he opened his coat-tails a leetle further,
he drug up his stool, he leaned over, and, sir, he just went
for that old pianner. He slapt her face, he boxed her
jaws, he pulled her nose, he pinched her ears, and he
scratched her cheeks, till she fairly yelled. He knockt her
down and he stompt on her shameful. She bellowed like

a bull, she bleated like a calf, she howled like a hound, she squealed like a pig, she shrieked like a rat, and then he wouldn't let her up. He run a quarter-stretch down the low grounds of the bass, till he got clean into the bowels of the earth, and you heard thunder galloping after thunder, through the hollows and caves of perdition; and then he fox-chased his right hand with his left till he got away out of the trible into the clouds, whar the notes was finer than the pints of cambric needles, and you couldn't hear nothin' but the shadders of 'em. And then he wouldn't let the old pianner go. He fetched up his right wing, he fetcht up his left wing, he fetcht up his center, he fetcht up his reserves. He fired by file, he fired by platoons, by company, by regiments, and by brigades. He opened his cannon, siege-guns down thar, Napoleons here, twelve-pounders yonder, big guns, little guns, middle-sized guns, round shot, shell, shrapnel, grape, canister, mortars, mines, and magazines, every livin' battery and bomb a-goin' at the same time. The house trembled, the lights danced, the walls shuk, the floor come up, the ceilin' come down, the sky split, the ground rockt—BANG!

"With that *bang!* he lifted hisself bodily into the ar', and he come down with his knees, his ten fingers, his ten toes, his elbows, and his nose, strikin' every single solitary key on that pianner at the same time. The thing busted and went off into seventeen hundred and fifty-seven thousand five hundred and forty-two hemi-demi-semi-quivers, and I know'd no mo'."

# FRANCIS HOPKINSON SMITH
## (1838–1915)

As engineer, as artist, and as novelist, Francis Hopkinson Smith left his mark upon his time; as lecturer he increased not only his influence but the circle, already large, of his admiring friends. With all this it would have seemed hard to determine his surest hold upon the hearts, and through them the memories, of his generation, if he had not settled the matter by giving us Colonel Carter of Cartersville.

Just how nearly this charming chivalric figure ever did come to cool actual fact, it is not to our present purpose to consider; enough that the North long since made up its mind that if there never were a Colonel Carter in the flesh there ought to have been. At any rate, he is here now, alive and lovable, one of the most sympathetic figures in our regional fiction, the despair of the reasonable and the delight of those who love their fellow men.

The still lovely Nancy Carter, though taking a gentlewoman's place in the picture and trained to "always let the gentlemen speak," makes quite as definite an impression upon the reader as her more exuberant relative. Through her love-story, hurriedly rehearsed by the Colonel to his friend, comes a glimpse of an Old South forever vanished, and through her part in the conduct of his present affairs one gets some idea of the way in which some of these ladies of the old *régime* met the responsibilities of the new, after their own gentle fashion and with a courage altogether magnificent.

The dwelling-place of Colonel Carter is identified and described in A. B. Maurice's "The New York of the Novelists," where a picture of it is added to prove to coming generations that once it was possible to carry on so idyllic an existence in the midst of brick walls and brownstone fronts. That it was possible to carry it on for so long on credit no one can doubt who has read the chapter in "Colonel Carter of Cartersville" in which he entertains the dazzled local grocer. To be sure he soon left this New York nest and went back to Virginia in a blaze of glory; the special providence that we like to think attends the fortunes of the pure in heart lived, on this occasion at least, up to its responsibilities. But something of the Colonel remains to sweeten the air of the time, and it is good to think that the metropolis once was visited by one who so truly bore the title of a "true Southern lady," who in Benèt's phrase

> "knew the whole duty of womankind,
> To take the burden and have the power
> And seem like the well-protected flower . . .
> And manage a gentleman's whole plantation
> In a manner befitting your female station."

F. Hopkinson Smith was born in Baltimore; he had, as we have seen, a wide choice of avocations, and it was not till he was forty-seven that his first novel appeared; he was fifty before he was well known as a writer. Most of his life he spent in New York, but he kept a clear eye and a good memory for the South and a sympathetic tenderness for days before the War.

# A TRUE SOUTHERN LADY

*By* F. Hopkinson Smith

"Mistress yer, sah! Come yistidd'y mawnin'."

How Chad beamed all over when this simple statement fell from his lips!

I had not seen him since the night when he stood behind my chair and with bated breath whispered his anxieties lest the second advent of "de grocerman" should bring dire destruction to the colonel's household.

To-day he looked ten years younger. His kinky gray hair, generally knotted into little wads, was now divided by a well-defined path starting from the great wrinkle in his forehead and ending in a dense tangle of underbrush that no comb dared penetrate. His face glistened all over. His mouth was wide open, showing a great cavity in which each tooth seemed to dance with delight. His jacket was as white and stiff as soap and starch could make it, while a cast-off cravat of the colonel's—double starched to suit Chad's own ideas of propriety—was tied in a single knot, the two ends reaching to the very edge of each ear. To crown all, a red carnation flamed away on the lapel of his jacket, just above an outside pocket, which held in check a pair of white cotton gloves bulging with importance and eager for use. Every time he bowed he touched with a sweep both sides of the narrow hall.

It was the first time in some weeks that I had seen the interior of the colonel's cosy dining-room by daylight. Of late my visits had been made after dark, with drawn curtains, lighted candles, and roaring wood fires. But this time it was in the morning,—and a bright, sunny, lovely spring morning at that,—with one window open in the L and the curtains drawn back from the other; with the honeysuckle beginning to bud, its long runners twisting themselves inquiringly through the half-closed shutters as if anxious to discover what all this bustle inside was about.

It was easy to see that some other touch besides that of the colonel and his faithful man-of-all-work had left its impress in the bachelor apartment. There was a general air of order apparent. The irregular line of foot gear which decorated the washboard of one wall, beginning with a pair of worsted slippers and ending with a wooden bootjack, was gone. Whisk brooms and dusters, that had never known a restful nail since they entered the colonel's service, were now suspended peacefully on convenient hooks. Dainty white curtains, gathered like a child's frock, flapped lazily against the broken green blinds, while some sprays of arbutus, plucked by Miss Nancy on her way to the railroad station, drooped about a tall glass on the mantel.

Chad has solved the mystery,—Aunt Nancy came yesterday.

I found the table set for four, its chief feature being a tray bearing a heap of eggshell cups and saucers I had not seen before, and an old-fashioned tea-urn humming a tune all to itself.

"De colonel's out, but he's comin' back d'rectly," Chad said eagerly, all out of breath with excitement. Then followed the information that Mr. Fitzpatrick was coming to breakfast, and that he was to tell Miss Nancy the moment we arrived. He then reduced the bulge in his outside pocket by thrusting his big hands into his white gloves, gave a sidelong glance at the flower in his buttonhole, and bore my card aloft with the air of a cup-bearer serving a princess.

A soft step on the stair, the rustle of silk, a warning word outside, "Look out for dat lower step, mistress—dat's it"; and Miss Nancy entered the room.

No, I am wrong. She became a part of it; as much so as the old andirons and the easy-chairs and the old-fashioned mantelpieces, the snowy curtains and the trailing vine. More so when she gave me the slightest dip of a curtsy and laid her dainty, wrinkled little hand in mine, and said in the sweetest possible voice how glad she was to see me after so many years, and how grateful she felt for all my kindness to the dear colonel. Then she sank into a quaint rocking-chair that Chad had brought down behind her, rested her feet on a low stool that mysteriously appeared from under the table, and took her knitting from her reticule.

She had changed somewhat since I last saw her, but

only as would an old bit of precious stuff that grew the more mellow and harmonious in tone as it grew the older. She had the same silky gray hair—a trifle whiter, perhaps; the same frank, tender mouth, winning wherever she smiled; the same slight, graceful figure; and the same manner—its very simplicity a reflex of that refined and quiet life she had always led. For hers had been an isolated life, buried since her girlhood in a great house far away from the broadening influences of a city, and saddened by the daily witness of a slow decay of all she had been taught to revere. But it had been a life so filled with the largeness of generous deeds that its returns had brought her the love and reverence of every living soul she knew.

While she sat and talked to me of her journey I had time to enjoy again the quaintness of her dress,—the quaintness of forty years before. There was the same old-fashioned, soft gray silk, with up-and-down stripe spotted with sprigs of flowers, the lace cap, with its frill of narrow pink ribbons and two wide pink strings that fell over the shoulders, and the handkerchief of India mull folded across the breast and fastened with an amethyst pin. Her little bits of feet—they were literally so —were incased in white stockings and heelless morocco slippers bound with braid.

But her dress was never sombre. She always seemed to remember, even in her bright ribbons and silks, the days of her girlhood, when half the young men in the county were wild about her. When she moved she wafted towards you a perfume of sweet lavender—the very smell that you remember came from your own mother's old-fashioned bureau drawer when she let you stand on tiptoe to see her pretty things. When you kissed her— and once I did—her cheek was as soft as a child's and fragrant with rose-water.

But I hear the colonel's voice outside, laughing with Fitz.

"Come in, suh, and see the dearest woman in the world."

The next instant he burst in, dressed in his gala combination,—white waistcoat and cravat, the old coat thrown wide open as if to welcome the world, and a bunch of red roses in his hand.

"Nancy, here's my dear friend Fitz, whom I have told you about,—the most extraord'nary man of modern times. Ah, Major! you here? Came in early, did you, so as to have Aunt Nancy all to yo'self? Sit down, Fitz, right alongside of her." And he kissed her hand gallantly. "Isn't she the most delightful bit of old porcelain you ever saw in all yo' bawn days?"

Miss Nancy rose, made another of her graceful curtsies, and begged that neither of us would mind the colonel's raillery; she never could keep him in order. And she laughed softly as she gave her hand to Fitz, who touched it very much as if he quite believed the colonel's reference to the porcelain to be true.

"There you go, Nancy, 'busin' me like a dog, and here I've been a-trampin' the streets for a' hour lookin' for flowers for you! You are breakin' my heart, Miss Caarter, with yo' coldness and contempt. Another word and you shall not have a single bud." And the colonel gayly tucked a rose under her chin with a loving stroke of his hand, and threw the others in a heap on her lap.

"Breakfast sarved, mistress," said Chad in a low voice.

The colonel gave his arm to his aunt with the air of a courtier; Fitz and I disposed ourselves on each side; Chad, with reverential mien, screwed his eyes up tight; and the colonel said grace with an increased fervor in his voice, no doubt remembering in his heart the blessing of the last arrival.

Throughout the entire repast the colonel was in his gayest mood brimming over with anecdotes and personal reminiscences and full of his rose-colored plans for the future.

Many things had combined to produce this happy frame of mind. There was first the Scheme, which had languished for weeks, owing to the vice-like condition of the money-market,—another of Fitz's mendacious excuses,—and which had now been suddenly galvanized into temporary life by an inquiry made by certain nabkers who were seeking an outlet for English capital, and who had expressed a desire to investigate the "Garden spot of Virginia." Only an "inquiry," but to the colonel the papers were already signed. Then there was the arrival of his distinguished guest, whom he loved devotedly, and with a certain old-school gallantry and tenderness as picturesque as it was interesting. Last of all there was that important episode of the bills. For Miss Nancy, the night she arrived, had collected all the household accounts, including the highly-esteemed pass-book, —they were all of the one kind, unpaid,—and had dispatched Chad early in the morning to the several creditors with his pocket full of crisp banknotes.

When Chad had returned from this liquidating tour, and the full meaning of that trust agent's mission had dawned upon the colonel, he had buttoned his coat tightly over his chest, straightened himself up, sought out his aunt, and, with some dignity and a slightly injured air, had said,—

"Nancy, yo' interfe'ence in my household affairs this mornin' was vehy creditable to yo' heart, and deeply touches me; but if I thought you regarded it in any other light except as a short tempo'ary loan, it would offend me keenly. Within a few days, however, I shall receive a vehy large amount of secu'ities from an English syndicate that is investigatin' my railroad. I shall then return the amount to you with interest, together with that other sum which you loaned me when I left Caarter Hall."

The little lady's only reply was to slip her hand into his and kiss him on the forehead.

And yet that very morning he had turned his pockets inside out for the remains of the last dollar of the money she had given him when he left home. When it had all been raked together, and its pitiable insufficiency had become apparent, this dialogue took place:—

"Chad, did you find any money on the flo' when you breshed my clothes?"

"No, Colonel."

"Look round on the mantelpiece; perhaps I left some bills under the clock."

"Ain't none dar, sah."

Then Chad, with that same anxious look suddenly revived in his face, went below into the kitchen, mounted a chair, took down an old broken teacup from the top shelf, and poured out into his wrinkled palm a handful of small silver coin,—his entire collection of tips, and all the money he had. This he carried to the colonel, with a lie in his mouth that the recording angel blotted out the moment it fell from his lips.

"Here's some change, Marsa George, I forgot to gib ye; been left ober from de marketin'."

And the colonel gathered it all in, and went out and spent every penny of it on roses for "dear Nancy!"

All of these things, as I have said, had acted like a tonic on the colonel, bracing him up to renewed efforts, and reacting on his guests, who in return did their best to make the breakfast a merry one.

Fitz, always delightful, was more brilliant than ever, his native wit, expressed in a brogue with verbal shadings so slight that it is hardly possible to give it in print, keeping the table in a roar; while Miss Nancy, encouraged by the ease and freedom of everybody about her, forgot for a time her quiet reserve, and was charming in the way she turned over the leaves of her own youthful experiences.

And so the talk went on until, with a smile to everybody, the little lady rose, called Chad, who stood ready with shawl and cushion, and, saying that she would retire to her room until the gentlemen had finished smoking, disappeared through the doorway.

The talk had evidently aroused some memory long buried in the colonel's mind; for when Fitz had gone, the dear old fellow picked up the glass holding the roses which he had given his aunt in the morning, and, while repeating her name softly to himself, buried his face in their fragrance. Something, perhaps, in their perfume stirred that haunting memory the deeper, for he suddenly raised his head and burst out,—

"Ah, Major, you ought to have seen that woman forty years ago! Why, suh, she was just a rose herself!"

And then followed in disconnected scraps, as if he were recalling it to himself, with long pauses between, that story which I had heard hinted at before,—a story never told the children, and never even whispered in Aunt Nancy's presence,—the one love affair of her life.

She and Robert had grown up together,—he a tall, brown-eyed young fellow just out of the university, and she a fair-haired, joyous girl, with half the county at her feet. Nancy had not loved him at first, nor ever until the day he had saved her life in that wild dash across country when her horse took fright, and he, riding neck and neck, had lifted her clear of her saddle. After that there had been but one pair of eyes and arms for her in the wide world. All of that spring and summer, as the colonel put it, she was like a bird pouring out her soul in one continuous song. Then there had come a night in Richmond,—the night of the ball,—followed by her sudden return home, hollow-eyed and white, and the mysterious postponement of the wedding for a year.

Everybody wondered, but no one knew, and only as the months went by did her spirits gain a little, and she began to sing once more.

It was at a great party on a neighboring estate, amid the swim of the music and the whirl of soft lace. Suddenly loud voices and threats, a shower of cards flung at a man's face, an uplifted arm caught by the host. Then a hall door thrust open and a half-frenzied man with disordered dress staggering out. Then the startled face of a young girl all in white, and a cry no one ever forgot,—

"Oh, Robert,—not again?"

Her long ride home in the dead of the night, Nancy alone in the coach, her escort—a distant cousin—on horseback behind.

Then the pursuit. The steady rise and fall of the hoof-beats back in the forest; the reining in of Robert's panting horse covered with foam; his command to halt; a flash, and then that sweet face stretched out in the road in the moonlight by the side of the overturned coach, the cousin bending over her with a bullet hole in his hat, and Robert, ghastly white and sobered, with the smoking pistol in his hand.

Then the long, halting procession homeward in the gray dawn.

It was not so easy after this to keep the secret shut away; so one day, when the shock had passed,—her arms about her uncle's neck,—the whole story came out. She told of that other night there in Richmond with Robert reeling and half crazed; of his promise of re-form, and the postponement of the wedding, while she waited and trusted: so sad a story that the old uncle forgot all the traditions that bound Southern families, and sustained her in her determination never to see Robert again.

For days the broken-hearted lover haunted the place, while an out-bound ship waited in Norfolk harbor.

Even Robert's father, crushed and humiliated by it all, had made no intercession for him. But now, he begged, would she see his son for the last time, only that he might touch her hand and say good-by?

That good-by lasted an hour, Chad walking his horse all the while before the porch door, until that tottering figure, holding to the railings and steadying itself, came down the steps.

A shutter thrown back, and Nancy at the open window watching him mount.

As he wheels he raises his hat. She pushes aside the climbing roses.

In an instant he has cleared the garden beds, and has

reined his horse just below her window-sill. Looking up into her face,—

"Nancy, for the last time, shall I stay?"

She only shakes her head.

"Then look, Nancy, look! This is your work!"

A gleam of steel in a clenched hand, a burst of smoke, and before Chad can reach him Nancy's lover lies dead in the flowers at her feet.

It had not been an easy story for the colonel. When he ceased he passed his hand across his forehead as if the air of the room stifled him. Then laying down his pipe, he bent once more over the slender vase, his face in the roses.

"May I come in?"

In an instant the colonel's old manner returned.

"May you come in, Nancy? Why, you dear woman, if you had stayed away five minutes longer I should have gone for you myself. What! Another skein of yarn?"

"Yes," she said, seating herself. "Hold out your hands."

The loop slipped so easily over the colonel's arms that it was quite evident that the role was not new to him.

"Befo' I forget it, Nancy, Mr. Fitzpatrick was called suddenly away to attend to some business connected with my railroad, and left his vehy kindest regards for you, and his apologies for not seein' you befo' he left."

Fitz had said nothing that resembled this, so far as my memory served me, but it was what he ought to have done, and the colonel always corrected such little slips of courtesy by supplying them himself.

"Politeness," he would sometimes say, "is becomin' rarer every day. I tell you, suh, the disease of bad manners is mo' contagious than the small-pox."

So the deception was quite pardonable in him.

"And what does Mr. Fitzpatrick think of the success of your enterprise, George?"

The colonel sailed away as usual with all his balloon topsails set, his sea-room limited only by the skein, while his aunt wound her yarn silently, and listened with a face expressive at once of deep interest and hope, mingled with a certain undefined doubt.

As the ball grew in size, she turned to me, and, with a penetration and practical insight into affairs for which I had not given her credit, began to dissect the scheme in detail. She had heard, she said, that there was lack of connecting lines and consequent absence of freight as well as insufficient harbor facilities at Warrentown.

I parried the question as well as I could, begging off on the plea that I was only a poor devil of a painter with a minimum knowledge of such matters, and ended by referring her to Fitz.

The colonel, much to my surprise, listened to every word without opening his lips,—a silence encouraged at first by his pride that she could talk so well, and maintained thereafter because of certain misgivings awakened in his mind as to the ultimate success of his pet enterprise.

When she had punctured the last of his little balloons, he laid his hand on her shoulder, and, looking into her face, said,—

"Nancy, you really don't mean that my railroad will *never* be built?"

"No, George; but suppose it should not earn its expenses?"

Her thoughts were new to the colonel. Nobody except a few foolish people in the Street, anxious to sell less valuable securities, and utterly unable to grasp the great merits of the Cartersville and Warrentown Air Line Railroad plan, had ever before advanced any such ideas in his presence. He loosened his hands from the yarn, and took a seat by the window. His aunt's misgivings had evidently so thoroughly disturbed him that for an instant I could see traces of a certain offended dignity coupled with a nervous anxiety lest her inquiries had shaken my own confidence in his schemes.

He began at once to reassure me. There was nothing to be uneasy about. Look at the bonds! Note the perfect safety of the plan of finance,—the earlier coupons omitted, the subsequent peace of the investor! The peculiar location of the road, with the ancestral estates dotted along its line! The dignity of the several stations! He could hear them now in his mind called out as they whistled down brakes, "Carter Hall!" "Barboursville!" "Talcott!" No; there was nothing about the road that should disturb his aunt. For all that, a still more anxious look came into his face. He began pacing the floor, buried in deep thought, his thumbs hooked behind his back. At last he stopped and took her hand.

"Dear Nancy, if anything should happen to you it would break my heart. Don't be angry, it is only the Major; but yo' talk with him has so disturbed me that I am determined to secure you against personal loss."

Miss Nancy raised her eyes wonderingly. She evidently did not catch his meaning.

"You have been good enough, my dear, to advance me certain sums of money which I still owe. I want to pay these now."

"But, George, you"—

"My dearest Nancy,"—and he stooped down, and kissed her cheek,—"I will have my way. Of co'se you didn't mean anything, only I cannot let another hour pass with these accounts unsettled. Think, Nancy; it is my right. The delay affects my honor."

The little lady dropped her knitting on the floor, and looked at me in a helpless way.

The colonel opened the table drawer, and handed me pen and ink.

"Now, Major, take this sheet of paper and draw a note of hand."

I looked at his aunt inquiringly. She nodded her head in assent.

"Yes, if it pleases George."

I began with the usual form, entering the words, "I promise to pay," and then stopped for instructions.

"Payable when, Colonel?" I asked.

"As soon as I get the money, suh."

"But you will do that anyhow, George."

"Yes, I know, Nancy; but I want to settle it in some safe way."

Then he gazed at the ceiling in deep thought.

"I have it, Major!" And the colonel seized the pen. The note ran as follows:—

On demand I promise to pay Ann Carter the sum of six hundred dollars, value received, with interest at the rate of six per cent. from January 1st.

Payable as soon as possible.

GEORGE FAIRFAX CARTER.

I looked to see what effect this unexpected influx of wealth would produce on the dear lady; but the trustful smile never wavered.

She read to the very end the modest scrap of paper so suddenly enriched by the colonel's signature, repeated in a whisper to herself, "Payable as soon as possible," folded it with as much care as if it had been a Bank of England note, then thanked the colonel graciously, and tucked it in her reticule.

From *Colonel Carter and other Tales of the South* by F. Hopkinson Smith. (New York, Scribner, 1902.)

# JOEL CHANDLER HARRIS
## (1848–1908)

"I am a journalist," said Joel Chandler Harris, "and nothing else. I have no literary training and know nothing at all of what is termed literary art." The negative statements may perhaps be set down, at least in part, to his life-long disposition not to make too much of himself, but as to his being a journalist born and trained there can be no manner of doubt. His training, however, was not only of the old school but in a department so unusual that it might almost be called unique; he began on *The Countryman*, the only plantation newspaper that has ever been published. One might have thought it impossible for a paper to thrive with the nearest post office nine miles away, but *The Countryman* had a circulation of two thousand. Here, at Hillsborough, Georgia, the boy learned the printing business, spent his spare time in an excellent library, and, above all, took part in the life of the old plantation and found there the inspiration for Uncle Remus. This folklore philosopher was not to come into literary existence until Harris was on the *Atlanta Constitution*, where one of the local staff had been writing since 1880 negro sketches that had made his "Uncle Si" locally famous. This worthy, however, suffered from the habits of his creator, and could not be depended upon to appear with unquestioned regularity, so Harris, then the paragrapher of the paper, was called in and created "Uncle Remus." Then, as always, he gave himself completely to his paper; as the sketches attracted ever more and wider attention, and as folklore began to be a feature of what was at first only local studies, readers from all over the State, and in time from all over the South, kept sending in legends and memories of their own young days and of tales told them then. Spinning all this and more into shape, and giving to legendry the direct human interest of his personality, was Uncle Remus, long since world-renowned.

It is worth the while of anyone interested in the technique of characterization in fiction to examine with some care the means by which the character of this old man is made to stand out clear. He is no mere mouth-piece for folk-tales. "He had always exercised authority over his fellow servants. He had been the captain of the corn-pile, the stoutest at the log-rolling, the swiftest with the hoe, the neatest with the plough, and the plantation hands still looked upon him as their leader." Now at eighty the "little boy" regards him as the fountain of wisdom and the perennial source of joy. Let anyone too lightly agreeing with his creator's disclaimer of "literary art" consider the fashion in which the figure of Uncle Remus and his little friend detach themselves from the stories and live so definitely that we think we have been told not only what goes on in the sessions reported but what goes on as it were between the acts. "Come down ter dat, an' dey ain't nuffin' dat ain't cu' us," muses the old man, and in a single sentence presents us with one secret of his undying youth.

This story of Mr. Jack Sparrow is chosen not only for its own sake but to indicate the disciplinary uses to which some of these tales were put. Uncle Remus was quite willing to tell stories on any terms and as the spirit moved, but he was no stickler for art for art's sake, and if he could thereby drive home a necessary moral, so much the better for a training for which he felt himself largely responsible. Much of the influence of his type was exercised through the cautionary tale.

# THE FATE OF MR. JACK SPARROW

## By Joel Chandler Harris

"You'll tromple on dat bark twel hit won't be fitten fer ter fling 'way, let 'lone make hoss-collars out'n," said Uncle Remus, as the little boy came running into his cabin out of the rain. All over the floor long strips of "wahoo" bark were spread, and these the old man was weaving into horse-collars.

"I'll sit down, Uncle Remus," said the little boy.

"Well, den, you better, honey," responded the old man, "kaze I 'spizes fer ter have my wahoo trompled on. Ef 'twuz shucks, now, hit mout be diffunt, but I'm a gittin' too ole fer ter be projickin' longer shuck collars."

For a few minutes the old man went on with his work, but with a solemn air altogether unusual. Once or twice he sighed deeply, and the sighs ended in a prolonged groan, that seemed to the little boy to be the result of the most unspeakable mental agony. He knew by experience that he had done something that failed to meet the approval of Uncle Remus, and he tried to remember what it was, so as to frame an excuse; but his memory failed him. He could think of nothing he had done calculated to stir Uncle Remus's grief. He was not exactly seized with remorse, but he was very un-

easy. Presently Uncle Remus looked at him in a sad
and hopeless way, and asked:

"W'at dat long rigmarole you bin tellin' Miss Sally
'bout yo' little brer dis mawnin?"

"Which, Uncle Remus?" asked the little boy, blush-
ing guiltily.

"Dat des w'at I'm a axin' un you now. I hear Miss
Sally say she's a gwineter stripe his jacket, en den I
knowed you bin tellin' on 'im."

"Well, Uncle Remus, he was pulling up your onions,
and then he went and flung a rock at me," said the child,
plaintively.

"Lemme tell you dis," said the old man, laying down
the section of horse-collar he had been plaiting, and
looking hard at the little boy—"lemme tell you dis—
der ain't no way fer ter make tattlers en tail-b'arers turn
out good. No, dey ain't. I bin mixin' up wid fokes now
gwine on eighty year, en I ain't seed no tattler come
ter no good een'. Dat I ain't. En ef ole man M'thoozlum
wuz livin' clean twel yit, he'd up'n tell you de same.
Sho ez youer settin' dar. You 'member w'at 'come er
de bird w'at went tattlin' 'roun' 'bout Brer Rabbit?"

The little boy didn't remember, but he was very
anxious to know, and he also wanted to know what kind
of a bird it was that so disgraced itself.

"Hit wuz wunner deze yer uppity little Jack Spar-
rers, I speck," said the old man; "dey wuz allers bod-
derin' n' longer udder fokes's bizness, en dey keeps at it
down ter dis day—peckin' yer, and pickin' dar, en

scratchin' out yander. One day, atter he bin fool by ole
Brer Tarrypin, Brer Rabbit wuz settin' down in de
woods studyin' how he wuz gwineter git even. He
feel mighty lonesome, en he feel mighty mad, Brer
Rabbit did. Tain't put down in de tale, but I speck he
cuest en r'ar'd 'roun' considerbul. Leas' ways, he wuz
settin' out dar by hisse'f, en dar he sot, en study en
study, twel bimeby he jump up en holler out:

"'Well, doggone my cats ef I can't gallop 'roun'
ole Brer Fox, en I'm gwineter do it. I'll show Miss
Meadows en de gals dat I'm de boss er Brer Fox,'
sezee.

"Jack Sparrer up in de tree, he hear Brer Rabbit, he
did, en he sing out:

"'I'm gwine tell Brer Fox! I'm gwine tell Brer Fox!
Chick-a-biddy-win'-a-blowin'-acuns-fallin'! I'm gwine
tell Brer Fox!'"

Uncle Remus accompanied the speech of the bird with
a peculiar whistling sound in his throat, that was a
marvellous imitation of a sparrow's chirp, and the little
boy clapped his hands with delight, and insisted on a
repetition.

"Dis kinder tarrify Brer Rabbit, en he skasely know
w'at he gwine do; but bimeby he study ter hisse'f dat de
man w'at see Brer Fox fus wuz boun' ter have de in-
turn, en den he go hoppin' off to'rds home. He didn't
got fur w'en who should he meet but Brer Fox, en den
Brer Rabbit, he open up:

"'W'at dis twix' you en me, Brer Fox?' sez Brer

Rabbit, sezee. 'I hear tell you gwine ter sen' me ter 'struckshun, en nab my fambly, en stroy my shanty,' sezee.

"Den Brer Fox he git mighty mad.

" 'Who bin tellin' you all dis?' sezee.

"Brer Rabbit make like he didn't want ter tell, but Brer Fox he 'sist en 'sist, twel at las' Brer Rabbit he up en tell Brer Fox dat he hear Jack Sparrer say all dis.

" 'Co'se,' sez Brer Rabbit, sezee, 'w'en Brer Jack Sparrer tell me dat I flew up, I did, en I use some langwidge w'ich I'm mighty glad dey weren't no ladies 'roun' nowhars so dey could hear me go on,' sezee.

"Brer Fox he sorter gap, he did, en say he speck he better be sa'nter'n on. But, bless yo' soul, honey, Brer Fox ain't sa'nter fur, 'fo' Jack Sparrer flip down on a 'simmon-bush by de side er de road, en holler out:

" 'Brer Fox! Oh, Brer Fox!—Brer Fox!'

"Brer Fox he des sorter canter 'long, he did, en make like he don't hear 'im. Den Jack Sparrer up'n sing out agin:

" 'Brer Fox! Oh, Brer Fox! Hole on, Brer Fox! I got some news fer you. Wait, Brer Fox! Hit'll 'stonish you.'

"Brer Fox he make like he don't see Jack Sparrer, ner needer do he hear 'im, but bimeby he lay down by de road, en sorter stretch hiss'f like he fixin' fer ter nap. De tattlin' Jack Sparrer he flew'd 'long, en keep on callin' Brer Fox, but Brer Fox, he ain't sayin' nuthin'. Den little Jack Sparrer, he hop down on de groun' en flutter 'roun' 'mongst de trash. Dis sorter 'track Brer Fox 'tenshun, en he look at de tattlin' bird, en de bird he keep on callin':

" 'I got sump'n fer ter tell you, Brer Fox.'"

" 'Git on my tail, little Jack Sparrer,' sez Brer Fox, sezee, 'Kaze I'm de'f in one year, en I can't hear out'n de udder. Git on my tail,' sezee.

"Den de little bird he up'n hop on Brer Fox's tail.

" 'Git on my back, little Jack Sparrer, kaze I'm de'f in one year, en I can't hear out'n de udder.'

"Den de little bird hop on his back.

" 'Hop on my head, little Jack Sparrer, kaze I'm de'f in bofe years.'

"Up hop de little bird.

" 'Hop on my toof, little Jack Sparrer, kaze I'm de'f in one year en I can't hear out'n de udder.'

"De tattlin' little bird hop on Brer Fox's toof, en den—"

Here Uncle Remus paused, opened wide his mouth and closed it again in a way that told the whole story.[1]

"Did the Fox eat the bird all-all-up?" asked the little boy.

---

[1] An Atlanta friend heard this story in Florida, but an alligator was substituted for the fox, and a little boy fcr the rabbit. There is another version in which the impertinent gosling goes to tell the fox something her mother has said, and is caught; and there may be other versions. I have adhered to the middle Georgia version, which is characteristic enough. It may be well to state that there are different versions of all the stories—the shrewd narrators of the mythology of the old plantation adapting themselves with ready tact to the years, tastes, and expectations of their juvenile audiences. AUTHOR'S NOTE.

"Jedge B'ar come 'long nex' day," replied Uncle Remus, "en he fine some fedders, en fum dat word went roun' dat ole man Squinch Owl done kotch nudder watzizname."

From *Uncle Remus, his Songs and Sayings, the Folk-Lore of the Old Plantation* by Joel Chandler Harris. (Appleton 1880.)

# MARY NOAILLES MURFREE
## (CHARLES EGBERT CRADDOCK)
### (1850–1922)

The delicate health of Miss Murfree had much to do with her reading but comparatively little with her writing. She was lame from her childhood and spent much of her time among books, especially novels—English, French and even Italian—but when she came to write it was with a vigor all her own and about a people as yet untouched by literature.

She was a city woman, born near Murfreesboro', and only her summers were spent at Beersheba in the Great Smoky Range; but she spent fifteen impressionable young summers there and they gave her the impulse and the material for short stories that she sent first to *Appleton's Journal,* then to the *Atlantic Monthly,* under the convincing name of Charles Egbert Craddock. In 1884 these were collected and given the title of "In the Tennessee Mountains," with this name upon the title page. A year later she called at the office of Thomas Bailey Aldrich at the *Atlantic* and provided our literary history with one of its outstanding dramatic surprises by revealing herself as the author of stories not Aldrich, Oliver Wendell Holmes, nor William Dean Howells had so much as suspected were the work of a woman.

It was more than the picturesque possibilities of the mountain country that made them an instant popular success, more even than the often grotesque features of existence hemmed in by these grim hills; their power was in the vitality of a people who seemed, for all their cramped conditions, at once to dominate and to personify the landscape. Her later novels, even the much-praised "Jerry," had not the drive and force of the first short stories, and it was indeed in this field that she was naturally more at home. As for the one here given, her father was a prosperous lawyer and she herself had begun to study law; it is possible that out of such experience the incidents of the story might have been drawn, but no evidence beyond that of the characters themselves is needed for the fidelity with which the conduct of the candidate and his constituency is sent down. There are feuds, revivals, raids, dancing, love-making, superstitions, in "In the Tennessee Mountains," one of the most striking of the collections of stories by which a region new to our literature was opened to us.

# ELECTIONEERIN' ON BIG INJUN MOUNTING

### By Mary Noailles Murfree [Charles Egbert Craddock]

"An' ef ye'll believe me, he hev hed the face an' grace ter come a-prowlin' up hyar on Big Injun Mounting, electioneerin' fur votes, an' a-shakin' hands with every darned critter on it."

To a superficial survey the idea of a constituency might have seemed incongruous enough with these rugged wilds. The July sunshine rested on stupendous crags; the torrent was bridged only by a rainbow hovering above the cataract; in all the wide prospect of valley and far-stretching Alleghany ranges the wilderness was broken by no field or clearing. But over this gloomy primeval magnificence of nature universal suffrage brooded like a benison, and candidates munificently endowed with "face an' grace" were wont to thread the tangled mazes of Big Injun Mounting.

The presence of voters in this lonely region was further attested by a group of teamsters, who had stopped at the wayside spring that the oxen might drink, and in the interval of waiting had given themselves over to the interest of local politics and the fervor of controversy.

"Waal, they tells me ez he made a powerful good 'torney-gineral las' time. An' it 'pears ter me ez the mounting folks oughter vote fur him agin them town cusses, 'kase he war born an' raised right down hyar on the slope of Big Injun Mounting. He never lef' thar till he war twenty year old, when he went ter live yander at Carrick Court House, an' arter a while tuk ter studyin' of law."

The last speaker was the most uncouth of the rough party, and poverty-stricken as to this world's goods. Instead of a wagon, he had only a rude "slide"; his lean oxen were thrust from the water by the stronger and better fed teams; and his argument in favor of the re-election of the attorney for the State in this judicial circuit—called in the vernacular "the 'torney-gineral" —was received with scant courtesy.

"Ye're a darned fool ter be braggin' that Rufus Chadd air a mounting boy!" exclaimed Abel Stubbs, scornfully. "He hev hed the insurance ter git ez thick ez he kin with them town folks down thar at Ephesus, an' he hev made ez hard speeches agin everybody that war tuk ter jail from Big Injun ez ef he hed never laid eyes on 'em till that minit; an' arter all that the mounting folks hev done fur him, too! 'T war thar vote that elected him the fust time he run, 'kase the convention put up that thar Taylor man, what nobody knowed nuthin' about an' jes' *de*spised; an' the t'other candidates wouldn't agree ter the convention, but jes' went before the people ennyhow, an' the vote war so split that

Big Injun kerried Rufe Chadd in. An' what do he do? Ef it hedn't hev been fur his term a-givin' out he would hev jailed the whole mounting arter a while!"

The dwellers on Big Injun Mounting are not the first rural community that have aided in the election of a prosecuting officer, and afterward have become wroth with a fiery wrath because he prosecutes.

"An' them town folks," Abel Stubbs continued, after a pause,—"at fust they war mightily interrupted 'bout the way that the election hed turned out, an' they promised the Lord that they would never butt agin a convention no more while they lived in this life. Hevin' a mounting lawyer over them town folks in Colbury an' Ephesus war mighty humbling ter thar pride, I reckon; nobody hed never hearn tell o' seck a thing afore. But when these hyar horsethieves an' mounting fellers gin-erally got ter goin' in sech a constancy ter the pen'tiary, them town folks changed thar tune 'bout Rufe Chadd. They 'lowed ez they hed never hed sech a good 'torney-gineral afore. An' now they air goin' ter hev a new election, an' hyar is Rufe a-leadin' off at the head of the convention ez graceful ez ef he hed never butted agin it in his life."

"Waal," drawled a heavy fellow, speaking for the first time,—a rigid soul, who would fain vote the straight ticket,—"I won't support Rufe Chadd; an' yit I dunno how I kin git my cornsent ter vote agin the nominee."

"Rufe Chadd air goin' ter be beat like hell broke loose," said Abel Stubbs, hopefully.

"He will ef Big Injun hev enny say so 'bout 'n it," rejoined the rigid voter. "I hev never seen a man ez onpopular ez he is nowadays on this mounting."

"I hev hearn tell that the kin-folks of some of them convicts, what he made sech hard speeches agin, hev swore ter git even with him yit," said Abel Stubbs. "Rufe Chadd hev been shot at twice in the woods sense he kem up on Big Injun Mounting. I seen him yestiddy, an' he tole me so; an' he showed me his hat whar a rifle ball hed done gone through. An' I axed him ef he warn't afeard of all them men what hed sech a grudge agin him. 'Mister Stubbs,' he say, sorter saft,—ye know them's the ways he hev l'arned in Ephesus an' Colbury an' sech, an' he hed, afore he ever left Big Injun Mounting, the sassiest tongue that ever wagged,—'Mister Stubbs,' Rufe say, mighty perlite, 'foolin' with me is like makin' faces at a rattlesnake: it may be satisfying to the feelin's, but 't ain't safe.' That's what Rufe tole ter me."

" 'T would pleasure me some ter see Rufe Chadd agin," said the driver of the slide. "Me an' him air jes' the same age,—thirty-three year. We used ter go huntin' tergether some. They tells me ez he hev app'inted ter speak termorrer at the Settlemint along of them t'other five candidates what air a-runnin' agin him. I likes ter hear him speak; he knocks things up somehow."

"He did talk mighty sharp an' stingin' the fust time

he war electioneerin' on Big Injun Mounting," the rigid voter reluctantly admitted; "but mebbe he hev furgot how sence he hev done been livin' with them town folks."

"Ef ye wants ter know whether Rufe Chadd hev furgot how ter talk, jes' take ter thievin' of horses an' sech, will ye!" exclaimed Abel Stubbs, with an emphatic nod. "Ye oughter hev hearn the tale my brother brung from the court-house at Ephesus when Josh Green war tried. He said Rufe jes' tuk that jury out 'n tharselves; an' he gits jes' sech a purchase on every jury he speaks afore. My brother says he believes that ef Rufe hed gin the word, that jury would hev got out 'n thar cheers an' throttled Josh. It's a mighty evil sort 'n gift,—this hyar way that Rufe talks."

"Waal, his tongue can't keep the party from bein' beat. I hates ter see it disgraced agin," said the rigid voter. "But law, I can't stand hyar all day jowin' 'bout Rufus Chadd! I hev got my wheat ter thrash this week, though I don't expec' ter make more 'n enough fur seed fur nex' year,—ef that. I must be joltin' along."

The ox-carts rumbled slowly down the steep hill, the slide continued its laborious ascent, and the forest was left once more to the fitful stir of the wind and the ceaseless pulsations of the falling torrent. The shadows of the oak leaves moved to and fro with dazzling effects of interfulgent sunbeams. Afar off the blue mountains shimmered through the heated air; but how cool was

this clear rush of emerald water and the bounding white
spray of the cataract! The sudden flight of a bird cleft
the rainbow; there was a flash of moisture on his swift
wings, and he left his wild, sweet cry echoing far behind
him. Beetling high above the stream, the crags seemed
to touch the sky. One glance up and up those towering,
majestic steeps,—how it lifted the soul! The Settlement, perched upon the apparently inaccessible heights,
was not visible from the road below. It cowered back af-
frighted from the verge of the great cliff and the grimly
yawning abysses. The huts, three or four in number,
were all silent, and might have been all tenantless, so
lonely was their aspect. Behind them rose the dense
forest, filling the background. In a rush-bottomed chair
before the little store was the only human creature to be
seen in the hamlet,—a man whose appearance was
strangely at variance with his surroundings. He had the
long, lank frame of the mountaineer; but instead of the
customary brown jeans clothes, he wore a suit of blue
flannel, and a dark straw hat was drawn over his brow.
This simple attire and the cigar that he smoked had
given great offense to the already prejudiced dwellers
on Big Injun Mounting. It was not deemed meet that
Rufe Chadd should "git tuk up with them town ways,
an' sot hisself ter wearin' of store-clothes." His face
was a great contrast to the faces of the stolid mountaineers. It was keenly chiseled; the constant friction of
thought had worn away the grosser lines, leaving sharply
defined features with abrupt turns of expression. The

process might be likened to the gradual denudation of those storied strata of his mountains by the momentum of their torrents.

And here was no quiet spirit. It could brook neither defeat nor control; conventional barriers went down before it; and thus some years ago it had come to pass that a raw fellow from the unknown wildernesses of the circuit was precipitated upon it as the attorney for the State. A startling sensation had awaited the dull court-rooms of the villages. The mountaineer seemed to have brought from his rugged heights certain subtle native instincts, and the wily doublings of the fox, the sudden savage spring of the catamount, the deadly sinuous approach of the copperhead, were displayed with a frightful effect translated into human antagonism. There was a great awakening of the somnolent bar; counsel for the defense became eager, active, zealous, but the juries fell under his domination, as the weak always submit to the strong. Those long-drawn cases that hang on from term to term because of faint-hearted tribunals, too merciful to convict, too just to acquit, vanished as if by magic from the docket. The besom of the law swept the country, and his name was a terror and a threat.

His brethren of the bar held him in somewhat critical estimation. It was said that his talents were not of a high order; that he knew no law; that he possessed only a remarkable dexterity with the few broad principles familiar to him, and a certain swift suppleness in their application, alike effectual and imposing. He was a natural orator, they admitted. His success lay in his influence on a jury, and his influence on a jury was due to a magnetic earnestness and so strong a belief in his own powers that every word carried conviction with it. But he did not see in its entirety the massive grandeur of that greatest monument of human intellect known as the common law of England.

In the face of all detraction, however, there were the self-evident facts of his success and the improvement in the moral atmosphere wrought during his term of office. He was thinking of these things as he sat with his absorbed eyes fastened upon the horizon, and of the change in himself since he had left his humble home on the slope of Big Injun Mounting. There he had lived seventeen years in ignorance of the alphabet; he was the first of his name who could write it. From an almost primitive state he had overtaken the civilization of Ephesus and Colbury,—no great achievement, it might seem to a sophisticated imagination; but the mountains were a hundred years behind the progress of those centres. His talents had burst through the stony crust of circumstance, like the latent fires of a volcano. And he had plans for the future. Only a short while ago he had been confident when he thought of them; now they were hampered by the great jeopardy of his reëlection, because of the egregious blindness that could not distinguish duty from malice, justice from persecution. He had felt the strength of education and civilization; he was beginning to feel the terrible strength of ignorance. His faith in his own powers was on the wane. He had experienced a suffocating sense of impotence when, in stumping Big Injun Mounting, he had been called upon by the meagre but vociferous crowd to justify the hard bearing of the prosecution upon Josh Green "fur stealin' of Squire Bibb's old gray mare, that ye knows, Rufe,—fur ye hev plowed with her,—warn't wuth more'n ten dollars. Ef Josh hedn't been in the dark, he wouldn't hev teched sech a pore old critter. Tell us 'bout'n seven year in the pen'tiary fur a mare wuth ten dollars." What possibility—even with Chadd's wordy dexterity—of satisfying such demands as this! He found that the strength of ignorance lies in its blundering brutality. And he found, too, that mental supremacy does not of its inherent nature always aspire, but can be bent downward to low ends. The opposing candidates made capital of these illogical attacks; they charged him with his most brilliant exploits as ingenious perversions of the law and attempts upon the liberties of the people. Chadd began to despair of dissipating the prejudice and ignorance so readily crystallized by his opponents, and the only savage instinct left to him was to die game. He justified his past conduct by the curt declaration that he had done his duty according to the law, and he asked the votes of his fellow-citizens with an arrogant *hauteur* worthy of Coriolanus.

The afternoon was wearing away; the lengthening shadows were shifting; the solitary figure that had been motionless in the shade was now motionless in the golden sunshine. A sound broke upon the air other than the

muffled thunder of the falls and the droning reitera-
tion of the katydid. There came from the rocky path
threading the forest the regular beat of horses' hoofs,
and in a few moments three men rode into the clearing
that sloped to the verge of the cliff. The first faint foot-
fall was a spell to wake the Settlement to sudden life:
sundry feminine faces were thrust out of the rude windows; bevies of lean-limbed, tow-headed, unkempt children started up from unexpected nooks; the store-keeper
strolled to the door, and stood with his pipe in his mouth,
leaning heavily against the frame; and Rufus Chadd
changed his position with a slow, lounging motion, and
turned his eyes upon the road.

"Waal," said the store-keeper, with frank criticism,
as the trio came in sight, "Isaac Boker's drunk agin. It's
the natur' of the critter, I'm a-thinkin.' He hev been ter
the still, ez sure ez ye air born. I hopes 'tain't a dancin'-
drunk he hev got. The las' time he hed a dancin'-drunk,
he jes' bounced up an' down the floor, an' hollered an'
sung an' sech, an' made sech a disturbament that the
Settle*mint* war kep' awake till daybreak, mighty nigh.
'T war mighty pore enjoymint for the Settle*mint*. 'T war
like sittin' up with the sick an' dead, stiddier along of a
happy critter like him. I'm powerful sorry fur his wife,
'kase he air mighty rough ter her when he air drunk;
he cut her once a toler'ble bad slash. She hev hed ter do
all the work fur four year,—plowin', an' choppin' wood,
an' cookin', an' washin', an' sech. It hev aged her some.
An' all her chillen is gals,—little gals. Boys, now,

mought grow some help, but gals is more no 'count the bigger they gits. She air a tried woman, surely. Isaac is drunk ez a constancy,—dancin' drunk mos'ly. Nuthin' kin stop him."

"A good thrashing would help him a little, I'm thinking," drawled the lawyer. "And if I lived here as a constancy I'd give it to him the first sober spell he had." His speech was slow; his voice was spiritless and languid; he still possessed the tone and idiom of the mountaineer, but he had lost the characteristic pronunciation, more probably from the influence of other associations than an appreciation of its incorrectness.

"That ain't the right sort o' sawder fur a candidate, Rufe," the store-keeper admonished him. "An' 'tain't safe no how fur sech a slim, stringy boy ez ye air ter talk that way 'bout'n Isaac Boker. He air a tremenjous man, an' ez strong ez an ox."

"I can thrash any man who beats his wife," protested the officer of the law. "I don't see how the Settlement gets its own consent to let that sort of thing go on."

"She air his wife," said the store-keeper, who was evidently of conservative tendencies. "An' she air powerful tuk up with him. I hev hearn her 'low ez he air better dancin'-drunk than other men sober. She could hev married other men; she didn't suffer with hevin' no ch'ice."

"He ought to be put under lock and key," said Chadd. "That would sober him. I wish these dancin'-drunk fellows could be sent to the state-prison. I could make a jury think ten years was almost too good for that wife-beating chap. I'd like to see him get away from me."

There was a certain calculating cruelty in his face as he said this. He was animated by no chivalric impulse to protect the weak and helpless; the spirit roused within him was rather the instinct of the beast of prey. The store-keeper looked askance at him. In his mental review of the changes wrought in the past few years there was one that had escaped Rufus Chadd's attention. The process was insinuating and gradual, but the result was bold and obvious. In the constant opposition in which he was placed to criminals, in the constant contemplation of the worst phases of human nature, in the active effort which his duty required to bring the perpetrators of all foul deeds to justice, he had grown singularly callous and pitiless. The individual criminal had been merged in the abstract idea of crime. After the first few cases he had been able to banish the visions of the horrors brought upon other lives than that of the prisoner by the verdict of guilty. Mother, wife, children,—these pale, pursuing phantoms were exorcised by prosaic custom, and his steely insensibility made him the master of many a harrowing court-room scene.

"That would be a mighty pore favor ter his wife," said the store-keeper, after a pause. "She hed ruther be beat."

The three men had dismounted, hitched their horses, and were now approaching the store. Rufus Chadd rose to shake hands with the foremost of the party. The quick fellow was easily schooled, and the store-keeper's comment upon his lack of policy induced him to greet the new-comers with a greater show of cordiality than he had lately practiced toward his constituents.

"I never looked ter find ye hyar this soon, Rufe," said one of the arrivals. "What hev ye done with the t'other candidates?"

"I left them behind, as I always do," said Chadd, laughing, "and as I expect to do again next Thursday week, if I can get you to promise to vote for me."

"I ain't a-goin' ter vote fur ye,—nary time," interpolated Boker, as he reeled heavily forward.

"Well, I'm sorry for that," said Chadd, with the candidate's long-suffering patience. "Why?"

Isaac Boker felt hardly equal to argument, but he steadied himself as well as he could, and looked vacantly into the eyes of his interlocutor for some pointed inspirations; perhaps he caught there an intimation of the contempt in which he was held. He still hesitated, but with a sudden anger inflaming his bloated face. Chadd waited a moment for a reply; then he turned carelessly away, saying that he would stroll about a little, as sitting still so long was fatiguing.

"Ef ye war whar ye oughter be, a-follerin' of the plow," said Isaac Boker, "ye wouldn't git a chance ter tire yerself a-sittin' in a cheer."

"I don't hold myself too high for plowing," replied Chadd, in a conciliatory manner. "Plowing is likely work for any able-bodied man." This speech was unlucky. There was in it an undercurrent of suggestion to Isaac Boker's suspicious conscience. He thought Chadd intended a covert allusion to his own indolence in the field, and his wife's activity as a substitute. "It was only an accident that took me out of the furrow," Chadd continued.

" 'T war a killin' accident ter the country," said Isaac Boker. "Fur they tells me that ye don't know no more law than a mounting fox." Chadd laughed, but he sneered too. His patience was evaporating. Still he restrained his irritation by an effort, and Boker went on: "Folks ez is bred ter the plow ain't got the sense an' the showin' ter make peart lawyers. An' that's why I ain't a-goin' ter vote fur ye."

This plain speaking was evidently relished by the others; they said nothing, but their low acquiescent chuckle demonstrated their opinion.

"I haven't asked you for your vote," said Chadd, sharply.

The burly fellow paused for a moment, in stupid surprise; then his drunken wrath rising, he exclaimed, "An' whyn't ye ax me fur my vote, then? Ye're the damnedest critter in this country, Rufe Chadd, ter come electioneerin' on Big Injun Mounting, an' a-makin' out ez I ain't good enough ter be axed ter vote fur ye! Ye hed better not be tryin' ter sot me down lower'n other folks. I'll break that empty cymlin' of a head of yourn," and he raised his clenched fist.

"If you come a step nearer I'll throw you off the bluff," said Chadd.

"That'll be a powerful cur'ous tale ter go the rounds o' the mounting," remarked one of the disaffected bystanders. "Ye hev done all ye kin ter torment yer own folks up hyar on Big Injun Mounting what elected ye afore; an' then ye comes up hyar agin, an' the fust man that says he won't vote fur ye must be flunged off'n the bluff."

" 'Pears ter me," said Isaac Boker, surlily, and still shaking his fist, "ez thar ain't all yit in the pen'tiary that desarves ter go thar. Better men than ye air, Rufe Chadd, hev been locked up, an' hung too, sence ye war elected ter office."

There was a sudden change in the lawyer's attitude; a strong tension of the muscles, as of a wild-cat ready to spring; the quickening of his blood showed in his scarlet face; there was a fiery spark in his darkening eyes.

"Oh, come now, Rufe," said one of the lookers-on hastily. "Ye oughtn't ter git ter fightin' with a drunken man. Jes' walk yerself off fur a while."

"Oh, he can *say* what he likes while he's drunk," replied Chadd, with a short, scornful laugh. "But I tell you, now, he had better keep his fists for his wife."

The others gathered about the great, massive fellow, who was violently gesticulating and incoherently asserting his offended dignity. Chadd strolled away toward the gloomy woods, his hands in his pockets, and his eyes bent upon the ground. Glances of undisguised aversion followed him,—from the group about the store, from the figures in the windows and doors of the poor dwellings, even from the half-clad children who paused in their spiritless play to gaze after him. He was vaguely conscious of these pursuing looks of hatred, but only once he saw the universal sentiment expressed in a face. As the long shadows of the forest fell upon his path, he chanced to raise his eyes, and encountered those of a woman, standing in Boker's cabin. He went on, feeling like a martyr. The thick foliage closed upon him; the sound of his languid footsteps died in the distance, and the figures on the cliff stood in the sunset glow, watching the spot where he had disappeared, as silent and as motionless as if they had fallen under some strange, uncanny spell.

The calm of the woodland, the refreshing aromatic odors, the rising wind after the heat of the sultry day, exerted a revivifying influence upon the lawyer's spirits, as he walked on into the illimitable solitudes of the forest. Night was falling before he turned to retrace his way; above the opaque, colorless leaves there was the lambent glinting of a star; the fitful plaint of a whip-poor-will jarred the dark stillness; grotesque black shadows had mustered strong among the huge boles of the trees. But he took no note of the gathering gloom; somehow, his heart had grown suddenly light. He had forgotten the drunken wrangler and all the fretting turmoils of the canvass; once he caught himself in making plans, with his almost impossible success in the election as a basis. And yet, inconsistently enough, he felt a dismayed astonishment at his unaccountable elation. The workings of his own mind and their unexpected developments were always to him strange phenomena. He was introspective enough to take heed of this inward tumult, and he had a shrewd suspicion that more activity was there than in all the mental exercitations of the combined bench and bar of the circuit. But he harbored a vague distrust of this uncontrollable power within, so much stronger than the untutored creature to whom it appertained. A harassing sense of doubleness often possessed him, and he was torn by conflicting counsels, —the inherent inertia and conservatism of the mountaineer, who would fain follow forever the traditional customs of his ancestry, and an alien overwhelming impetus, which carried him on in spite of himself, and bewildered him with his own exploits. He was helpless under this unreasonable expectation of success, and regarded the mental gymnastic of joyous anticipation with perplexed surprise. "I'm fixing a powerful disappointment for myself," he said.

He could now see, through the long vista of the road, the open space where the Settlement was perched upon the crag. The black, jagged outline of the rock serrated the horizon, and was cut sharply into the delicate, indefinable tints of the sky. Above it a great red moon was rising. There was the gleam of the waterfall; how did it give the sense of its emerald green in the darkness?

The red, rising moon showed, but did not illumine, the humble cluster of log huts upon the great cliff. Here and there a dim yet genial flare of firelight came broadly. The men at the store sprang to their feet, shaken by a speechless agitation, when Isaac Boker rushed in among them, suddenly sobered, and covered with blood.

"I hev done it!" he exclaimed, with a pallid anguish upon his bloated face. "I met him in the woods, an' slashed him ter pieces."

The red moon turned to gold in the sky, and the world was flooded with a gentle splendor; and as the hours went by no louder sound broke upon the gilded dusk than the throb of the cataract, pulsing like the heart of the mountains, and the stir of the wind about the rude hut where the wounded man had been carried.

When Rufus Chadd opened his eyes upon the awe-stricken faces that clustered about the bed, he had no need to be reminded of what had happened. The wave of life, which it seemed would have carried him so far, had left him stranded here in the ebb, while all the world sailed on.

"They hev got Isaac Boker tied hard an' fast, Rufe," said the store-keeper, in an attempt to reply to the complex changes of expression that flitted over the pale face.

Chadd did not answer. He was thinking that no adequate retribution could be inflicted upon Isaac Boker. The crime was not only the destruction of merely sensuous human life, but, alas, of that subtler entity of human schemes, and upward-reaching ambitions, and the immeasurable opportunity of achievement, which after all is the essence of the thing called life. He was to die at the outset of his career, which his own steadfast purpose and unaided talent had rendered honorable and brilliant, for the unreasoning fury of a drunken mountaineer. And this was an end for a man who had turned his ambitious eyes upon a chief-justice's chair,—an absurd ambition but for its splendid effrontery! In all this bitterness, however, it was some comfort to know that the criminal had not escaped.

"Are you able to tell how it happened, Chadd?" asked one of the lawyers.

As Chadd again opened his eyes, they fell upon the face of a woman standing just within the door,—so drawn and piteous a face, with such lines of patient endurance burnt into it, with such a woeful prophecy in the sunken, horror-stricken eyes, he turned his head that he might see it no more. He remembered that face with another expression upon it. It had given him a look like a stab from the door of Boker's hut, when he had passed in the afternoon. He wished never to see it again, and yet he was constrained to glance back. There it was, with its quiver of a prescient heart-break. He felt a strange inward thrill, a bewildering rush of emotion. That sense of doubleness and development which so mystified him was upon him now. He was surprised at himself when he said, distinctly, so that all might hear, "If I die— don't let them prosecute Isaac Boker."

There was a sudden silence, so intense that it seemed

as if the hush of death had already fallen, or that the primeval stillness of creation was never broken. Had his soul gone out into the night? Was there now in the boundless spaces of the moonlit air some mysterious presence, as incomprehensible to this little cluster of overawed humanity as to the rocks and woods of the mighty, encompassing wilderness? How did the time pass? It seemed hours before the stone-like figure stirred again, and yet the white radiance on the puncheon floor had not shifted. His consciousness was coming back from those vague border-lands of life and death. He was about to speak once more. "Nobody can know how it happened except me." And then again, as he drifted away, "Don't let them prosecute."

There was a fine subject of speculation at the Settlement the next morning, when the country-side gathered to hear the candidates speak. The story of Isaac Boker's attack upon Rufus Chadd was repeated to every newcomer, and the astonishment created by the victim's uncharacteristic request when he had thought he was dying revived with each consecutive recital. It presently became known that no fatal result was to be anticipated. The doctor, who lived twenty miles distant, and who had just arrived, said that the wounds, though painful, were not dangerous, and his opinion added another element of interest to the eager discussion of the incident.

Thus relieved of the shadow of an impending tragedy, the knots of men congregated on the great cliff gradually gave themselves up to the object of their meeting.

Candidates of smiling mien circulated among the saturnine, gravefaced mountaineers. In circulation, too, were other genial spirits, familiarly known as "applejack." It was a great occasion for the store-keeper; so pressing and absorbing were his duties that he had not a moment's respite, until Mr. Slade, the first speaker of the day, mounted a stump in front of the store and began to address his fellow-citizens. He was a large, florid man, with a rotund voice and a smooth manner, and he was considered Chadd's most formidable competitor. The mountaineers hastily concentrated in a semicircle about him, listening with the close attention singularly characteristic of rural audiences. Behind the crowd was the immensity of the unpeopled forests; below, the mad fret of the cataract; above, the vast hemisphere of the lonely skies; and far, far away was the infinite stretching of those blue ranges that the Indians called The Endless.

Chadd had lain in a sort of stupor all the morning, vaguely conscious of the distant mountains visible through the open window,—vaguely conscious of numbers of curious faces that came to the door and gazed in upon him,—vaguely conscious of the candidate's voice beginning to resound in the noontide stillness. Then he roused himself.

The sensation of the first speech came at its close. As Chadd lay in expectation of the stentorian "Hurrah for Slade!" which should greet his opponent's peroration, his face flushed, his hands trembled; he lifted himself on his elbow, and listened again. He could hardly trust his senses, yet there it was once more,—his own name, vibrating in a prolonged cheer among the mountain heights, and echoing far down the narrow valley.

That sympathetic heart of the multitude, so quick to respond to a noble impulse, had caught the true interpretation of last night's scene, and to-day all the barriers of ignorance and misunderstanding were down.

The heaviest majority ever polled on Big Injun Mounting was in the reëlection of the attorney for the State. And the other candidates thought it a fine electioneering trick to get one's self artistically slashed; they became misanthropic in their views of the inconstancy of the people, and lost faith in saving grace and an overruling Providence.

This uncharacteristic episode in the life of Rufus Chadd was always incomprehensible to his associates. He hardly understood it himself. He had made a keen and subtle distinction in a high moral principle. As Abel Stubbs said, in extenuation of the inconsistency of voting for him, "I knows that this hyar Rufe Chadd air a powerful hard man, an' evil-doers ez offends agin the law ain't got no mercy ter expect from him. But then he don't hold no grudge agin them ez hev done *him* harm. An' that's what I'm a-lookin' at."

From *In the Tennessee Mountains* by Mary N. Murfree. (Houghton Mifflin, 1884.)

# RUTH McENERY STUART
## (1856–1917)

Arkansas is the state in which Ruth McEnery Stuart spent her married life, and here the scene of "Sonny," perhaps her best-known book, is laid; but she was born and raised in Louisiana, and could not only recall the humor and pathos of the plantation but set it down simply and with sympathy and affection. Joel Chandler Harris told her, "You have got nearer the heart of the negro than any of us," and it is not without reason that she was called in her time "the laureate of the lowly." Surely no title could have pleased her more.

According to the supposed narrator of "Sonny," the hero is the boy who has just come into the family in this, the opening story in a loosely connected series making the book. This boy has, to be sure, uncommon qualities, including a sweetness of disposition that not only resists but thrives on the spoiling of a devoted pair overtaken late in life by the ecstasy of parenthood. But the interest of the reader is centered throughout upon the father, the lovable backwoodsman whose hold on the hearts of the reading public was so strong that he was forced to make another appearance in book form. It would be hard to find for a story a situation that has happened oftener in real life than the one here so tenderly and truthfully treated, but just as every

first baby comes to its parent trailing clouds of glory, so everything about this simple story keeps a glow of breathless wonder
and surprise. It is, to be sure, a story of Arkansas, dialect and all,
but it drives deep down through that soil to the springs of human
emotion.

# A CHRISTMAS GUEST

## *By* Ruth McEnery Stuart

A BOY, you say, doctor? An' she don't know it yet? Then what're you tellin' *me* for? No, sir—take it away. I don't want to lay my eyes on it till she's saw it—not if I *am* its father. She's its *mother*, I reckon!

Better lay it down somew'eres an' go to *her*—not there on the rockin'-cheer, for somebody to set on—'n' not on the trunk, please. That ain't none o' yo' ord'nary new-born bundles, to be dumped on a box that'll maybe be opened sudden d'rec'ly for somethin' needed, an' be dropped ag'in the wall-paper behin' it.

*It's hers,* whether she knows it or not. *Don't,* for *gracious* sakes, lay 'im on the *table! Anybody* knows *that's* bad luck.

You think it might bother her on the bed? She's that bad? An' they ain't no fire kindled in the settin'-room, to lay it in there.

*S-i-r?* Well, yas, I-I reck'n I'll *haf* to hold it, ef you say so—that is—of co'se—

*Wait,* doctor! *Don't* let go of it *yet!* Lordy! but I'm thess *shore* to drop it! Lemme set down first, doctor, here by the fire an' git het th'ugh. Not yet! My ol' shin-bones stan' up thess like a pair o' dog-irons. Lemme bridge 'em over first 'th somethin' soft. That'll do. She patched that quilt herself. Hold on a minute, 'tel I git the aidges of it under my ol' boots, to keep it f'om saggin' down in the middle.

There, now! Merciful goodness, but I never! I'd ruther trus' myself with a whole playin' fountain in blowed glass'n sech ez this.

Stoop down there, doctor, please, sir, an' shove the end o' this quilt a leetle further under my foot, won't you? Ef it was to let up sudden, I wouldn't have no more lap'n what any other fool man's got.

'N' now—you go to *her*.

I'd feel a heap safer ef this quilt was nailed to the flo' on each side o' my legs. They're trimblin' so I dunno what minute my feet'll let go their holt.

An' she don't know it yet! An' he layin' here, dressed up in all the little clo'es she sewed! She mus' be purty bad. I dunno, though: maybe that's gen'ally the way.

They're keepin' mighty still in that room. Blessed ef I don't begin to feel 'is warmth in my ol' knee-bones! An' he's a-breathin' thess ez reg'lar ez that clock, on'y quicker. Lordy! An' she don't know it yet! An' he a boy! He takes that after the Joneses; we've all been boys in our male branch. When that name strikes, seem like it comes to stay. Now for a girl—

Wonder if he ain't covered up mos' too clos't. Seem like he snuffles purty loud—for a beginner.

Doctor! *oh*, doctor! I say, *doctor!*

Strange he don't hear—'n' I don't like to holler no louder. Wonder ef she could be worse? Ef I could thess

reach somethin' to knock with! I daresn't lif' my feet,
less'n the whole business'd fall through.

Oh, doc! Here he comes now— *Doctor*, I say, don't
you think maybe he's covered up too—

How's *she*, doctor? "Thess the same," you say? 'n'
she don't know yet—about him? "In a couple o' hours,"
you say? Well, don't lemme keep you, doctor. But, tell
me, don't you think maybe he's covered up a leetle too
close-t?

That's better. An' now I've saw him befo' she did!
An' I didn't want to, neither.

Poor, leetle, weenchy bit of a thing! Ef he ain't the
*very* littlest! Lordy, Lordy, Lordy! But I s'pose all
thet's needed in a baby is a startin'-p'int big enough to
hol' the fam'ly characteristics. I s'pose maybe he is, but
the po' little thing mus' feel sort o' scrouged with 'em,
ef he's got 'em all—the Joneses' an' the Simses'. Seems
to me he favors her a little thess aroun' the mouth.

An' she don't know it yet!

Lord! But my legs ache like ez if they was bein'
wrenched off. I've got 'em on sech a strain, somehow.
An' he on'y a half hour ol', an' two hours mo' 'fo' I can
budge! Lord, Lord! how *will* I stand it!

*God bless 'im!* Doc! He's a-sneezin'! Come quick!
Shore ez I'm here, he snez twice-t!

Don't you reckon you better pile some mo' wood on
the fire an—

What's that you say? "Fetch 'im along"? An' has she
ast for 'im? Bless the Lord! I say. But a couple of you'll

have to come help me loosen up 'fo' I can stir, doctor.

Here, you stan' on that side the quilt, whiles I stir my foot to the flo' where it won't slip—an' Dicey—, where's that nigger Dicey? Yo, Dicey, come on here, an' tromp on the other side o' this bedquilt till I h'ist yo' young marster up on to my shoulder.

No, you don't take 'im, neither. I'll tote him myself.

Now, go fetch a piller till I lay 'im on it. That's it. And now git me somethin' stiff to lay the piller on. There! That lapbo'd'll do. Why didn't I think about that befo'? It's a heap safeter 'n my ole knee-j'ints. Now, I've got 'im *se*cure. *Wait*, doctor—hold on! I'm afeered you'll haf to ca'y 'im in to her, after all? I'll cry ef I do it. I'm trimblin' like ez ef I had a 'ager, thess a-startin' in with 'im—an' seein' me give way might make her nervous. You take 'im to her, and lemme come in sort o' unconcerned terreckly, after she an' 'im 've kind o' got acquainted. Dast you hold 'im that-a-way, doctor, 'thout no support to 'is spinal colume? I s'pose he *is* too sof' to snap, but I wouldn't resk it. Reckon I can slip in the other do' where she won't see me, an' view the meetin'.

Yas, I'm right here, honey! (The idea o' her a-callin' for me an' *him* in 'er arms!) I'm right here, honey— mother! Don't min' me a-cryin'! I'm all broke up, some- how; but don't you fret. I'm right here by yo' side on my knees, in pure thankfulness.

Bless His name, I say! You know he's a boy, don't

yer? I been a holdin' 'im all day—'t least ever sence
they dressed 'im, purty nigh a' hour ago. An' he's slep'
—an' waked up—an' yawned—an' snez—an' wunk—
an' sniffed—'thout me sayin' a word. Opened an' shet
his little fist, once-t, like ez ef he craved to shake hands,
howdy! He cert'n'ly does perform 'is functions wonderful.

Yas, doctor; I'm a-comin', right now.

Go to sleep now, honey, you an' him, an' I'll be right
on the spot when needed. Lemme whisper to her thess a
minute, doctor?

I thess want to tell you, honey, thet you never, even
in yo' young days, looked ez purty to my eyes ez what
you do right now. An' that boy is *yo' boy*, an' I ain't
a-goin' to lay no mo' claim to 'im 'n to see thet you have
yo' way with 'im—you hear? An' now good night, honey,
an' go to sleep.

They wasn't nothin' lef' for me to do but to come out
here in this ol' woodshed where nobody wouldn't see
me ac' like a plumb baby.

An' now, seem like I *can't* git over it! The idea o'
me, fifty year ol', actin' like this!

An' she knows it! An' she's *got* 'im—*a boy*—layin' in
the bed 'longside 'er.

"Mother an' child doin' well!" Lord, Lord! How
often I've heerd that said! But it never give me the all-
overs like it does now, some way.

Guess I'll gether up a' armful o' wood, an' try to act

unconcerned—an' laws-a-mercy-me! Ef—to-day— ain't-been-Christmas! My! my! my! An' it come an' gone befo' I remembered!

I'll haf to lay this wood down ag'in *an' think.*

I've had many a welcome Christmas gif' in my life, but the idee o' the good Lord a-timin' *this* like that!

Christmas! An' a boy! An' she doin' well!

No wonder that ol' turkey-gobbler sets up on them rafters blinkin' at me so peaceful! He knows he's done passed a critical time o' life—

You've done crossed another bridge safe-t, ol' gobbly, an' you can *afford* to blink—an' to set out in the clair moonlight, 'stid o' roostin' back in the shadders same ez you been doin'.

You was to've died by accident las' night, but the new visitor thet's dropped in on us ain't cut 'is turkey teeth yet, an' his mother—

Lord, how that name sounds! Mother! I hardly know 'er by it, long ez I been tryin' to fit it to 'er—an' fearin' to, too, less'n somethin' might go wrong with either one.

I even been callin' him "it" to myse'f, all along, so 'feerd thet ef I set my min' on either the "he" or the "she" the other one might take a notion to come—an' I didn't want any disappointment mixed in with the arrival.

But now he's come—an' registered, ez they say at the polls,—I know I sort o' counted on the boy, some way.

Lordy! but he's little! Ef he hadn't 'a' showed up so many of his functions spontaneous, I'd be oneasy less'n he mightn't have 'em; but they're there! Bless goodness, they're there!

An' he snez prezac'ly, for all the world, like my po' ol' pap—a reg'lar little cat sneeze, thess like all the Joneses.

Well, Mr. Turkey, befo' I go back into the house, I'm a-goin' to make you a solemn promise.

You go free till about this time next year, *anyhow*. You an' me'l celebrate the birthday between ourselves with that contrac'. You needn't git oneasy Thanksgivin', or picnic-time, or Easter, or no other time 'twixt this an' nex' Christmas—less'n, of co'se, you stray off an' git stole.

An' this here reprieve, I want you to understand, is a present from the junior member of the firm.

Lord! but I'm that tickled! This here wood ain't much needed in the house,—the wood-boxes 're all full, —but I can't *de*vise no other excuse for vacatin'—thess at this time.

S'pose I *might* gether up some eggs out'n the nests, but it'd look sort o' flighty to go egg-huntin' here at midnight—an' he not two hours ol'.

I dunno, either, come to think; she might need a new-laid egg—sof'-b'iled. Reckon I'll take a couple in my hands—an' one or two sticks o' wood—an' I'll draw a bucket o' water too—an' tote *that* in.

Goodness! but this back yard is bright ez day! Goin'

to be a clair, cool night—moon out, full an' white. Ef this ain't the *stillest* stillness!

Thess such a night, for all the world, I reckon, ez the first Christmas, when HE come—

> When shepherds watched their flocks by night,
> All seated on the ground,
> The angel o' the Lord come down,
> En' glory shone around—

thess like the hymn says.

The whole o' this back yard is full o' glory this minute. Th' ain't nothin' too low down an' mean for it to shine on, neither—not even the well-pump or the cattle-trough—'r the pig-pen—'r even me.

Thess look at me, covered over with it! An' how it does shine on the roof o' the house where they lay—her an' him!

I suppose that roof has shined that-a-way frosty nights 'fo' to-night; but some way I never seemed to see it.

Don't reckon the creakin' o' this windlass could disturb her—or him.

Reckon I might go turn a little mo' cotton-seed in the troughs for them cows—an' put some extry oats out for the mules an' the doctor's mare—an' onchain Rover, an' let 'im stretch 'is legs a little. I'd like everythin' on the place to know he's come, an' to feel the diff'ence.

Well, now I'll load up—an' I do hope nobody won't notice the *re*dic'lousness of it.

You say she's asleep, doctor, an' th' ain't nothin' mo' needed to be did—an' yo' goin'?

Don't, fr' gracious sakes! go, doctor, an' leave me!
I won't know what on top o' the round earth to do,
ef-ef— You know she—she might wake up—or he!

You say Dicey she knows. But she's on'y a nigger,
doctor. Yes: I know she's had exper'ence with the common rin o' babies, but—

Lemme go an' set down this bucket, an' lay this stick
o' wood on the fire, an' put these eggs down, so's I can
talk with you free-handed.

Step here to the do', doctor. I say, doc, ef it's a question o' the size o' yo' bill, you can make it out to suit
yo'self—or, I'll tell you what I'll do? You stay right
along here a day or so—tell to-morrow or nex' day, anyhow—an' I'll sen' you a whole bale o' cotton—an' you
can sen' back any change you see fit—or none—*or none*,
I say. Or, ef you'd ruther take it out in perpaters an'
corn an' sorghum, thess say so, an' how much of each.

But *what?* "It wouldn't be right? Th' ain't no use,"
you say? An' you'll *shore* come back to-morrer? Well.
But, by-the-way, doctor, did you know to-day was
Christmas? Of co'se I might've knew you did—but I
never. An' now it seems to me like Christmas, an' fo'th o'
July, an' "Hail Columbia, happy lan' " all b'iled down
into one big jubilee!

But tell me doctor, confidential—Sh!—step here a
little further back—tell me, don't you think he's to say a
leetle bit undersized? Speak out, ef he is.

Wh—how'd you say? "Mejun," eh? Thess mejun!
An' they do come even littler yet? An' you say mejum

babies 're thess ez liable to turn out likely an' strong ez over-sizes, eh? Mh—hm! Well, I reckon you *know*— an' maybe the less they have to contend with at the start the better.

Oh, thanky, doctor! Don't be afeerd o' wrenchin' my wris'! A thousand thankies! Yo' word for it, he's a fine boy! An' you've inspected a good many, an' of co'se you know—yas, yas! Shake ez hard ez you like—up an' down—up an' down!

An' now I'll go git yo' horse—an' don't ride 'er too hard to-night, 'cause I've put a double po'tion of oats in her trough ahile ago. The junior member he give instructions that everything on the place was to have a' extry feed to-night—an' of co'se I went and obeyed orders.

Now—'fo' you start, doctor—I ain't got a thing stronger 'n raspberry corjal in the house—but ef you'll drink a glass o' that with me? (Of co'se he will!)

She made this 'erself, doctor—picked the berries an' all—an' I raised the little sugar thet's in it. Well, good-night, doctor! To-morrer, shore!

SH-H!

How that do' latch does click! Thess like thunder!

Sh-h! Dicey, you go draw yo' pallet close-t outside the do', an' lay down—an' I'll set here by the fire an' keep watch.

How my ol' stockin'-feet do tromp! So lemme hurry an' set down! Seem like this room's awful rackety, the fire a-poppin' an' tumblin', an' me breathin' like a por-

poise. Even the clock ticks ez excited ez I feel. Wonder
how they sleep through it all! But they do. He beats
her a-snorin' a'ready, blest ef he don't! Wonder ef he
knows he's born into the world, po' little thing! I reckon
not; but they's no tellin'. Maybe that's th' one thing
the good Lord gives 'em *to* know, so's they'll realize
what to begin to study about—theirselves an' the world
—how to fight it an' keep friends with it at the same
time. Ef I could giggle an' sigh both at once-t, seem like
I'd be relieved. Somehow I feel sort o' tight 'round the
heart—an' wide awake an'—

How that clock *does* travel—an' how they all keep
time, he an' she—an' it—an' me—an' the fire a roa'in'
up the chimbley, playin' a tune all around us like a'
organ, an' he—an' she—an' he—an' it—an' he—an'.

Blest ef I don't hear singing—an' how white the
moonlight is! They's angels all over the house—an'
their robes is breshin' the roof whiles they sing—

His head had fallen. He was dreaming.

From *Sonny: a Christmas Guest* by Ruth
McEnery Stuart. (Century, 1897.)

# WILLIAM SIDNEY PORTER
## (O. HENRY)
### (1862–1910)

"I was born and raised in No'th Ca'lina," said O. Henry, "and at eighteen came to Texas and ran wild on the prairies." In Texas he punched cattle and followed, rapidly and cheerfully, a variety of trades; here he was a draughtsman, a bookkeeper; here he sang in church; here he married, and here he met his life's tragedy. It is useful for our present purpose to recall that here he was a member of a military company such as figures in "The Moment of Victory."

His later years were spent in New York, and his best-known stories were written about Bagdad-on-the Subway; he never returned to Texas, though the scene of more than one famous tale is laid there. The Lone Star State is more than a scene and background; it is a pervading spirit. A state so vast and varied could not be represented by a single story, were this to depend for its distinction upon local color, manners or customs. There are too many kinds of weather in Texas, too many counties, too many types of landscape and ways of making a living between the northern boundary and the Gulf and the Mexican border, for one story to stand for them all. But this story stands

for one conviction held in common, well based on experience—
that in the matter of a war it will save time to let Texas attend
to it, and to let her alone while she does.

There are men who trained in Texas for a war more deadly
than that with Spain, who will recognize in the man-to-man
protest of the soldier to his officer and in the manner of the
officer's reply, accents familiar and respected. They may even
sound familiar to one who has read "The Militia Company
Drill," earlier in this collection. Democracy had a long time to
work in early days in Georgia, while the section was separated
from more aristocratic neighbors; Texas too had a long time to
herself, in which democracy was working. The great American
experiment takes on a bracing character when something of the
West sharpens the air of the South. No one, it seems to me, knows
America who knows nothing of Texas. If he knows even a little,
he will soon recognize something familiar in this tale.

# THE MOMENT OF VICTORY

*By* O. HENRY

BEN GRANGER is a war veteran aged twenty-nine—which should enable you to guess the war. He is also principal merchant and postmaster of Cadiz, a little town over which the breezes from the Gulf of Mexico perpetually blow.

Ben helped to hurl the Don from his stronghold in the Greater Antilles; and then, hiking across half the world, he marched as a corporal-usher up and down the blazing tropic aisles of the open-air college in which the Filipino was schooled. Now, with his bayonet beaten into a cheese slicer, he rallies his corporal's guard of cronies in the shade of his well-whittled porch, instead of in the matted jungles of Mindanao. Always have his interest and choice been for deeds rather than for words; but the consideration and digestion of motives is not beyond him, as this story, which is his, will attest.

"What is it," he asked me one moonlit eve, as we sat among his boxes and barrels, "that generally makes men go through dangers, and fire, and trouble, and starvation, and battle, and such recourses? What does a man do it for? Why does he try to outdo his fellow-humans, and be braver and stronger and more daring and showy than even his best friends are? What's his game? What does he expect to get out of it? He don't do it just for the fresh air and exercise. What would you say, now, Bill, that an ordinary man expects, generally speaking, for his efforts along the line of ambition and extraordinary hustling in the market-places, forums, shooting-galleries, lyceums, battlefields, links, cinder-paths, and arenas of the civilized and *vice versa* places of the world?"

"Well, Ben," said I, with judicial seriousness, "I think we might safely limit the number of motives of a man who seeks fame to three—to ambition, which is a desire for popular applause; to avarice, which looks to the material side of success; and to love of some woman whom he either possesses or desires to possess."

Ben pondered over my words while a mocking-bird on the top of a mesquite by the porch trilled a dozen bars.

"I reckon," said he, "that your diagnosis about covers the case according to the rules laid down in the copy-books and historical readers. But what I had in my mind was the case of Willie Robbins, a person I used to know. I'll tell you about him before I close up the store, if you don't mind listening.

"Willie was one of our social set up in San Augustine. I was clerking there then for Brady & Murchison, whole-sale dry-goods and ranch supplies. Willie and I belonged to the same german club and athletic association and military company. He played the triangle in our serenading and quartet club that used to ring the welkin three nights a week somewhere in town.

"Willie jibed with his name considerable. He weighed

about as much as a hundred pounds of veal in his summer suitings, and he had a 'Where-is-Mary' expression on his features so plain that you almost could see the wool growing on him.

"And yet you couldn't fence him away from the girls with barbed wire. You know that kind of young fellows —a kind of mixture of fools and angels—they rush in and fear to tread at the same time; but they never fail to tread when they get the chance. He was always on hand when 'a joyful occasion was had,' as the morning paper would say, looking as happy as a king full, and at the same time as uncomfortable as a raw oyster served with sweet pickles. He danced like he had hind hobbles on; and he had a vocabulary of about three hundred and fifty words that he made stretch over four germans a week, and plagiarized from to get him through two ice-cream suppers and a Sunday-night call. He seemed to me to be a sort of a mixture of Maltese kitten, sensitive plant, and member of a stranded 'Two Orphans' company.

"I'll give you an estimate of his physiological and pictorial make-up and then I'll stick spurs into the sides of my narrative.

"Willie inclined to the Caucasian in his coloring and manner of style. His hair was opalescent and his conversation fragmentary. His eyes were the same blue shade as the china dog's on the right-hand corner of your Aunt Ellen's mantelpiece. He took things as they came, and I never felt any hostility against him. I let him live, and so did others.

"But what does this Willie do but coax his heart out of his boots and lose it to Myra Allison, the liveliest, brightest, keenest, smartest, and prettiest girl in San Augustine. I tell you, she had the blackest eyes, the shiniest curls, and the most tantalizing— Oh, no you're off—I wasn't a victim. I might have been, but I knew better. I kept out. Joe Granberry was *It* from the start. He had everybody else beat a couple of leagues and thence east to a stake and mound. But, anyhow, Myra was a nine-pound, full-merino, fall-clip fleece, sacked and loaded on a four-horse team for San Antone.

"One night there was an ice-cream sociable at Mrs. Colonel Spraggin's in San Augustine. We fellows had a big room upstairs opened up for us to put our hats and things in, and to comb our hair and put on the clean collars we brought along inside the sweat-bands of our hats —in short, a room to fix up in just like they have everywhere at high-toned doings. A little farther down the hall was the girls' room, which they used to powder up in, and so forth. Downstairs we—that is, the San Augustine Social Cotillion and Merrymakers' Club—had a stretcher put down in the parlor where our dance was going on.

"Willie Robbins and me happened to be in our— cloak-room, I believe we called it—when Myra Allison skipped through the hall on her way downstairs from the girls' room. Willie was standing before the mirror, deeply interested in smoothing down the blond grass-

plot on his head, which seemed to give him lots of
trouble. Myra was always full of life and devilment.
She stopped and stuck her head in our door. She certainly was good-looking. But I knew how Joe Granberry stood with her. So did Willie; but he kept on
ba-a-a-ing after her and following her around. He had
a system of persistence that didn't coincide with pale
hair and light eyes.

" 'Hello, Willie!' says Myra. 'What are you doing to
yourself in the glass?'

" 'I'm trying to look fly,' says Willie.

" 'Well, you never could *be* fly,' says Myra with her
special laugh, which was the provokingest sound I ever
heard except the rattle of an empty canteen against my
saddle horn.

"I looked around at Willie after Myra had gone.
He had a kind of lily-white look on him which seemed to
show that her remark had, as you might say, disrupted
his soul. I never noticed anything in what she said that
sounded particularly destructive to a man's ideas of self-
consciousness; but he was set back to an extent you could
scarcely imagine.

"After we went downstairs with our clean collars on,
Willie never went near Myra again that night. After
all, he seemed to be a diluted kind of a skim-milk sort of
a chap, and I never wondered that Joe Granberry beat
him out.

"The next day the battleship *Maine* was blown up,

and then pretty soon somebody—I reckon it was Joe Bailey, or Ben Tillman, or maybe the Government—declared war against Spain.

"Well, everybody south of Mason & Hamlin's line knew that the North by itself couldn't whip a whole country the size of Spain. So the Yankees commenced to holler for help, and the Johnny Rebs answered the call. 'We're coming, Father William, a hundred thousand strong—and then some,' was the way they sang it. And the old party lines drawn by Sherman's march and the Kuklux and nine-cent cotton and the Jim Crow street-car ordinances faded away. We became one undivided country, with no North, very little East, a good-sized chunk of West, and a South that loomed up as big as the first foreign label on a new eight-dollar suitcase.

"Of course the dogs of war weren't a complete pack without a yelp from the San Augustine Rifles, Company D, of the Fourteenth Texas Regiment. Our company was among the first to land in Cuba and strike terror into the hearts of the foe. I'm not going to give you a history of the war; I'm just dragging it in to fill out my story about Willie Robbins, just as the Republican party dragged it in to help out the election in 1898.

"If anybody ever had heroitis, it was that Willie Robbins. From the minute he set foot on the soil of the tyrants of Castile he seemed to engulf danger as a cat laps up cream. He certainly astonished every man in our company, from the captain up. You'd have expected him to gravitate naturally to the job of an orderly to the colonel, or typewriter in the commissary—but not any. He created the part of the flaxen-haired boy hero who lives and gets back home with the goods, instead of dying with an important dispatch in his hands at his colonel's feet.

"Our company got into a section of Cuban scenery where one of the messiest and most unsung portions of the campaign occurred. We were out every day capering around in the bushes, and having little skirmishes with the Spanish troops that looked more like kind of tired-out feuds than anything else. The war was a joke to us, and of no interest to them. We never could see it any other way than as a howling farce-comedy that the San Augustine Rifles were actually fighting to uphold the Stars and Stripes. And the blamed little señors didn't get enough pay to make them care whether they were patriots or traitors. Now and then somebody would get killed. It seemed like a waste of life to me. I was at Coney Island when I went to New York once, and one of them down-hill skidding apparatuses they call 'roller-coasters' flew the track and killed a man in a brown sack-suit. Whenever the Spaniards shot one of our men, it struck me as just about as unnecessary and regrettable as that was.

"But I'm dropping Willie Robbins out of the conversation.

"He was out for bloodshed, laurels, ambition, medals, recommendations, and all other forms of military glory. And he didn't seem to be afraid of any of the recognized forms of military danger, such as Spaniards, cannon-balls, canned beef, gunpowder, or nepotism. He went forth with his pallid hair and china-blue eyes and ate up Spaniards like you would sardines *à la* canopy. Wars and rumbles of wars never flustered him. He would stand guard-duty, mosquitoes, hardtack, treat, and fire with equally perfect unanimity. No blondes in history ever come in comparison distance of him except the Jack of Diamonds and Queen Catherine of Russia.

"I remember, one time, a little *caballard* of Spanish men sauntered out from behind a patch of sugar-cane and shot Bob Turner, the first sergeant of our company, while we were eating dinner. As required by the army regulations, we fellows went through the usual tactics of falling into line, saluting the enemy, and loading and firing, kneeling.

"That wasn't the Texas way of scrapping; but, being a very important addendum and annex to the regular army, the San Augustine Rifles had to conform to the red-tape system of getting even.

"By the time we had got out our 'Upton's Tactics,' turned to page fifty-seven, said 'one-two-three-one-two-three' a couple of times, and got blank cartridges into our Springfields, the Spanish outfit had smiled repeatedly, rolled and lit cigarettes by squads, and walked away contemptuously.

"I went straight to Captain Floyd, and says to him, 'Sam, I don't think this war is a straight game. You know as well as I do that Bob Turner was one of the whitest fellows that ever threw a leg over a saddle, and now these wire-pullers in Washington have fixed his clock. He's politically and ostensibly dead. It ain't fair. Why should they keep this thing up? If they want Spain licked, why don't they turn the San Augustine Rifles and Joe Seely's ranger company and a carload of West Texas deputy-sheriffs on to these Spaniards, and let us exonerate them from the face of the earth? I never did,' says I, 'care much about fighting by the Lord Chesterfield ring rules. I'm going to hand in my resignation and go home if anybody else I am personally acquainted with gets hurt in this war. If you can get somebody in my place, Sam,' says I, 'I'll quit the first of next week. I don't want to work in an army that don't give its help a chance. Never mind my wages,' says I; 'let the Secretary of the Treasury keep 'em.'

" 'Well, Ben,' says the captain to me, 'your allegations and estimations of the tactics of war, government, patriotism, guard-mounting, and democracy are all right. But I've looked into the system of international arbitration and the ethics of justifiable slaughter a little closer, maybe, than you have. Now, you can hand in your resignation the first of next week if you are so minded. But if you do,' says Sam, 'I'll order a corporal's guard to take you over by that limestone bluff on the creek and shoot enough lead into you to ballast a submarine airship. I'm captain of this company, and I've sworn allegiance to the Amalgamated States regardless of sectional, secessional, and Congressional differences. Have you got any smoking-tobacco?' winds up Sam. 'Mine got wet when I swum the creek this morning.'

"The reason I drag all this *non ex parte* evidence in is because Willie Robbins was standing there listening to us. I was a second sergeant and he was a private then, but among us Texans and Westerners there never was as much tactics and subordination as there was in the regular army. We never called our captain anything but 'Sam' except when there was a lot of major-generals and admirals around, so as to preserve the discipline.

"And says Willie Robbins to me, in a sharp construction of voice much unbecoming to his light hair and previous record:

" 'You ought to be shot, Ben, for emitting any such sentiments. A man that won't fight for his country is worse than a horse-thief. If I was a cap, I'd put you in the guard-house for thirty days on round steak and tamales. War,' says Willie, 'is great and glorious. I didn't know you were a coward.'

" 'I'm not,' says I. 'If I was, I'd knock some of the pallidness off of your marble brow. I'm lenient with you,' I says, 'just as I am with the Spaniards, because you have always reminded me of something with mushrooms on the side. Why, you little Lady of Shalott,' says I, 'you underdone leader of cotillions, you glassy fashion and moulded form, you white-pine soldier made in the Cisalpine Alps in Germany for the late New-Year trade, do you know of whom you are talking to? We've been in the same social circle,' says I, 'and I've put up with you because you seemed so meek and self-unsatisfying. I don't understand why you have so sudden taken a personal interest in chivalrousness and murder. Your nature's undergone a complete revelation. Now, how is it?'

" 'Well, you wouldn't understand, Ben,' says Willie, giving one of his refined smiles and turning away.

" 'Come back here!' says I, catching him by the tail of his khaki coat. 'You've made me kind of mad, in spite of the aloofness in which I have heretofore held you. You are out for making a success in this here business, and I believe I know what for. You are doing it either because you are crazy or because you expect to catch some girl by it. Now if it's a girl, I've got something here to show you.'

"I wouldn't have done it, but I was plumb mad. I pulled a San Augustine paper out of my hip-pocket, and showed him an item. It was a half a column about the marriage of Myra Allison and Joe Granberry.

"Willie laughed, and I saw I hadn't touched him.

" 'Oh,' says he, 'everybody knew that was going to happen. I heard about that a week ago.' And then he gave me the laugh again.

" 'All right,' says I. 'Then why do you so recklessly chase the bright rainbow of fame? Do you expect to be elected President, or do you belong to a suicide club?'

"And then Captain Sam interferes.

" 'You gentlemen quit jawing and go back to your quarters,' says he, 'or I'll have you escorted to the guard-house. Now, scat, both of you! Before you go, which one of you has got any chewing-tobacco?'

"'We're off, Sam,' says I 'It's supper-time, anyhow. But what do you think of what we was talking about? I've noticed you throwing out a good many grappling hooks for this here balloon called fame— What's ambition, anyhow? What does a man risk his life day after day for? Do you know of anything he gets in the end that can pay him for the trouble? I want to go back home,' says I. 'I don't care whether Cuba sinks or swims, and I don't give a pipeful of rabbit tobacco whether Queen Sophia Christina or Charlie Culberson rules these fairy isles; and I don't want my name on any list except the list of survivors. But I've noticed you, Sam,' says I, 'seeking the bubble notoriety in the cannon's larynx a number of times. Now, what do you do it for? Is it ambition, business, or some freckle-faced Phoebe at home that you are heroing for?'"

"'Well, Ben,' says Sam, kind of hefting his sword out from between his knees, 'as your superior officer I could court-martial you for attempted cowardice and desertion. But I won't. And I'll tell you why I'm trying for promotion and the usual honors of war and conquest. A major gets more pay than a captain, and I need the money.'

"'Correct for you!' says I. 'I can understand that. Your system of fame-seeking is rooted in the deepest soil of patriotism. But I can't comprehend,' says I, 'why

Willie Robbins, whose folks at home are well off, and who used to be as meek and undesirous of notice as a cat with cream on his whiskers, should all at once develop into a warrior bold with the most fire-eating kind of proclivities. And the girl in his case seems to have been eliminated by marriage to another fellow. I reckon,' says I, 'it's a plain case of just common ambition. He wants his name, maybe, to go thundering down the coroners of time. It must be that.'

"Well, without itemizing his deeds, Willie sure made made good as a hero. He simply spent most of his time on his knees begging our captain to send him on forlorn hopes and dangerous scouting expeditions. In every fight he was the first man to mix it at close quarters with the Don Alfonsos. He got three or four bullets planted in various parts of his autonomy. Once he went off with a detail of eight men and captured a whole company of Spanish. He kept Captain Floyd busy writing out recommendations of his bravery to send to headquarters; and he began to accumulate medals for all kinds of things —heroism and target-shooting and valor and tactics and uninsubordination, and all the little accomplishments that look good to the third assistant secretaries of the War Department.

"Finally, Cap Floyd got promoted to be a major-general, or a knight commander of the main herd, or something like that. He pounded around on a white horse, all desecrated up with gold-leaf and hen-feathers and a

Good Templar's hat, and wasn't allowed by the regulations to speak to us. And Willie Robbins was made captain of our company.

"And maybe he didn't go after the wreath of fame then! As far as I could see it was him that ended the war. He got eighteen of us boys—friends of his, too—killed in battles that he stirred up himself and that didn't seem to me necessary at all. One night he took twelve of us and waded through a little rill about a hundred and ninety yards wide, and climbed a couple of mountains, and sneaked through a mile of neglected shrubbery and a couple of rock-quarries and into a rye-straw village, and captured a Spanish general named, as they said, Benny Veedus. Benny seemed to me hardly worth the trouble, being a blackish man without shoes or cuffs, and anxious to surrender and throw himself on the commissary of his foe.

"But that job gave Willie the big boost he wanted. The San Augustine *News* and the Galveston, St. Louis, New York and Kansas City papers printed his picture and columns of stuff about him. Old San Augustine simply went crazy over its 'gallant son.' The *News* had an editorial tearfully begging the Government to call off the regular army and the national guard, and let Willie carry on the rest of the war single-handed. It said that a refusal to do so would be regarded as a proof that the Northern jealousy of the South was still as rampant as ever.

"If the war hadn't ended pretty soon, I don't know to

what heights of gold braid and encomiums Willie would
have climbed; but it did. There was a secession of hostil-
ities just three days after he was appointed a colonel,
and got in three more medals by registered mail, and
shot two Spaniards while they were drinking lemonade
in an ambuscade.

"Our company went back to San Augustine when the
war was over. There wasn't anywhere else for it to go.
And what do you think? The old town notified us in
print, by wire cable, special delivery, and a nigger named
Saul sent on a gray mule to San Antone, that they was
going to give us the biggest blowout, complimentary,
elimentary, and elementary, that ever disturbed the kil-
dees on the sand-flats outside of the immediate conti-
guity of the city.

"I say 'we,' but it was all meant for ex-Private, Captain *de facto*, and Colonel-elect Willie Robbins. The
town was crazy about him. They notified us that the re-
ception they were going to put up would make the
Mardi Gras in New Orleans look like an afternoon tea
in Bury St. Edmonds with a curate's aunt.

"Well, the San Augustine Rifles got back home on
schedule time. Everybody was at the depot giving forth
Roosevelt-Democrat—they used to be called Rebel—
yells. There was two brass-bands, and the mayor, and
schoolgirls in white frightening the street-car horses by
throwing Cherokee roses in the streets, and—well,
maybe you've seen a celebration by a town that was in-
land and out of water.

"They wanted Brevet-Colonel Willie to get into a carriage and be drawn by prominent citizens and some of the city aldermen to the armory, but he stuck to his company and marched at the head of it up Sam Houston Avenue. The buildings on both sides was covered with flags and audiences, and everybody hollered 'Robbins!' or 'Hello, Willie!' as we marched up in files of fours. I never saw an illustriouser looking human in my life than Willie was. He had at least seven or eight medals and diplomas and decorations on the breast of his khaki coat; he was sunburnt the color of a saddle, and he certainly done himself proud.

"They told us at the depot that the courthouse was to be illuminated at half-past seven, and there would be speeches and chili-con-carne at the Palace Hotel. Miss Delphine Thompson was to read an original poem by James Whitcomb Ryan, and Constable Hooker had promised us a salute of nine guns from Chicago that he had arrested that day.

"After we had disbanded in the armory, Willie says to me:

" 'Want to walk out a piece with me?'

" 'Why, yes,' says I, 'if it ain't so far that we can't hear the tumult and the shouting die away. I'm hungry myself,' says I, 'and I'm pining for some home grub, but I'll go with you.'

"Willie steered me down some side streets till we came to a little white cottage in a new lot with a twenty-by-thirty-foot lawn decorated with brickbats and old barrel-staves.

" 'Halt and give the counter sign,' says I to Willie. 'Don't you know this dugout? It's the bird's-nest that Joe Granberry built before he married Myra Allison. What you going there for?'

"But Willie already had the gate open. He walked up the brick walk to the steps, and I went with him. Myra was sitting in a rocking-chair on the porch, sewing. Her hair was smoothed back kind of hasty and tied in a knot. I never noticed till then that she had freckles. Joe was at one side of the porch, in his shirt-sleeves, with no collar on, and no signs of a shave, trying to scrape out a hole among the brickbats and tin cans to plant a little fruit-tree in. He looked up but never said a word, and neither did Myra.

"Willie was sure dandy-looking in his uniform, with medals strung on his breast and his new gold-handled sword. You'd never have taken him for the little white-headed snipe that the girls used to order about and make fun of. He just stood there for a minute, looking at Myra with a peculiar little smile on his face; and then he says to her, slow, and kind of holding on to his words with his teeth:

" *'Oh, I don't know! Maybe I could if I tried!'*

"That was all that was said. Willie raised his hat, and we walked away.

"And, somehow, when he said that, I remembered,

all of a sudden, the night of that dance and Willie brushing his hair before the looking-glass, and Myra sticking her head in the door to guy him.

"When we got back to Sam Houston Avenue, Willie says:

" 'Well, so long, Ben. I'm going down home and get off my shoes and take a rest.'

" 'You?' says I. 'What's the matter with you? Ain't the courthouse jammed with everybody in town waiting to honor the hero? And two brass-bands, and recitations and flags and jags, and grub to follow waiting for you?'

"Willie sighs.

" 'All right, Ben,' says he. 'Darned if I didn't forget all about that.'

"And that's why I say," concluded Ben Granger, "that you can't tell where ambition begins any more than you can where it is going to wind up."

From *Options by O. Henry*.

# EDWARD LUCAS WHITE

Though Edward Lucas White was born in Baltimore and still lives there, and though his family before him lived there for three generations, his literary fame rests less upon anything written about the city, or indeed about the United States, than upon a novel of a Roman nobleman of the days of the Empire, "Andivius Hedulio," whose realism has shouldered its way through the centuries and set him and the time before us with the distinctness of a dream. "The Unwilling Vestal," too, and "Helen," spring from his close acquaintance with the classics— he has taught Greek and Latin in boys' schools and is a member of the Classical Association of the Middle States and Maryland —and "El Supremo" comes from farther South than our America. But this short story here presented, which appeared first in the *Atlantic Monthly*, has found its way far beyond its original circle of readers through more than one reprint, and kept a longer life than is often granted to a single separate magazine story. It needs no explanation, no introduction: it is clearly based on fact, and it rings true. Since it first appeared, a war more terrible than that it commemorates has set little flags on American graves here and oversea, but the spirit it celebrates has not faded.

# THE LITTLE FADED FLAG

*By* EDWARD LUCAS WHITE

"ANY objections to graveyards?" the American inquired.

"I should object to taking up my permanent abode in one unnecessarily soon," the Frenchman replied, his black eyes twinkling, his thin lips smiling between his jetty mustache and his pointed sable beard.

"Monseer Daypurtwee," said his host, "I'm not joking, you understand. I've showed you most of this neighborhood, and I rather like to drive through our cemetery, myself. I'm trying to find out how the idea strikes you."

"I should be charmed, I'm sure," Des Pertuis answered in his unexceptionable English.

"Some people don't like to go to a graveyard," Wade resumed, "any oftener or any sooner than they have to. Sure you're not just being polite?"

"Quite sure," René replied, smiling again.

"Honor bright, no reservations?" Wade queried anxiously, half turning, and glancing into his guest's eyes.

"None whatever," René answered him smilingly.

"Then we'll drive through the cemetery," Wade informed him, settling back comfortably, not a muscle showing effort, except his outstretched arms, tense against the taut reins.

"I shall be charmed, I am sure," René repeated.

"You may think it queer," Wade remarked, "my taking you to the cemetery, but I'll explain afterwards, you understand, or perhaps you'll find out for yourself, before we leave it, why I took you there. I want to try an experiment, want to see whether something is going to strike you the way it strikes me, you understand."

"You are very kind, I am sure," said Des Pertuis. "I shall be interested to learn the result of your experiment."

"Ferris wrote me," Wade went on, "that what you wanted was real American atmosphere, and he thought I could let you into some at Middleville. I believe you've found some, haven't you?"

"Yes," the Frenchman agreed, "I have been in what I am sure is a genuinely American atmosphere."

"I've watched you absorbing it, you understand," Wade chuckled. "You've had to take in quite an amount of hot air with your American atmosphere."

Des Pertuis smiled deprecatingly.

"Oh yes," his host continued. "You've been polite about it. I could appreciate that, you understand. You've smiled and looked interested when Uncle George talked bushels-to-the-acre and all that, while Tupper talked tons of tomatoes and the rest of it, while Bowe talked reapers and thrashers and iron fences and cutlery, while

Parks talked tonnage-per-mile and tonnage-per-land-ing; you've taken it all in: farm-brag, trade-brag, railroad-brag, and steamboat-brag; you've appeared charmed, but you've got everlastingly tired of the brag all the same."

"I have not heard you brag, Mr. Wade," René re-minded him quietly, his twinkling black eyes fixed on his host's plump, smooth-shaven visage.

"Perhaps I'm going to brag," Wade replied. "Brag is part of what you came after, part of the American atmosphere, you understand, and I brag myself, but not about the same things, nor in just the same way. I love the Eastern Shore, I like to hear it called 'God's Foot-stool', or 'The Garden Spot of the World'. But I've quit using those terms myself,—to foreigners, anyhow. I never run down my home state or my home country, you understand, but when I meet a man like you, who has seen Holland and Belgium and Luxembourg and Saxony and Provence and Lombardy, let alone other places I haven't seen, I let others do the bragging about density of population and fertility and productivity and all that. I don't call them down, I sit and smoke and look on. But I'm not saying much, you understand."

"I quite comprehend," René assured him. "Enthusi-asm for one's own is not by any means unpleasant."

"Not unless you get too much of it," his host com-mented, "or unless the enthusiasm is for the wrong things, you understand. Enthusiasm for the wrong thing makes me mad. We Americans have plenty to brag of;

things really worth boasting of. But it makes me hot to hear these half-baked countrymen blat about the area of the United States, which is an accident; or our coal and iron and copper and petroleum and what not, which are quite as accidental; or our population, which is the result of the other accidents; or the volume of immigration, which is a menace. I want them to distinguish what we really ought to be proud of from what we have no call to boast of. And I bet you feel that way, too. I've been watching you, you understand."

"Boasting about one's own country is an amiable foible," René remarked. "I do not object to such chauvinism, as we call it."

"But you are a trifle uneasy," Wade put in, "when they begin to draw comparisons,—especially if they are undeserved, you understand,—and to run down France and French things. Is that what you mean?"

"Precisely," Des Pertuis replied. "You have penetrated my meaning; and I may remind you that you yourself have done nothing of the kind, nor Madame Wade."

"It's good of you to notice it," his host said. "Naturally she wouldn't any more than I. We've been in France, you understand. But perhaps I'm going to do that, too, as well as brag. No offense, you understand. But I'm commercial. I take a commercial view of things. I fail to see through a great many things other people seem to comprehend, you understand, and one thing they told me in France surprised me. I thought I heard

Mary asking you about it last night. But I wasn't sure, what with Humphreys and all the other fellows talking at once, you understand. Anyhow, I want to ask you about it."

"What is it?" his guest queried civilly.

"What was the name of that part of France, over toward England, where there was no end of a civil war during your revolution?"

"You mean La Vendée?" René asked.

"That's it," his host replied. "I never can remember that sort of a name. I'm commercial, you understand. Well, somebody told us while we were in Paris (I think it was the Rogerses, who live there, but I'm not sure), that the descendants of the people who fought on opposite sides in that war won't sit down to table together this minute, nor be under the same roof. Is that true?"

"Not wholly," René responded; "two might be in the same theatre or in the same public building, and neither think it necessary to leave after recognizing the other. But certainly it is true of not dining together. No one would invite a Charette to meet a Hoche; neither would remain in any house a moment after learning the presence of the other. Still less would a Cathelineau or Rochejaquelein consent to spend an instant in a drawing-room with a Turreau or a Carrier; no, nor in a restaurant or hotel."

"Don't you think that is carrying personal hostility pretty far?" Wade asked.

Des Pertuis stroked his short spike of a beard.

"You do not comprehend," he said, "how fierce, how implacable, how ferocious was the fighting in that war. You have never heard of the devastations and counter-devastations, of the massacres and retaliatory massacres, of the savageries, the tortures, the insults, the ingenious horrors inflicted on the vanquished by the victors on both sides; of the brutal ruthlessness and refined cruelties."

"Perhaps not," Wade rejoined. "But when did all that happen?"

"From sometime in 1793," René replied, "to sometime in 1796."

"All over a hundred and ten years ago," his host commented. "No offense, you understand, but speaking as between friends, don't you think that is a long time to hold a grudge?"

"The families concerned," Des Pertuis made answer, "do not take that view of it. They still smart under the reciprocal wrongs inflicted, they still recall the gloating fiendishness of their foes, and apart from any recollections of outrage, they rather make a point of honor of their inflexibility. Why, not only the families involved on one side or the other of the war in La Vendée, but the old legitimist nobility generally and the descendants of the revolutionists at large, stand upon the same punctilio. No son of a noble house which never bowed to Bonapartism or to the Orleanist ascendancy, or to the party of the Citizen King, no member of any such noble family would ever meet socially any descendant of a Bonapartist, still less of a regicide, were he Montagnard, Jacobin, or Girondist. No La Rochefoucauld or Château-Repnaud would unbend to any Murat or Carnot."

"Don't you think yourself,—no offense, you understand," Wade suggested, "that that is rather a peevish and childish way to behave?"

René again stroked his beard, even more slowly.

"They do not so look upon it," he said; "they take pride in their tenacity."

"What's that national motto of yours on your coins," Wade asked argumentatively. "What does it mean in English?"

"Liberty, Equality, and Fraternity is the translation of that motto," Des Pertuis answered, a trifle stiffly.

"Do you call that fraternity?" Wade queried triumphantly.

"You do not comprehend," the Frenchman began ardently.

"I allow that," his host cut in. "I'm commercial, you know, and miss the fine points. No offense, Daypurtwee, go on."

"Indeed, you do not comprehend," René declared. "Our national motto is for us as the—what do you call it?—Golden Rule for all Christians; the ideal which is aimed at rather than an injunction which all live up to. The Golden Rule has not made all Christians always treat others as they wish themselves to be treated. We strive for fraternity. But a motto cannot make human nature otherwise than it is."

"Human nature," Wade remarked, "varies with the race and country, you understand. Some kinds don't need to be made over."

"I see," said his guest shortly.

"No offense, I hope, Daypurtwee"; his host spoke anxiously. "No offense meant, you understand."

"Yes, I understand," René replied, smiling again.

"Here's the cemetery," Wade proclaimed. "We've driven miles around. I wanted to talk before we reached it."

He pointed with his whip to one gravestone after another, telling of the families, their characteristics, and their relationships to one another and to his own. The horse walked slowly. René, his hat in his hand, listened affably.

Wade halted his team under four big wide-spreading maples.

"That's my father's grave," he said, pointing.

René bowed in silence.

"And that's my uncle's," Wade went on, "my mother's brother, Colonel William Spence."

"He was a soldier in the Federal armies during your late war," René remarked.

"What makes you think that?" Wade inquired.

"I have visited many of your cemeteries," René

answered, "at Boston, New York, Philadelphia, Baltimore, and other cities. I have learned your customs in respect to the graves of all such soldiers."

"So you think he fought for the Union?" Wade queried.

"I am sure of it," René replied confidently.

"Well," said his host, "you never were more mistaken in your life. My father's brothers both fought for the Union, but my mother's kin were all fire-eating rebels. Colonel William Spence fought under Lee."

"What!" the Frenchman cried, "the Union flag on a Confederate soldier's grave!"

"You'll find," Wade told him, "that this is not the only part of the country where they put the Stars and Stripes on the graves of ex-Confederates."

The Frenchman said nothing. They sat silent, side by side, the stout, blond, jolly-faced, red-cheeked, smooth-shaven American, his gray felt hat on the back of his head, looking sideways with quizzical blue eyes at his guest; the compact, black-haired, black-bearded Frenchman gazing steadily down at the white headstone, the narrow grass-mound, the month-old withered flowers, the draggled, mud-streaked, rain-bleached muslin flag, no bigger than a handkerchief. One of the geldings tossed his head and champed at his bit, and the reins tinkled and clanked softly.

"Who put it there?" René queried at last.

"The veterans," Wade answered lightly.

"When?" René inquired.

"The thirtieth of last May," his host replied.

"Why," Des Pertuis exclaimed, "that is your national Decoration Day. I was told that the Confederates had a different decoration day of their own; in June, I think."

"Yes," Wade responded. "They observe it all over the South, you understand. But here and in many of the border districts, in small towns, where there are not many veterans, they all walk out here, blue and gray together, and put Old Glory on every grave indifferently."

"I had been led to think," René ruminated, "that there was much rancor after your civil war; but I fancy from what you tell me that there was less animosity than I had conceived."

"There was much rancor," his host declared. "The animosity at the time of the war cannot be exaggerated, could not be conveyed to you by any description, you understand. There is rancor yet, mostly among the Southern women, particularly those born since the war, or those whose families really suffered least or whose men did not fight at all,—a sort of artificial cult of rancor. But the families who lost everything, whose estates were trampled by the armies, whose homes were burned, whose best men died in battle, who were left beggars when it was all over,—well, they and theirs talk now as they acted then, like the thoroughbreds they are. Not a complaint then, not a recrimination now. And the Northern families who gave most lives on the field are as mute on their side. As for the men who did the fighting, their animosity has all faded away. They forgive and forget."

"If the bitterness of feeling has so soon effaced itself," the Frenchman argued, "the war must have been waged without any exasperating atrocities on either side."

"If you mean by atrocities," Wade replied, "such massacres of prisoners by the regular authorities as you spoke of a while ago, or such butchery of surrendered adversaries as goes on in the South American revolutions, nothing of the kind occurred. But the bushwhackers and jayhawkers who hung about the armies and infested the border were often worse than Apache Indians. The Confederate raiders burned some buildings, the devastation of the Shenandoah Valley caused much suffering and venom. But that is about the list of what you might call atrocities. Yet without any unnecessary ferocity, the mere inevitable horrors of fair, honorable, open warfare roused enough exasperation and bitterness and animosity and rancor, you understand. The hatred on both sides was at white heat while it lasted."

"I can scarcely credit," René said, "that what has cooled so soon could have been so fierce."

"You are comparing our forty years," Wade conjectured, "with your hundred and ten after the war in what's-its-name?"

"Just so," his guest replied. "It seems the hatred can scarcely have been so intense as you claim, nor the provocations so frightful."

"You ought to have heard the veterans last Decoration Day," Wade told him. "They had a sort of reunion of both sides here. Several of them stayed at my house and they made my porch their headquarters. You ought to have heard the stories they told."

"For instance," the Frenchman suggested.

"Oh, I can't begin to tell them," Wade disclaimed. "I'm commercial, you understand. I never can remember the names of the battles and generals and colonels, nor the number of the regiments, nor the dates either, for that matter; any more than I can remember the names of all those high-and-mighty families you were telling me about, you understand. But I took in the gist of their talk, you bet. I just sat there and smoked and listened, and when they ran dry I'd take 'em out in the pantry for a little ammunition. One evening in particular, I think it was the 29th of May, they got going.

"There were two of them staying with me, my uncle, General Tom Wade of Milwaukee, and Colonel Melrose of Boston, an uncle of my wife's. They were both born in Middleville, you understand, but one went west and one went north, and they live there yet. They were back in Middleville for a visit. Then there was Captain Tupper, cousin of the farmer you met, and Captain

Bowe, uncle of the storekeeper. They both live here, came back after they made their pile, but they were out west when the war broke out. They were Union men too, you understand.

"We had five Confeds. Captain John Spence, my mother's youngest brother, Colonel Parks, father of the Parks you met, and old General Humphreys, Dick Humphreys's father. They live here, and with them were Colonel Janney, Henry Tupper's father-in-law, and Colonel Rhett, my sister-in-law's uncle.

"They were all right there on my porch, where you and I were sitting this morning. It was a beautiful night, hot for May and still. They had had a snifter or two all around and had rather limbered up to each other and warmed up to their talk. They talked war, of course, talked it good-naturedly. They had all been in it, had all lost near relatives in battle: Colonel Rhett had lost most,—never heard of such a connection as the Rhetts. But Colonel Janney had lost nearly as many. The five Confeds had all come out of the war beggars, lost every cent they ever had. Yet they all talked good-naturedly, you understand. They got to talking about a cornfield; not the cornfield at Gettysburg, but one famous in some small battle, early in the war, soon after Bull Run, I think. Anyhow they called it Rumbold's cornfield. I can't remember the name of the battle or of the locality, but they remembered it all right, you understand. They talked about the first charge and the second charge, and the second day's fighting, and the third charge across that same cornfield.

"Colonel Melrose said nothing.

"Uncle Wade asked, 'Weren't you there, Melrose?'"

"Melrose tugged at his curly gray beard.

" 'Yes, I was there,' he said. 'The most fearful moment of my life was in Rumbold's cornfield.'

"We expected him to tell a story, but he said no more.

"General Humphreys launched into an account of the difficulties the Confederates labored under, their shortness of supplies, and all that. He told how they got five field-guns in position to cover that cornfield, and he made a good story of it too. You could just feel what an exploit it was merely to plant those guns after all they had to overcome. Then, when they were in position, they found they had just three shells. Only three shells, you understand. And before they could get more the first charge across the cornfield began.

"You ought to have heard Humphreys describe just how they felt, how they could not see the men charging, but could see the movement in the corn, how they made each one of those shells tell, and at short range too. How the shells failed to stop the charge, how the rifle-fire failed to stop the charge, how they barely saved their guns, how they lost one and recaptured it next day. He made you feel the fierceness, the hurry, the sweat of it all, you understand. He had sighted one of the guns himself for the second shot.

"When he stopped every cigar was out. They all started to light up. After they settled down again, Colonel Melrose began:—

" 'So you sighted the gun that fired that second shell, Humphreys! I was a private then. It was my third fight. When we scrambled over the rail-fence Nathan Adams was next me. We were on one end of the line. I was strong runner then and must have drawn ahead of him farther than I thought as we forced ourselves through the tall corn. The second shell burst midway of the company a little toward the rear. The force of the explosion knocked me flat on my face, though I was not hit. When I scrambled to my feet I glanced behind me, could not see Nathan, and ran back to look for him. I had heard of the horrors of war, but then I first realized them.

" 'A fragment of shell had torn him open from hip to hip. His heart could scarcely have ceased beating, his flesh must still have been quivering. But what I saw was already a loathsome carcass, not a man.

" 'I turned away. Gentlemen, there was nothing there for me to help. Nothing but carrion, what an instant before had been my dearest friend, the man I most admired, the most promising youth I ever knew. I bore my part in that charge, did my utmost in the fight. But I was a mere maniac with the riot of my feelings, the turmoil of my thoughts. I was surprised at the clearness of those same thoughts. The rush of the charge, the fury of the fight, the confusion of the retreat were

enough to occupy the whole of any man's faculties. The
mere physical horror of what I had seen was sufficient
to benumb any conceivable intellect. Yet I went through
everything like a wound-up automaton, not needing
any faculties seemingly, for what I did, thinking inde-
pendently of what I was doing, and observing my own
sensations as one does in the double-consciousness of a
dream. I remember what I thought, for I went over it
a hundred times, a thousand times in the next year.

" 'First of all there was a sort of incredulous amaze-
ment at the intensity of the internal, physical sensation of overwhelming grief. It amazed me that it could
hurt so atrociously, and I was more amazed that a
spiritual smart could feel so entirely corporeal, like a
scald or burn. It was as if I had swallowed hell-fire and
it blazed in me without consuming me, a suffocating
agony.

" 'Then there was the bewilderment at my lone-
liness, the inability to realize that he would never speak
to me again, that we should never again exchange con-
fidences. I had gone to college very unformed. There
was not much to form a lad on the Eastern Shore in
those days. And at Harvard my mind and soul had
developed rapidly. But my intellectual growth had
been less the effect of Harvard than of Nathan Adams.
He had been not so much my guiding star as the sun
of my existence from the moment I first saw him. My
other interests had been swallowed up in the fascina-
tion he exercised over me, and always for good. He was

the prophet, preacher, and poet of my college days. My devotion to him was the first passion of my life, its only passion up to his death. To please him, to strive after the ideals he held before himself, to aspire with his aspirations, had been the sum of my aims. Behold, the idol had vanished from my heart's shrine. Life was empty.

" 'Also I was dazed with a sense of the loss to the commonwealth. Not only I but all who knew him had regarded Nathan as a natural leader of men, as possessed of transcendent powers, capacities and abilities, as born to a high destiny, as a precious possession of his state, his nation, of the world. I quailed at the irretrievable annihilation of his potentialities for good, of all he was certain to have done had he lived.

" 'Likewise I was overwhelmed with the sense of the waste of life the war entailed, of its frightful cost to humanity, and with that sense a crushing weight of my part of the duty to win for the country all his blood had been spilled for, all that was to be bought at the price of such lives as his. I had an access of partisan patriotism.

" 'And yet I felt not only that flare of ardor, but the lofty intellectual exaltation of devotion to the cause which had led us to enlist, swamped utterly by a torrent of personal animosity, of revengefulness, throughout that charge. I felt that life's most precious prize would be to have the man who fired that shell helpless before me, to feel my bayonet pierce his breast. That feeling haunted me for months. After I was an officer, after I had my sword and had used my sword, after I knew that gritty, friable, yielding grind of bone under my sabre-point, no other desire so consumed me as to meet in fair fight the man who fired that shell and feel tingle all up my arm the crunching, clinging drag of my sabre-edge cleaving his skull. I was astonished at the elemental fury of my inward savagery. I was as primitive as Agamemnon praying to Jupiter to let him feel his spear-point rend Hector's corselet and pierce his breast-bone. I was as primitive as a Sioux brave at a war-dance.'

"When Melrose stopped, nobody thought of cigars. They sat so still you could hear the breath whistle in Colonel Park's asthmatic wind-pipe. And they were still for some time.

"At last Humphreys asked:—

" 'And now?'

" 'And now,' Melrose took him up, 'there is not even the ghost of that acrimony left. We meet and you tell of it and I hear of it and know that you are the man. But all that volcano of hatred is burned out in me. I tell of how I felt, but the telling does not revive the feeling it recalls. I have no more animus against you than if those horrors had happened in some past lifetime, or to other men altogether.' "

Wade paused.

"And then?" René queried.

"And then," Wade enlightened him, "they shook hands and we all went out and took a drink."

"Do you know," René remarked, "for a man who calls himself commercial, you tell a story very well?"

"So my wife says," Wade replied shortly.

"Also," René went on, "for a man who disclaims a memory for names you have some rather pat. Agamemnon is not a commercial word."

"Oh," Wade laughed, "I remember names I learned at school. But I get so lost among names of battles, commanders and numbers of regiments, you understand, that I give up altogether. I can repeat a conversation pretty well, though. My wife says it's a wonder that a man who can remember another man's language so exactly can find so few words to express his own ideas. But that's the way I'm built. I remember what impresses itself on me, you understand.

"After we got out on the porch again they were all a little uncomfortable. Melrose's story had been too real. Captain Tupper started in to create a diversion; you could hear that in his tone.

" 'Speaking of sighting a shell,' he said, 'the best shot I ever saw was fired from a battery I commanded on the march to the sea. It was just before we reached Columbia. There was really no force in front of us, but they behaved as if they had a substantial body of men, and fooled us for some hours. We got our guns well within range and well-masked. Through my binoculars I could see the enemy's staff as pompous as if they had an army of a hundred thousand men intrenched.

" 'There was an officer with a gray goatee seated at a little table, two younger officers, with black goatees, standing on his left, and five or six men on his right, one in front with a long dark beard. They were as cool as if they controlled the situation, orderlies galloping up and galloping off and all that.

" 'We had a German named Krebs, a barrel of a man, but a wonderful artillerist: I called him and he sighted our best gun through the scrub pines.

" 'He plunked the shell square on that table, I saw the table smash, and the shell exploded as it struck the ground. That was the best cannon-shot I ever saw or heard of.'

"The instant Tupper ceased Colonel Rhett cleared his throat. He spoke in a muffled, choked voice.

" 'Strange,' he said, 'a second recognition the same evening. I was one of the half-dozen men on that general's right hand. I was the only one not killed of the nine by the table. The general was my father, and the man with the long black beard my brother-in-law. Two of the others were my cousins.'

"You may be sure we were all uncomfortable after that. And it didn't seem to me another drink was in order, just then, either.

"Colonel Tupper spoke like a man.

" 'It was all in the course of duty, Rhett,' he said.

'I wouldn't hold a personal grudge for it against you, if our places were changed, not if the shell had killed all my family and friends.'

"That sort of relieved the tension and we all felt less nervous when Rhett answered,—

" 'I hold no grudge, Tupper. We're all friends together, now. And since you mention it, it would have taken an almighty big shell to kill all my kin at one shot.'

"We laughed at that and felt better.

"Captain Bowe cut in. He thought he could change the line of thought.

" 'Duty led to some pretty unpalatable acts being forced on a fellow in wartime,' he said. 'Sometimes I think some of the duties that resulted in no bloodshed at all were worse to have to do than any kind of killing. I was in the Shenandoah Valley, and I can tell you turning ladies and children out of doors and burning their homes before their eyes took all a man's resolution and devotion to duty. It took all a man's resolve not to bolt and desert rather than carry out orders. I had some horrible days then.

" 'The worst of all was near Red Post, at an estate named Tower Hill, belonging to some people named Archibald. Of course there were women at home, only the women. Mrs. Archibald was not over twenty-six. She had four children, a beautiful little girl of about five years, twin boys, not any too sure on their feet, and a baby not six weeks old. She had two sisters, handsome dark girls, about seventeen and nineteen; Rannie their name was, or something like it. Her mother was an exquisite old lady, all quiet dignity. They were not hard and cold and scornful like some of the women I had had to leave houseless; they acquiesced without protests. Mrs. Archibald said she realized how distasteful my task must be to me. Indeed, I had tears in my eyes when I talked to her, I know. They huddled together just beyond the heat of the fire, and watched the barn and quarters burn and the house catch. They clung to each other, and the girls cried softly. By the Lord, gentlemen, that hurt more than any loss by death, and death took some of my dear ones during the war. That tried my soul more than danger or privations. It was bitter hard to have to do, and it is not agreeable to recall, even now.'

"Janney swore out loud.

" 'This seems to be a day of recognitions,' he said. 'Their name was not Rannie, it was Janney. They were my sisters and my mother. I was not two miles away, and I saw the house go. I vowed to kill the man that burned it, if I ever met him, and I meant it too.'

" 'Does that vow hold good?' Bowe asked quietly, never stirring in his chair.

" 'Time has canceled all the rash vows of those years,' Melrose put in before Janney could speak. 'All the rash vows and all the old hatreds.'

" 'Yes,' Janney agreed, 'that is my view too. I consider that vow as completely annulled as if I had never taken it. But if we had captured you, Bowe, among the prisoners we made out of the stragglers then, and if I had known you for the man who burnt Tower Hill, I'd have shot you like a dog, sir; murdered you in cold blood without a qualm, sir!'"

Wade sat silent. The near horse pawed at the turf-grown carriage track and turned his head toward the buggy, wickering softly.

"And what followed?" Des Pertuis queried.

"I don't remember any more that evening," Wade replied. "But next day the nine of them walked down here, arm in arm, Humphreys with Melrose, Rhett with Tupper, Janney with Bowe, and Captain Spence and Parks and Uncle Wade, with seven or eight more veterans. Colonel Melrose stuck that flag on Colonel Spence's grave, himself."

René looked at the flag as if he had never seen it before.

"I perceive the point," he said. "Your experiment is entirely successful. I agree with you. I have seen nothing in America as wonderful as that little faded flag. I understand what it is of which you especially boast. You conceive that here in the United States exists a kind of fraternity more genuine than anything anywhere else in the world. It is this of which you brag."

"Exactly so," Wade affirmed. "That's what I brag of, that's worth bragging of, you understand. What do area and population and wealth and manufactures and trade-balances and prosperity and all that sort of thing amount to, after all? Other nations have had them, and have them, and will have them. But what other nation ever had what the flag stands for? I don't know much history, you understand, but my wife spends her life reading, and I listen when she talks. I'm dead sure no nation ever produced anything to compare with the spirit in which our differences have resulted. I'm sure no nation has it to-day. And if it ever overspreads the world in the future, we made it, we started it, we had it first. That's something worth being proud of."

"I comprehend indeed," René told him. "And I do not wonder at your pride in it."

"Bully for you," Wade cried. "It's some satisfaction talking to somebody who is appreciative, you understand. Now I don't mean to run down the old countries. I acknowledge their culture and manners, their music and poetry and literature, their painting and sculpture and architecture. They've all that and we haven't; we can't compete with them in any of those things. Let them brag of their cathedrals, and art-galleries, and court-balls, and all the rest of it. They are wonderful. But that flag stands for the most wonderful thing in all the world, for the finest thing the world has ever produced yet. Not for talk about brotherhood, but for the real thing. That's my view, you understand."

"I comprehend indeed," René repeated. "And how long will that flag stay there?"

"Till the thirtieth of next May," his host replied.

"What will they do with it then?" Des Pertuis queried.

"Throw it away, I suppose," Wade answered easily. "It will be pretty well used up by then, you see, and they'll stick down a fresh one."

"Shall you be there then?" the Frenchman inquired.

"Sure," said the American. "Why?"

"Could you get it for me?" René queried. "If you could I should like to put it up over the fireplace at Pertuis."

"With What's-his-name's stirrup and Thing-em-a-bob's glove?" Wade asked.

"Yes," René answered, "with the gauntlet left by Du Guesclin with that hostess who had nursed him back to life; with the stirrup-iron from the saddle which Gaston de Foix gave his boyhood crony, my ancestor; with the other like relics, not a few."

"My wife went wild over that chimney-piece," Wade affirmed. "She said it was the finest she had seen in France and the most wonderful collection of mementos she ever saw in a private house."

"Madame Wade is very kind," René replied. "If you will be so good I should like to place among them this very flag."

From *The Atlantic Monthly*, vol. 101, 1908.

# IRVIN S. COBB

When Irvin S. Cobb was fourteen he had already begun to send out jokes to the papers of his native state, Kentucky; by the time he was seventeen he was a reporter on one of them and for a time at least an editor in Paducah, Kentucky; he was columnist on the *Louisville Post* till 1901, and then a war correspondent. Then he moved on to the North.

"In the midst of the hottest summer of the Christian Era," he says, he came to New York and hastened the process of looking for a job by sending to the managing editor of every newspaper in town a copy of so provocative a letter that within two days he had six offers. Of these he chose the one from the *Evening Sun*, going later to the *World*. His story is so well told by himself in Thomas Masson's "Our American Humorists" (Dodd, Mead) and his personality shows so clearly in the admiration of his friend, that the student of his career or of the course of American humor should not miss it.

It is not by a funny story, however, that he is represented in this volume, and by which the swamp land of Kentucky and the ragged soaring scavenger so much a part of the Southern landscape will live in our literature. For "The Belled Buzzard" will live. The quivering silence of the swamp, the hovering presence of the bird whose eye no spot of corruption can escape, the slight successive jerks by which the noose tightens about the murderer's neck, all give the tale, whether or not anything like it ever "really happened," a sense of the undeniable. No wonder it has been so often reprinted, more often than any of the excellent studies of Kentucky life and character in his "Old Judge Priest" and "The Escape of Mr. Trimm," from the second of which collections this story is taken. It has the "sacred shiver," the thrill with which we recognize the presence of something working through humanity but existing beyond it, a thrill heightened at the last by the grotesque contrast between its catastrophe and the means by which this is brought about.

Every established humorist likes to stake out a claim to immortality in some other field than that in which his public expects to find him. In this field there can be no doubt that the creator of old Judge Priest struck gold.

# THE BELLED BUZZARD

*By* IRVIN COBB

THERE was a swamp known as Little Niggerwool, to distinguish it from Big Niggerwool, which lay across the river. It was traversable only by those who knew it well—an oblong stretch of tawny mud and tawny water, measuring maybe four miles its longest way and two miles roughly at its widest; and it was full of cypress and stunted swampoak, with edgings of canebreak and rank weeds; and in one place, where a ridge crossed it from side to side, it was snaggled like an old jaw with dead tree trunks, rising close-ranked and thick as teeth. It was untenanted of living things— except, down below, there were snakes and mosquitoes, and a few wading and swimming fowl, and up above, those big woodpeckers that the country people called logcocks—larger than pigeons, with flaming crests and spiky tails—swooping in long, loping flight from snag to snag, always just out of gunshot of the chance invader and uttering a strident cry which matched the surroundings so fitly that it might well have been the voice of the swamp itself.

On one side Little Niggerwool drained its saffron waters off into a sluggish creek, where summer ducks bred, and on the other it ended abruptly at a natural bank of high ground, along which the country turn-pike was. The swamp came right up to the road and thrust its fringe of reedy, weedy undergrowth forward as though in challenge to the good farm lands that were spread beyond the barrier. At the time I was speaking of it was midsummer, and from these canes and weeds and waterplants there came a smell so rank as almost to be overpowering. They grew thick as a curtain, making a blank green wall taller than a man's head.

Along the dusty stretch of road fronting the swamp nothing living had stirred for half an hour or more. And so at length the weed-stems rustled and parted, and out from among them a man came forth silently and cautiously. He was an old man—an old man who had once been fat, but with age had grown lean again, so that now his skin was by odds too large for him. It lay on the back of his neck in folds. Under the chin he was pouched like a pelican and about the jowls was wattled like a turkey gobbler.

He came out upon the road slowly and stopped there, switching his legs absently with the stalk of a horseweed. He was in his shirtsleeves—a respectable, snuffy old figure; evidently a man deliberate in words and thoughts and actions. There was something about him suggestive of an old staid sheep that had been engaged in a clandestine transaction and was afraid of being found out.

He had made amply sure no one was in sight before he came out of the swamp, but now, to be doubly cer-

tain, he watched the empty road—first up, then down
—for a long half minute, and fetched a sighing breath
of satisfaction. His eyes fell upon his feet, and, taken
with an idea, he stepped back to the edge of the road
and with a wisp of crabgrass wiped his shoes clean of
the swamp mud, which was of a different color and tex-
ture from the soil of the upland. All his life Squire H.
B. Gathers had been a careful, canny man, and he had
need to be doubly careful on this summer morning.
Having disposed of the mud on his feet, he settled his
white straw hat down firmly upon his head, and, crossing the road, he climbed a stake-and-rider fence labori-
ously and went plodding sedately across a weedfield
and up a slight slope toward his house, half a mile away,
upon the crest of the little hill.

He felt perfectly natural—not like a man who had
just taken a fellowman's life—but natural and safe,
and well satisfied with himself and with his morning's
work. And he was safe; that was the main thing—
absolutely safe. Without hitch or hindrance he had
done the thing for which he had been planning and
waiting and longing all these months. There had been
no slip or mischance; the whole thing had worked out
as plainly and simply as two and two make four. No
living creature except himself knew of the meeting
in the early morning at the head of Little Niggerwool,
exactly where the squire had figured they should meet;
none knew of the device by which the other man had
been lured deeper and deeper in the swamp to the

exact spot where the gun was hidden. No one had seen the two of them enter the swamp; no one had seen the squire emerge, three hours later, alone.

The gun, having served its purpose, was hidden again, in a place no mortal eye would ever discover. Face downward, with a hole between his shoulderblades, the dead man was lying where he might lie undiscovered for months or for years, or forever. His pedler's pack was buried in the mud so deep that not even the probing crawfishes could find it. He would never be missed probably. There was but the slightest likelihood that inquiry would ever be made for him—let alone a search. He was a stranger and a foreigner, the dead man was, whose comings and goings made no great stir in the neighborhood, and whose failure to come again would be taken as a matter of course—just one of those shiftless, wandering Dagoes, here today and gone tomorrow. That was one of the best things about it— these Dagoes never had any people in this country to worry about them or look for them when they disappeared. And so it was all over and done with, and nobody the wiser. The squire clapped his hands together briskly with the air of a man dismissing a subject from his mind for good, and mended his gait.

He felt no stabbings of conscience. On the contrary, a glow of gratification filled him. His house was saved from scandal; his present wife would philander no more—before his very eyes—with these young Dagoes, who came from nobody knew where, with packs on their backs and persuasive, wheedling tongues in their heads. At this thought the squire raised his head and considered his homestead. It looked good to him—the small white cottage among the honey locusts, with beehives and flower beds about it; the tidy whitewashed fence; the sound outbuildings at the back, and the well-tilled acres roundabout.

At the fence he halted and turned about, carelessly and casually, and looked back along the way he had come. Everything was as it should be—the weedfield steaming in the heat; the empty road stretching along the crooked ridge like a long gray snake sunning itself; and beyond it, massing up, the dark, cloaking stretch of swamp. Everything was all right, but— The squire's eyes, in their loose sacs of skin, narrowed and squinted. Out of the blue arch away over yonder a small black dot had resolved itself and was swinging to and fro, like a mote. A buzzard—hey? Well, there were always buzzards about on a clear day like this. Buzzards were nothing to worry about—almost any time you could see one buzzard, or a dozen buzzards if you were a mind to look for them.

But this particular buzzard now—wasn't he making for Little Niggerwool? The squire did not like the idea of that. He had not thought of the buzzards until this minute. Sometimes when cattle strayed the owners had been known to follow the buzzards, knowing mighty well that if the buzzards led the way to where the stray was, the stray would be past the small salvage of hide and hoofs—but the owner's doubts would be set at rest for good and all.

There was a grain of disquiet in this. The squire shook his head to drive the thought away—yet it persisted, coming back like a midge dancing before his face. Once at home, however, Squire Gathers deported himself in a perfectly normal manner. With the satisfied proprietorial eye of an elderly husband who has no rivals, he considered his young wife, busied about her household duties. He sat in an easy-chair upon his front gallery and read his yesterday's Courier-Journal which the rural carrier had brought him; but he kept stepping out into the yard to peer up into the sky and all about him. To the second Mrs. Gathers he explained that he was looking for weather signs. A day as hot and still as this one was a regular weather breeder; there ought to be rain before night.

"Maybe so," she said; "but looking's not going to bring rain."

Nevertheless the squire continued to look. There was really nothing to worry about; still at midday he did not eat much dinner, and before his wife was half through with hers he was back on the gallery. His paper was cast aside and he was watching. The original buzzard—or, anyhow, he judged it was the first one he had seen—was swinging back and forth in great pendulum swings, but closer down toward the swamp—closer and closer—until it looked from that distance as though the buzzard flew almost at the level of the tallest snags there. And on beyond this first buzzard, coursing above him, were other buzzards. Wère there four of them? No; there were five—five in all.

Such is the way of the buzzard—that shifting black question mark which punctuates a Southern sky. In the woods a shoat or a sheep or a horse lies down to die. At once, coming seemingly out of nowhere, appears a black spot, up five hundred feet or a thousand in the air. In broad loops and swirls this dot swings round and round and round, coming a little closer to earth at every turn and always with one particular spot upon the earth for the axis of its wheel. Out of space also other moving spots emerge and grow larger as they tack and jibe and drop nearer, coming in their leisurely buzzard way to the feast. There is no haste—the feast will wait. If it is a dumb creature that has fallen stricken the grim coursers will sooner or later be assembled about it and alongside it, scrouging ever closer and closer to the dying thing, with awkward out-thrustings of their naked necks and great dust-raising flaps of the huge, unkempt wings; lifting their feathered shanks high and stiffly like old crippled grave-diggers in overalls that are too tight—but silent and patient all, offering no attack until the last tremor runs through the stiffening carcass and the eyes glaze over. To humans the buzzard pays a deeper meed of respect—he hangs aloft longer; but in the end he comes. No scavenger shark, no carrion

crab, ever chambered more grisly secrets in his diges-
tive processes than this big charnel bird. Such is the
way of the buzzard.

.     .     .     .     .     .     .     .

The squire missed his afternoon nap, a thing that
had not happened in years. He stayed on the front gallery and kept count. Those moving distant black specks
typified uneasiness for the squire—not fear exactly, or
panic or anything akin to it, but a nibbling, nagging
kind of uneasiness. Time and again he said to himself
that he would not think about them any more; but he
did—unceasingly.

By supper time there were seven of them.

.     .     .     .     .     .     .     .

He slept light and slept badly. It was not the thought
of that dead man lying yonder in Little Niggerwool
that made him toss and fume while his wife snored
gently alongside him. It was something else altogether.
Finally his stirrings roused her and she asked him drow-
sily what ailed him. Was he sick? Or bothered about
anything?

Irritated, he answered her snappishly. Certainly
nothing was bothering him, he told her. It was a hot
enough night—wasn't it? And when a man got a little
along in life he was apt to be a light sleeper—wasn't
that so? Well, then? She turned upon her side and slept
again with her light, purring snore. The squire lay
awake, thinking hard and waiting for day to come.

At the first faint pink-and-gray glow he was up and

out upon the gallery. He cut a comic figure standing there in his shirt in the half light, with the dewlap at his throat dangling grotesquely in the neck opening of the unbuttoned garment, and his bare bowed legs showing, splotched and varicose. He kept his eyes fixed on the skyline below, to the south. Buzzards are early risers too. Presently, as the heavens shimmered with the miracle of sunrise, he could make them out—six or seven, or maybe eight.

An hour after breakfast the squire was on his way down through the weedfield to the county road. He went half eagerly, half unwillingly. He wanted to make sure about those buzzards. It might be that they were aiming for the old pasture at the head of the swamp. There were sheep grazing there—and it might be that a sheep had died. Buzzards were notoriously fond of sheep, when dead. Or, if they were pointed for the swamp, he must satisfy himself exactly what part of the swamp it was. He was at the stake-and-rider fence when a mare came jogging down the road, drawing a rig with a man in it. At sight of the squire in the field the man pulled up.

"Hi, squire!" he saluted. "Goin' somewheres?"

"No; jest knockin' about," the squire said—"jest sorter lookin' the place over."

"Hot agin—ain't it?" said the other.

The squire allowed that it was, for a fact, mighty hot. Commonplaces of gossip followed this—county politics and a neighbor's wife sick of breakbone fever down the road a piece. The subject of crops succeeded inevitably. The squire spoke of the need of rain. Instantly he regretted it, for the other man, who was by way of being a weather wiseacre, cocked his head aloft to study the sky for any signs of clouds.

"Wonder whut all them buzzards are doin' yonder, squire," he said, pointing upward with his whipstock.

"Whut buzzards—where?" asked the squire with an elaborate note of carelessness in his voice.

"Right yonder, over Little Niggerwool—see 'em there?"

"Oh, yes," the squire made answer. "Now I see 'em. They ain't doin' nothin', I reckin—jest flyin' round same as they always do in clear weather."

"Must be somethin' dead over there!" speculated the man in the buggy.

"A hawg probably," said the squire promptly—almost too promptly. "There's likely to be hawgs usin' in Niggerwool. Bristow, over on the other side from here—he's got a big drove of hawgs."

"Well, mebbe so," said the man; "but hawgs is a heap more apt to be feedin' on high ground, seems like to me. Well, I'll be gittin' along towards town. G'day, squire." And he slapped the lines down on the mare's flank and jogged off through the dust.

He could not have suspected anything—that man couldn't. As the squire turned away from the road and headed for his house he congratulated himself upon that stroke of his in bringing in Bristow's hogs; and yet there remained this disquieting note in the situation, that buzzards flying, and especially buzzards flying over Little Niggerwool, made people curious—made them ask questions.

He was half-way across the weedfield when, above the hum of insect life, above the inward clamor of his own busy speculations, there came to his ear dimly and distantly a sound that made him halt and cant his head to one side the better to hear it. Somewhere, a good way off, there was a thin, thready, broken strain of metallic clinking and clanking—an eery ghost-chime ringing. It came nearer and became plainer—tonk-tonk-tonk; then the tonks all running together briskly.

A sheep bell or a cowbell—that was it; but why did it seem to come from overhead, from up in the sky, like? And why did it shift so abruptly from one quarter to another—from left to right and back again to left? And how was it that the clapper seemed to strike so fast? Not even the breachiest of breachy young heifers could be expected to tinkle a cowbell with such briskness. The squire's eye searched the earth and the sky, his troubled mind giving to his eye a quick and flashing scrutiny. He had it. It was not a cow at all. It was not anything that went on four legs.

One of the loathly flock had left the others. The orbit of his swing had carried him across the road and over Squire Gathers' land. He was sailing right toward and over the squire now. Craning his flabby neck, the squire could make out the unwholesome contour of the huge bird. He could see the ragged black wings—a buzzard's wings are so often ragged and uneven—and the naked throat; the slim, naked head; the big feet folded up against the dingy belly. And he could see a bell too—an under-sized cowbell—that dangled at the creature's breast and jangled incessantly. All his life nearly Squire Gathers had been hearing about the Belled Buzzard. Now with his own eye he was seeing him.

Once, years and years and years ago, some one trapped a buzzard, and before freeing it clamped about its skinny neck a copper band with a cowbell pendent from it. Since then the bird so ornamented has been seen a hundred times—and heard oftener—over an area as wide as half the continent. It has been reported, now in Kentucky, now in Texas, now in North Carolina —now anywhere between the Ohio River and the Gulf. Crossroads correspondents take their pens in hand to write to the country papers that on such and such a date, at such a place, So-and-So saw the Belled Buzzard. Always it is the Belled Buzzard, never a belled buzzard. The Belled Buzzard is an institution.

There must be more than one of them. It seems hard to believe that one bird, even a buzzard in his prime, and protected by law in every Southern state and known to be a bird of great age, could live so long and range so far and wear a clinking cowbell all the time! Probably other jokers have emulated the original joker; probably if the truth were known there have been a dozen such; but the country people will have it that there is only one Belled Buzzard—a bird that bears a charmed life and on his neck a never silent bell.

.    .    .    .    .    .    .    .

Squire Gathers regarded it a most untoward thing that the Belled Buzzard should have come just at this time. The movements of ordinary, unmarked buzzards mainly concerned only those whose stock had strayed; but almost anybody with time to spare might follow this rare and famous visitor, this belled and feathered junkman of the sky. Supposing now that some one followed it today—maybe followed it even to a certain thick clump of cypress in the middle of Little Niggerwool!

But at this particular moment the Belled Buzzard was heading directly away from that quarter. Could it be following him? Of course not! It was just by chance that it flew along the course the squire was taking. But, to make sure, he veered off sharply, away from the footpath into the high weeds so that the startled grasshoppers sprayed up in front of him in fan-like flights.

He was right; it was only a chance. The Belled Buzzard swung off too, but in the opposite direction, with a sharp tonking of its bell, and, flapping hard, was in a minute or two out of hearing and sight, past the trees to the westward.

Again the squire skimped his dinner, and again he spent the long drowsy afternoon upon his front gallery. In all the sky there were now no buzzards visible, belled or unbelled—they had settled to earth somewhere; and this served somewhat to soothe the squire's pestered mind. This does not mean, though, that he was by any means easy in his thoughts. Outwardly he was calm enough, with the ruminative judicial air befitting the oldest justice of the peace in the county; but, within him, a little something gnawed unceasingly at his nerves like one of those small white worms that are to be found in seemingly sound nuts. About once in so long a tiny spasm of the muscles would contract the dewlap under his chin. The squire had never heard of that play, made famous by a famous player, wherein the murdered victim was a pedler too, and a clamoring bell the voice of unappeasable remorse in the murderer's ear. As a strict churchgoer the squire had no use for players or for play actors, and so was spared that added canker to his conscience. It was bad enough as it was.

That night, as on the night before, the old man's sleep was broken and fitful and disturbed by dreaming, in which he heard a metal clapper striking against a brazen surface. This was one dream that came true. Just after daybreak he heaved himself out of bed, with a flop of his broad bare feet upon the floor, and stepped to the window and peered out. Half seen in the pinkish light, the Belled Buzzard flapped directly over his roof and flew due south, right toward the swamp—drawing a direct line through the air between the slayer and the victim—or, anyway, so it seemed to the watcher, grown suddenly tremulous.

. . . . . . . .

Knee deep in yellow swamp water the squire squatted, with his shotgun cocked and loaded and ready, waiting to kill the bird that now typified for him guilt and danger and an abiding great fear. Gnats plagued him and about him frogs croaked. Almost overhead a logcock clung lengthwise to a snag, watching him. Snake doctors, limber, long insects with bronze bodies and filmy wings, went back and forth like small living shuttles. Other buzzards passed and repassed, but the squire waited, forgetting the cramps in his elderly limbs and the discomfort of the water in his shoes.

At length he heard the bell. It came nearer and nearer, and the Belled Buzzard swung overhead not sixty feet up, its black bulk a fair target against the blue. He aimed and fired, both barrels bellowing at once and a fog of thick powder smoke enveloping him. Through the smoke he saw the bird career and its bell jangled furiously; then the buzzard righted itself and was gone, fleeing so fast that the sound of its bell was hushed almost instantly. Two long wing feathers drifted slowly down; torn disks of gunwadding and shredding green scraps of leaves descended about the squire in a little shower.

He cast his empty gun from him so that it fell in the water and disappeared; and he hurried out of the

swamp as fast as his shaky legs would take him, splash-
ing himself with mire and water to his eyebrows.
Mucked with mud, breathing in great gulps, trembling,
a suspicious figure to any eye, he burst through the
weed curtain and staggered into the open, his caution
all gone and a vast desperation fairly choking him—
but the gray road was empty and the field beyond the
road was empty; and, except for him, the whole world
seemed empty and silent.

As he crossed the field Squire Gathers composed
himself. With plucked handfuls of grass he cleansed
himself of much of the swamp mire that coated him
over; but the little white worm that gnawed at his
nerves had become a cold snake that was coiled about
his heart, squeezing it tighter and tighter!

.    .    .    .    .    .    .    .

This episode of the attempt to kill the Belled Buzzard occurred in the afternoon of the third day. In
the forenoon of the fourth, the weather being still
hot, with cloudless skies and no air stirring, there was
a rattle of warped wheels in the squire's lane and a hail
at his yard fence.

Coming out upon his gallery from the innermost darkened room of his house, where he had been stretched
upon a bed, the squire shaded his eyes from the glare
and saw the constable of his own magisterial district
sitting in a buggy at the gate waiting.

The old man went down the dirtpath slowly, almost
reluctantly, with his head twisted up sidewise, listening,

watching; but the constable sensed nothing strange about the other's gait and posture; the constable was full of the news he brought. He began to unload the burden of it without preamble.

"Mornin', Squire Gathers. There's been a dead man found in Little Niggerwool—and you're wanted."

He did not notice that the squire was holding on with both hands to the gate; but he did notice that the squire had a sick look out of his eyes and a dead, pasty color in his face; and he noticed—but attached no meaning to it—that when the squire spoke his voice seemed flat and hollow.

"Wanted—fur—what?" The squire forced the words out of his throat, pumped them out fairly.

"Why, to hold the inquest," explained the constable. "The coroner's sick abed, and he said you bein' the nearest jestice of the peace you should serve."

"Oh," said the squire with more ease. "Well, where is it—the body?"

"They taken it to Bristow's place and put it in his stable for the present. They brought it out over on that side and his place was the nearest. If you'll hop in here with me, squire, I'll ride you right over there now. There's enough men already gathered to make up a jury, I reckin."

"I—I ain't well," demurred the squire. "I've been sleepin' porely these last few nights. It's the heat," he added quickly.

"Well, suh, you don't look very brash, and that's a

fact," said the constable; "but this here job ain't goin' to keep you long. You see it's in such shape—the body is—that there ain't no way of makin' out who the feller was nor whut killed him. There ain't nobody reported missin' in this county as we know of, either; so I jedge a verdict of a unknown person dead from unknown causes would be about the correct thing. And we kin git it all over mighty quick and put him underground right away, suh—if you'll go along now."

"I'll go," agreed the squire, almost quivering in his newborn eagerness. "I'll go right now." He did not wait to get his coat or to notify his wife of the errand that was taking him. In his shirtsleeves he climbed into the buggy, and the constable turned his horse and clucked him into a trot. And now the squire asked the question that knocked at his lips demanding to be asked —the question the answer to which he yearned for and yet dreaded.

"How did they come to find—it?"

"Well, suh, that's a funny thing," said the constable. "Early this mornin' Bristow's oldest boy—that one they call Buddy—he heared a cowbell over in the swamp and so he went to look; Bristow's got cows, as you know, and one or two of 'em is belled. And he kept on followin' after the sound of it till he got way down into the thickest part of them cypress slashes that's near the middle there; and right there he run acrost it—this body.

"But, suh, squire, it wasn't no cow at all. No, suh; it was a buzzard with a cowbell on his neck—that's whut it was. Yes, suh; that there same old Belled Buzzard he's come back agin and is hangin' round. They tell me he ain't been seen round here sence the year of the yellow fever—I don't remember myself, but that's whut they tell me. The niggers over on the other side are right smartly worked up over it. They say—the niggers do—that when the Belled Buzzard comes it's a sign of bad luck for somebody, shore!"

The constable drove on, talking on, garrulous as a guinea hen. The squire didn't heed him. Hunched back in the buggy, he harkened only to those busy inner voices filling his mind with thundering portents. Even so, his ear was first to catch above the rattle of the buggy wheels the far-away, faint tonk-tonk! They were about half-way to Bristow's place then. He gave no sign, and it was perhaps half a minute before his companion heard it too.

The constable jerked the horse to a standstill and craned his neck over his shoulder.

"Well, by doctors!" he cried, "if there ain't the old scoundrel now, right here behind us! I kin see him plain as day—he's got an old cowbell hitched to his neck; and he's shy a couple of feathers out of one wing. By doctors, that's somethin' you won't see every day! In all my born days I ain't never seen the beat of that!"

Squire Gathers did not look; he only cowered back

farther under the buggy top. In the pleasing excitement of the moment his companion took no heed, though, of anything except the Belled Buzzard.

"Is he followin' us?" asked the squire in a curiously flat, weighted voice.

"Which—him?" answered the constable, still stretching his neck. "No, he's gone now—gone off to the left —jest a-zoonin', like he'd done forgot somethin'."

And Bristow's place was to the left! But there might still be time. To get the inquest over and the body underground—those were the main things. Ordinarily humane in his treatment of stock, Squire Gathers urged the constable to greater speed. The horse was lathered and his sides heaved wearily as they pounded across the bridge over the creek which was the outlet to the swamp and emerged from a patch of woods in sight of Bristow's farm buildings.

The house was set on a little hill among cleared fields and was in other respects much like the squire's own house except that it was smaller and not so well painted. There was a wide yard in front with shade trees and a lye hopper and a well-box, and a paling fence with a stile in it instead of a gate. At the rear, behind a clutter of outbuildings—a barn, a smokehouse and a corncrib—was a little peach orchard, and flanking the house on the right there was a good-sized cowyard, empty of stock at this hour, with feedracks ranged in a row against the fence. A two-year-old negro child, bareheaded and barefooted and wearing but a single garment, was grubbing busily in the dirt under one of these feedracks.

To the front fence a dozen or more riding horses were hitched, flicking their tails at the flies; and on the gallery men in their shirtsleeves were grouped. An old negro woman, with her head tied in a bandanna and a man's old slouch hat perched upon the bandanna, peeped out from behind a corner. There were gaunt hound dogs wandering about, sniffing uneasily.

Before the constable had the horse hitched the squire was out of the buggy and on his way up the footpath, going at a brisker step than the squire usually traveled. The men on the porch hailed him gravely and ceremoniously, as befitting an occasion of solemnity. Afterward some of them recalled the look in his eye; but at the moment they noted it—if they noted it at all—subconsciously.

For all his haste the squire, as was also remembered later, was almost the last to enter the door; and before he did enter he halted and searched the flawless sky as though for signs of rain. Then he hurried on after the others, who clumped single file along a narrow little hall, the bare, uncarpeted floor creaking loudly under their heavy farm shoes, and entered a good-sized room that had in it, among other things, a high-piled feather bed and a cottage organ—Bristow's best room, now to be placed at the disposal of the law's representatives for the inquest. The squire took the largest chair and drew it to the very center of the room, in front of a fireplace, where the grate was banked with withering asparagus ferns. The constable took his place formally at one side of the presiding official. The others sat or stood about where they could find room— all but six of them, whom the squire picked for his coroner's jury, and who backed themselves against the wall.

The squire showed haste. He drove the preliminaries forward with a sort of tremulous insistence. Bristow's wife brought a bucket of fresh drinking water and a gourd, and almost before she was out of the room and the door closed behind her the squire had sworn his jurors and was calling the first witness, who it seemed likely would also be the only witness—Bristow's oldest boy. The boy wriggled in confusion as he sat on a cane-bottomed chair facing the old magistrate. All there, barring one or two, had heard his story a dozen times already, but now it was to be repeated under oath; and so they bent their heads, listening as though it were a brand-new tale. All eyes were on him; none were fastened on the squire as he, too, gravely bent his head, listening—listening.

The witness began—but had no more than started when the squire gave a great, screeching howl and sprang from his chair and staggered backward, his eyes popped and the pouch under his chin quivering as though it had a separate life all its own. Startled, the constable made toward him and they struck together heavily and went down—both on their all fours—right in front of the fireplace.

The constable scrambled free and got upon his feet, in a squat of astonishment, with his head craned; but the squire stayed upon the floor, face downward, his feet flopping among the rustling asparagus greens—a picture of slavering animal fear. And now his gagging screech resolved itself into articulate speech.

"I done it!" they made out his shrieked words. "I done it! I own up—I killed him! He aimed fur to break up my home and I tolled him off into Nigger-wool and killed him!

"There's a hole in his back if you'll look for it. I done it—oh, I done it—and I'll tell everything jest like it happened if you'll jest keep that thing away from me! Oh, my lawdy! Don't you hear it? It's a-comin' clos'ter and clos'ter—it's a-comin' after me! Keep it away—" His voice gave out and he buried his head in his hands and rolled upon the gaudy carpet.

And now they all heard what he had heard first— they heard the tonk-tonk-tonk of a cowbell, coming nearer and nearer toward them along the hallway without. It was as though the sound floated along. There was no creak of footsteps upon the loose, bare boards— and the bell jangled faster than it would dangling from a cow's neck. The sound came right to the door and Squire Gathers wallowed among the chair legs.

The door swung open. In the doorway stood a negro

child, barefooted and naked except for a single garment, eyeing them with serious, rolling eyes—and, with all the strength of his two puny arms, proudly but solemnly tolling a small rusty cowbell he had found in the cowyard.

From *The Escape of Mr. Trimm* by Irvin Cobb. (Doran, N. Y.)

# JAMES WELDON JOHNSON

In 1915 James Weldon Johnson left Nicaragua and returned to New York. He had spent seven years in the consular service, first at Puerto Caballo, Venezuela, then at Corinto, and had seen three revolutions—including the one that overthrew Castro—and the bubonic plague. Many an American sheltered then by the consulate remembered with gratitude and respect the colored man who represented his country.

He was born in Jacksonville, Florida. As there were then only grammar schools for colored boys there, he was sent to Atlanta and graduated from Atlanta University. Then he taught school in his home city. Here he changed the grammar school of which he was principal into a high school by a process which goes far to explain why he was later so successful, not only in diplomacy abroad, but in more difficult and delicate situations in his own country. Mary White Ovington, in her "Portraits in Color" (Viking), says: "At the end of three years, the graduating class proving a promising one, the principal persuaded twenty of his pupils to stay. After one year, they stayed for two. The board of education granted another teacher, and at the end of four years there was a high school with a graduating class. All this had been done without friction and without anyone but the principal realizing what was happening."

From Mrs. Ovington's book one learns also that he was

meanwhile writing the words for the songs of his brother Rosamond, who had studied at Boston Conservatory. They had the gift of popular song; they wrote "Lift Ev'ry Voice and Sing," for a chorus of children to sing on Lincoln's Birthday, and it went on, on its own momentum, until there is reason why it is now called the Negro National Anthem. Then they took their talent to Broadway, wrote some of the most popular songs of the opening century, went into vaudeville, and then into musical comedy. J. W. Johnson was in musical comedy for seven years; after his seven years in the consular service he used his knowledge of Spanish in the translation of the libretto of "Goyescas" used at the Metropolitan Opera House. Besides assured success in the theatrical world, it seemed likely that he would make his mark as a writer. Then J. E. Spingarn asked him to become field secretary of the National Association for the Advancement of Colored People, and his real work began.

In the midst of this work "The Book of Negro Spirituals" came quietly into the publishing season of 1925 and found itself straightway among the ten best sellers. It was the work of J. Rosamond Johnson, with an introduction by his brother so valuable that no student of American music or social history should neglect it. Three years later a slender volume of inspirational sermons by old-time Negro preachers, cast in free and flowing verse-form, appeared as "God's Trombones." A book of poems seldom makes so wide and so deep an impression in America. It was everywhere recognized as the ideal memorial to the Negro preacher until then usually treated in literature only as a grotesque and amusing feature of plantation life. Since then the old-time preacher has found in "Green Pastures" what amounts to apotheosis upon the stage, but the book in which he first came into his own is "God's Trombones."

In the introduction Mr. Johnson tells of listening to a famous visiting preacher in Kansas City who broke off in the midst of a formal sermon and started intoning the old folk-sermon that

begins with the creation of the world and ends with Judgment
Day. He was at once a changed man, free, at ease and masterful.
The change in the congregation was instantaneous. An electric
current ran through the crowd. It was in a moment alive
and quivering; and all the while the preacher held it in the palm
of his hand. He was wonderful in the way he employed his
conscious and unconscious art. He strode the pulpit up and
down in what was actually a very rhythmic dance, and he
brought into play the full gamut of his wonderful voice, a voice
—what shall I say?—not of an organ or a trumpet, but rather
of a trombone, the instrument possessing above all others the
power to express the wide and varied range of emotions encom-
passed by the human voice—and with greater amplitude. He
intoned, he moaned, he pleaded—he blared, he crashed, he thun-
dered. I sat fascinated; and more, I was, perhaps against my
will, deeply moved; the emotional effect upon me was irresistible. Before he had finished I took a slip of paper and somewhat surreptitiously jotted down some ideas for the first poem,
"The Creation."

# THE CREATION

James Weldon Johnson

And God stepped out on space,
   And he looked around and said:
   I'm lonely—
   I'll make me a world.

And far as the eye of God could see
   Darkness covered everything,
   Blacker than a hundred midnights
   Down in a cypress swamp.

Then God smiled,
   And the light broke,
   And the darkness rolled up on one side,
   And the light stood shining on the other,
   And God said: That's good!

Then God reached out and took the light in his hands,
   And God rolled the light around in his hands
   Until he made the sun;
   And he set that sun a-blazing in the heavens.
   And the light that was left from making the sun
   God gathered it up in a shining ball
   And flung it against the darkness,

Spangling the night with the moon and stars.
Then down between
The darkness and the light
He hurled the world;
And God said: That's good!

Then God himself stepped down—
And the sun was on his right hand,
And the moon was on his left;
The stars were clustered about his head,
And the earth was under his feet.
And God walked, and where he trod
His footsteps hollowed the valleys out
And bulged the mountains up.

Then he stopped and looked and saw
That the earth was hot and barren.
So God stepped over to the edge of the world
And he spat out the seven seas—
He batted his eyes, and the lightnings flashed—
He clapped his hands, and the thunders rolled—
And the waters above the earth came down,
The cooling waters came down.

Then the green grass sprouted,
And the little red flowers blossomed,
The pine tree pointed his finger to the sky,
And the oak spread out his arms,
The lakes cuddled down in the hollows of the ground,

And the rivers ran down to the sea;
And God smiled again,
And the rainbow appeared,
And curled itself around his shoulder.

Then God raised his arm and he waved his hand
Over the sea and over the land,
And he said: Bring forth! Bring forth!
And quicker than God could drop his hand,
Fishes and fowls
And beasts and birds
Swam the rivers and the seas,
Roamed the forests and the woods,
And split the air with their wings,
And God said: That's good!

Then God walked around,
And God looked around
On all that he had made.
He looked at his sun,
And he looked at his moon,
And he looked at his little stars;
He looked on his world
With all its living things,
And God said: I'm lonely still.

Then God sat down—
On the side of a hill where he could think;
By a deep, wide river he sat down;

With his head in his hands,
God thought and thought,
Till he thought: I'll make me a man!

Up from the bed of the river
God scooped the clay;
And by the bank of the river
He kneeled him down;
And there the great God Almighty
Who lit the sun and fixed it in the sky,
Who flung the stars to the most far corner of the
    night,
Who rounded the earth in the middle of his hand;
This Great God,
Like a mammy bending over her baby,
Kneeled down in the dust
Toiling over a lump of clay
Till he shaped it in his own image;
Then into it he blew the breath of life,
And man became a living soul.
Amen. Amen.

From *God's Trombones: Seven Negro Sermons
in Verse* by James Weldon Johnson. (Viking
Press, 1927.)

# DON MARQUIS

No one with a birthplace set down in *Who's Who* as Walnut, Bureau County, Illinois, need fear that it will be forgotten. Yet without this information some American readers might perhaps have taken Don Marquis for a native Southerner, he writes with such sympathy of life in Georgia. He did not come from that state however; he went there as a young editorial writer, first on the *Atlanta News*, then on the *Atlanta Journal*, after trying his hand at being printer's devil, clerk in the Census Office, art student, and newspaper man. When *Uncle Remus's Magazine* was started in 1906 he became assistant to Joel Chandler Harris and remained three years, till he came to New York. From this point on he is known to everyone in America who reads newspapers or goes to the play.

Now and again he has plunged an arm into the files of the "Sun Dial" and brought up a bookful, thus granting a place in our literature as well as in our affections to his column-creations, Hermione, Archy and Mehitabel, or The Old Soak, or adding to the world's Utopias "The Almost Perfect State." He writes plays and poetry; he writes stories for the magazines, and from one of the volumes in which these are collected, "A Variety of People," this story has been taken. I think Mark Twain would have relished its grim good humor.

# A MEAN JOKE

*By* Don Marquis

"Why is old Noah always stopping in his tracks like that, to take a look around him, every hundred yards or so?" I asked old Noah's brother, Jack Williams.

"Old Noah, he's got a kind of a notion some of the boys is layin' to shoot him," said Jack, looking after his brother with a faint smile.

"Shoot him?"

"Uh-huh. From in behint a tree or a rock or some place," said Jack. "Hit's a joke the boys has got onto old Noah; and in my opinion hit's a joke that has been carried too far in this heah settle*ment*."

I was in the hill country of northwest Georgia, camping out with a friend who knew the natives well. Jack had come over to the camp to "set by for a spell," as he called it, and gossip.

"Old Noah, there," he said, "is like as not goin' to turn the tables onto the boys one of these heah days. He's a dead shot with that theah old rifle of his'n, ef he kin get his eyes sot on anythin' to shoot at."

Old Noah was a fascinating figure to me. He must have been well over seventy, and he had a long, dirty, yellowish-white beard that had evidently never been trimmed in his life. He carried, always, a heavy,

octagon-barrelled, muzzle-loading rifle, such as Daniel
Boone himself must have carried; and I had once seen
him "bark" a squirrel with it. When you bark a squirrel
you do not shoot the squirrel himself; you put a bullet
just beneath the bark of the tree limb the squirrel is
clinging to, right under the squirrel's heart; the bullet
"explodes" the bark against his chest, so to speak, and
he falls dead from the shock, without a mark on him.
It takes extraordinarily good shooting.

"Why are the boys laying to shoot Noah?" I asked.

"They ain't, really," said Jack. "Hit's a notion they
give him some yeahs ago. That's the joke of hit."

He frowned and took a chew of tobacco. He had
some difficulty getting into his story. Presently I realized it was a difficulty concerning liquor.

"About fifteen yeahs ago," began Jack, "some of the
boys in the settle*ment* heah went to jail foh quite a
spell on a charge they had been makin' whiskey."

He paused. I respected his silence. Pretty soon he
resumed: "None of us hadn't made no whiskey."

At the bottom of the slope on which we sat was an
old-fashioned gristmill, turned by a considerable creek
that came down out of the hills. And farther up the
creek was a moonshine still. Jack knew that I knew
it was there, and only three days before had brought
me a jug of liquor manufactured there. But never, at
any time, would he admit that he had made liquor.
He'd give it to you or sell it to you, if you were a
friend; he'd tell about having been to jail on three

separate occasions on charges of making it; he would even discuss processes of making it, and methods of attempting to remove some of the cruder oils by running the liquor through charred logs—but he would always wind up by saying: "Of course, hit's a thing none of us around this heah settle*ment* ever made."

"Of course not, Jack," was the proper answer, always; and I gave it to him. Then we had a drink from the jug that he had brought me, from the still that he knew I knew was up the creek, and he proceeded:

"No, sir, none of we-uns ever made it around heah. But the United States gov'ment convicted us, and after we had laid around jail quite a spell the word come to us that it was old Noah had went and info'med onto us.

"Well, sir, we helt a caucus as to what was the right and fittin' thing to do when we got back to the settle*ment*. The most nacheral thing to do was to shoot old Noah. The' wasn't no argyment I could make again' hit. I knowed hit was the right thing and the moral thing. Still and all, old Noah he was my brother; and you don't take no pleasure in thinkin' of yo' own kinsfolk bein' shot thataway.

"But hit was, most p'intedly, a case wheah hit wasn't my turn to speak. Ef hit had been anyone else exceptin' of my brother, I mought 'a' put in a word for Noah. But hit would 'a' looked like I was prejudice' in his favoh ef I had been the one to say he wasn't wo'th killin'. Hit was a mos' delicate p'int foh me to speak to, and I didn't speak. And the plain moral facks was, he had hit comin' to him.

"And then one of the boys—Bud Hightower, hit was —laughs of a sudden, and he says: 'Hell's pepper,' he says, 'old Noah, he ain't wo'th killin', and never was. S'pose we-all just keep him *thinkin'* we-all is goin' to shoot him?'"

"Well, sir, they all laughed at that; and that's what's been done ever since. Fo' the last fifteen yeahs, sir, every six or eight weeks one of the boys shoots *near* to old Noah, out'n the bushes, or from behint a rock. It's a joke that everybody knows in this heah settle-*ment* but old Noah himself.

"And tha's why he's always stoppin', and lookin' over his shoulder, and swingin' that theah old gun of his'n this way or that—like he is now."

He was standing in a level place beside the creek bank, near the mill, looking about him. As I gazed on the old man he took on, for me, a look of pathos, for the first time. He must have died fifty—a hundred!— deaths in the last fifteen years, on account of the primi- tive sense of humor of his neighbors.

"Hit's gettin' to be a kind of a mean joke, I opin- ionate," mused Jack. "The last fo' or five yeahs, old Noah, he's done aged considerable. Hit's my opinion hit's been carried too far. I'm lookin' to see him shoot himself, one of these heah days, just fo' to get hit ovah with."

As he spoke there was a report of a gun from farther up the hill, twenty yards from where Jack and I were sitting, and a bullet tore up the sod five feet beyond old Noah.

"Bud Hightower's gun, by the sound of her," commented Jack.

Just then old Noah lifted his ancient rifle and fired. And with a cry Bud Hightower pitched headforemost forward from a clump of bushes, and lay still.

"I reckoned I'd git him sooner or later, Jack," squeaked old Noah excitedly, running up the slope toward us. "He's been poppin' away at me fo' fifteen yeahs!"

Not then, nor at any previous time, it appeared, had old Noah taken the matter as the pleasantry it was intended for.

From *A Variety of People* by Don Marquis. (Doubleday, Doran, 1928, 1929.)

# PERNET PATTERSON

It is seldom that so young a man as Pernet Patterson writes so understandingly and so charmingly of a past phase in the South. "Buttin' Blood" appeared in the *Atlantic Monthly* in 1928; it was at once greeted as a story of unusual importance and promise and its writer marked as one whose work was by all means to be watched. The story was chosen for the O. Henry prize volume of the year, and generally noticed by those who reviewed this book as a sympathetic study of life in the older South. The little black boy has, of course, a special athletic distinction and accomplishment, but the friendship between the white boy and the black, expressed though it may be with the bluff unsentimentality of boyhood, the protecting affection on one side and the unhesitating devotion on the other, belong to youth in general. The landscape, the atmosphere, is of a rural Virginia that seldom reaches the reader of magazine fiction and has never done so more graciously.

# BUTTIN' BLOOD

### By Pernet Patterson

THE canvas-covered tobacco-wagon had been jolting over the frozen track of Little North Road since before dawn. On the seat huddled two small figures, almost submerged in a welter of old quilts. Silent they sat, swaying instinctively to the pitch and roll of the wagon, as the steel tires climbed screechingly from rut to rut.

The larger, a white boy, held the reins loosely, in one hand, allowing the mules their own way. His eyes were fixed abstractedly on the road ahead; his shoulders bowed, as if under weighty responsibility.

The clink of the breast chains, in soft accompaniment to the *clack-clack* of the mules' shoes on the frozen ground, and the rumble and creak of the heavily loaded wagon came vaguely to him as homely, comfortable sounds, in the deserted stillness of early morning. And the intimate mellow-peach fragrance of Virginia sun-cured tobacco, together with the everyday mule-and-harness smell, drifted over him comfortably, too.

With a sigh he roused from his reverie and quickened the lagging team. Glancing at the small head resting on his shoulder, muffled in an old slouch hat brought down about his ears with a fragment of blanket, his face softened into a whimsical smile. He gave a vigorous shrug, and shouted:

"Wake up, Nubbin! Sun's up, nigger!"

The little form straightened with a start. An ashy-black hand came out from the chaos of covers and pulled off the headpiece. Slowly he rubbed his face, scratched his head, and rolled his big eyes at his companion.

"Huccome you 'niggah' me?" he demanded, frowning. "I got big graveyard in de woods full o' white boys what call me 'niggah'."

The white boy threw back his head and laughed; then, turning suddenly, with an explosive "Baa!" butted his coonskin cap roundly against the black ear.

"Ba-a! Phut! Phut!" went the little darky, jumping from the seat; and bridling like an angry goat, sent his bullet head thump against the white boy's ribs.

"Ouch! I give up! I give up!" capitulated the latter.

"You ain' gwine call me 'niggah no mo'?"

"No! No!" acceded the white boy, shrinking into his corner. "Cross my heart—and double cross," and his mittened hand made youth's inviolable sign of the double cross.

"Dat's mo' like hit—an' you member hit too, Luther Patten," grinned the Negro. With a final admonitory "Baa!" and a half-dancing shuffle of his big-shod feet on the wagon bottom, he dived to the seat and snatched the quilts about him.

"Huccome you don' git col' like me? Huccome don'

no white folks git col' like niggah?" he asked queru-
lously.

Luther smiled at the forbidden word; but of course
it carried a vastly different meaning when used by Nubbin's race—an intangible, shadowy difference to the
white mind, but to the black a difference as clear cut as
a cameo.

He answered with an imitative question:

"Huccome nig—colored folks' heads harder than
white folks'?" Wrinkling his brow, he pondered, "I
rully do wonder what makes yo' head so tough. Don't
it hurt you, Nub, buttin' ol' calves and things? Just
buttin' a pile of bags hurts me somep'n awful. I don't
reckon," he continued resignedly, "I ever will be a
butter. But," he added, brightening, "I can drive
tobacco to Richmond—that's more'n you can do."

"Hunh!" disparaged Nubbin. "Drivin' ol' 'bacca
down ain' nothin', but buttin' is buttin'."

Pausing, he continued as if in soliloquy: "But I ain'
no buttah a-tall. You des oughter see my grand'pa. He
war de buttin'es' one in de county—in de whole worl',
I reckon. He kill hese'f buttin'—"

"Killed himself buttin'!"

"Yeah. A white man offer 'im two dollah ef he butt
de sto' do'. Well, de wo'd wan't more'n outen he mouf
'fo' gran'pa had back hese'f 'back, an' wid a shake er
he haid, 'way he went, buckin' an' jumpin', scerse
touchin' de groun'; and when putty nigh de do' he give
a 'Baa!' an' des nachully sailed th'u' de air, an'—blam!

He hit it, an' went clear th'u' it, mon, up to he shoulders.

"Dey had a hard time gettin' 'im out, an' de man put de two dollah in he han', an' say he war de buttin'es' niggah in de county; but gran'pa des give one puny 'Baa' an' pass out, right dar. De hole stay in de do' fo' fifty—fo' hund'ed year; an' 't would be dar yit if de sto' hadn't bu'ned. I reckon I got buttin' blood."

Luther sat musing, without comment.

After a silence Nubbin continued prophetically, "One dese days I gwina be de buttin'es' niggah in Louisa County—maybe in de whole worl'."

He added the last words softly, as if almost afraid to disclose such an overpowering vision. Sighing, he pulled the quilts to his chin, squirmed closer to Luther, and drifted into reverie. No word broke the silence as the wagon rocked on down Little North Road.

Suddenly Nubbin exclaimed, "Dar Jesus! Look who heah!"

Abreast of the wagon, just out of sight, trotted a diminutive black-and-white beagle. With his mouth lolling in a satisfied grin he jogged placidly along, seemingly intent on his own affairs.

"Git! Git home, you ol' sneaker, 'fore I tan you!" yelled Luther, hurrying to dismount.

But the short stubby legs of the hound had suddenly developed surprising speed. Before either boy could find a loose clod in the roadway, the dog was facing his enemies well out of range. Slowly he sank to his haunches, head cocked to one side questioningly. A barrage of frozen clods forced him to dive into the thick woods, where he vanished.

The victors meandered back toward the wagon. They skipped, galloped, and pushed each other into ruts. Nubbin, in his cracked man's shoes that seemed merely to dangle on his small splay feet, half shuffled, half waltzed, a big sack coat flopping grotesquely about his knees, the long sleeves completely hiding his hands.

Suddenly he became a buzzard. Holding his arms out rigidly the sleeve ends dangling like broken pinions, he sailed and circled, swooped and banked down the road. Another, less natural buzzard materialized behind the first, following its track, reproducing its every movement. The buzzards came up to the wagon with such a grandiose sweep that the drooping mules were startled from their dozing.

Jolting along again, the boys chuckled and giggled. They certainly had scared 'at ol' Spot dog. Guess he was home by now. But wa'n't he some kind of a rabbit dog, though! And didn't he have sense? And he was a nice ol' dog. A hundred dollars—no, ten hundred dollars—wouldn't buy 'at ol' Spot. No sir-re-e!

II

As the morning wore on, Nubbin's imagination began to picture the contents of the big lunch basket under the seat. He wiped his lips frequently, but they would not stay dry. Feeling he had reached the limit of all human endurance, he leaned far over the dashboard and carefully scrutinized the sun.

"Unhu-n-h! Gittin' close tow'ds dinnah time," he asserted.

Luther cut a mischievous eye at him: "You're crazy! 'Tain't 'leven yet. Don' guess we'll eat till we get to Coleman's store."

Nubbin frowned: "*You* nevah could tell time by de sun—an' you know hit."

The argument was waxing vehement when a man on horseback drew up to inquire after Mr. Patten. Luther was much obliged to Mr. Thorpe: Yes, his father was a lot better, but a broken leg was a tedious thing. Yes, sir, they were taking the tobacco down. Yes, Luther knew the roads—he'd been down before with his father. Anyway, they hoped to pick up other wagons after they turned into the Big Road—at least to find them about sundown at the Deep Run Camping Ground.

"Well, you're a pretty spunky boy, taking the tobacco down with just that little nigger. Yo' pa ought to be proud of you," praised the man.

Luther flushed, but belittled the undertaking. Nubbin rolled his eyes at the white man.

Thorpe asked if Luther wasn't afraid he'd lose his dog in the big town.

"Dog?" asked the boy in surprise. "What dog?"

"Ain't that yo li'l hound under the wagon?"

With a flurry of quilts the boys were out on the ground. Slowly wagging his drooping tail, Spot looked up beseechingly from under his lids, and, rolling gently over on his back, held up his front paws, crooked at the joints like little hands.

"Now ain't dat de beatin'es!" Nubbin exclaimed, mouth spreading in a wide grin. " 'Tain't no use whup 'im now," he interposed hastily, as Luther flourished the whip. "He too fur fo' drive 'im home."

"The nigger is right, Luther; you'll have to take him along," chuckled Thorpe.

"Oh, darn the ol' dog!" exclaimed Luther. He sprang to the seat and started the team so abruptly that the little Negro was caught with one leg over the dashboard. Scrambling in, glaring white eyed at his partner, he tucked the covers about himself in silence.

Finally Luther drew in the team beside a small brook and ordered Nubbin to unhitch and water while he built a fire. With the coffee pot steaming away and the heaping lunch basket before him, Luther's irritation melted. Nubbin, happy at his friend's softening mood, and utterly unable to watch quietly the arrangement of the mouth-watering biscuits, sausage, and apple puffs, shuffle-stepped in circles and, patting his hands, eyes half closed, sang softly in jig tempo:

> "Sif' de meal an' gi' me de hus',
> Bake de bread an' gi' me de crus',
> Ho mart de Juba, Juba.
> Juba dis an' Juba dat,

Eat de lean an' leave de fat,
Ho mart de Juba."

Spot was in the near background, keeping one eye on the basket, the other alert for any wild thing he might nose out of the brush piles. Suddenly a rabbit jumped from under his very feet! The basket was forgotten, the boy's yelling commands unheeded. Fainter and fainter grew the dog's yaps as the rabbit lured him on into the tangles of the deep woods.

With intermittent discussion of rabbit dogs in general—but particularly of ol' Spot and his qualities— biscuits, sausage, and puffs disappeared with alarming rapidity. Nubbin's jaws stopped working only after Luther had tied tight the basket cover.

The boys' prolonged calls and shrill whistles brought no Spot. Though thoroughly anxious, they could wait no longer. As it was, the sun would be low before they reached Deep Run Camp.

Both were silent as the wagon rolled down the long hill behind the trotting mules. Time must be made up on every down grade now.

At the foot of the hill a small black-and-white animal slipped out of the woods ahead of the team and, giving one self-assuring glance toward the wagon, trotted unconcernedly down the middle of the road toward Richmond.

"Look!" exclaimed Luther.

Nubbin chuckled. "Dat ol' dog!" he said admiringly. "Ain't he de beatin'es'?"

The other boy chuckled, too: "Ain't he some kinda smart ol' dog though!"

The wagon lurched on and finally turned into the Big Road. Surely there should be other wagons now! But none were in sight. Perhaps they'd come up with one at the Forks. Gazing down the long deserted road, Luther's thoughts insistently turned to depressing possibilities Suppose there were no wagons at the camp? His back crept. Deep Run was so ha'nty in late evening —with its black creek, winding like a monstrous snake into the blacker depths of the slash. And Nubbin wasn't much comfort—he was too scary. They must hurry on.

Evening approached, and still no wagons. Of all the tobacco that must be going down, why couldn't they pick up one single wagon? Both boys tried valiantly to keep the talk going, but after each fresh effort the periods of silence grew longer.

The sun was down before they became aware of it. The world went suddenly all dusky and fearsome. Luther was glad to feel Nubbin snuggling close to him again. He thought they should be close to Deep Run, but wasn't sure. He whipped up the jaded mules.

The way grew unfamiliar as dark settled over the road. The wagon seemed only to creep.

Nubbin shuddered: " 'Tis gittin' so dark! Le's stop heah 'fo' we git in any mo' ol' black woods."

"Oh, we pretty near there now!" encouraged Luther. " 'Twon't be no time 'fore we see a fire," but his voice trembled slightly.

He was tired—so tired with responsibility—and the mules were tired. Was it maybe three, or four miles yet to Deep Run Hill? Persistently he beat away the thought that the camp ground might be vacant. The thing was to reach it!

Then, pulling up a grade that seemed interminable, the off mule fell to his knees.

"Oh, Jesus!" whimpered Nubbin. "Ol' Rock down! We can't go no fudder." He began to sob.

But Rock regained his feet and the wagon strained on again.

"You shut up, you ol' cry-baby!" admonished Luther scathingly. "I bet I won't bring any more ol' cry-babies with me!"

"Oh, I's so skeered! Hit all—so dark—an' skeery. . . . Oh, please! Le's stop an' buil' a fiah, Luther, please. . . ." The little black head went suddenly under the quilts and down on Luther's lap, the little arms grasped Luther's leg.

Suddenly the team quickened its pace, the wagon rolled more easily. The seat slanted forward, and the mules broke into a tired jog-trot.

"Man, we're here! We're on the big hill!" Luther shouted.

They tossed down the slope, Nubbin holding fast to Luther. Then Rock nickered, and a flickering light showed ahead.

Big Buck Smith, the boys' idea of a veritable paragon of a tobacco man, welcomed Luther, and the roaring fire welcomed Nubbin. Buck's frank, bluff praise embarrassed Luther almost to speechlessness:

"So you an' the little nigger jus' set out to carry the Ol' Man's 'bacca down, did you? Well, now, ain't that the beatin'es'!" and he slapped Luther so bearishly on the back that the boy swallowed his breath. "Well, you jus' foller ol' Buck; he'll p'int you down—a-rollin'," and he bellowed such a loud, assured guffaw that Luther felt the devil himself couldn't scare him now. Nubbin's white teeth glistened bravely across the fire.

Luther was treated almost as a man; and he swaggered a little as he spoke knowingly of the roads, the weather, and the color of this year's crop "up our way." Nubbin swaggered too—silently, in reflected glory, as he struttingly ordered Spot hither and yon, to the little hound's great discomfort. Buck even passed his plug of tobacco over to Luther.

"Don't believe I'll chew right now," he declined casually. "Maybe I'll take a bite later on."

Nubbin gave him so searching a stare that his eyes fell.

After the cheering supper about the big fire, his last bone sucked, Nubbin rubbed his face well over with the pork grease on his hands and rinsed them thoroughly in the residue. He cocked his old hat more assuredly and drew forth a small battered harmonica. Softly, tentatively, he sounded a chord or two. Buck looked up: Could the nigger play?

"Play!" bristled Luther. "Why, he can make a ol'

harp fairly talk, man. Play 'im 'Nelly Gray,' Nub."

Lovingly the little darky's hands wrapped themselves about the harmonica; slowly his eyes closed; gently his big shoes began patting a subdued accompaniment. The strains of the old ballad rose softly, then swelled into the double-tonguing roll of the born master. Through "Minstick Town," "The Bob-tailed Nag," through ballad and reel, breakdown and jig, moaned and laughed the battered harmonica.

Without pause it swept into the finale, the time-honored air of the tobacco trains, the men humming the chorus:

> "Car' my 'bacca down,
> Car' my 'bacca down,
> Car'y it down Richmon' town,
> Car' my 'bacca down."

"Nigger, you sho' can play!" exclaimed Buck, as they rose to go to their wagons. "But a player like you oughter have a good harp—a big one. Maybe," and his eyes twinkled, "Santa Claus will bring you a new one." Then, turning to Luther, he laughingly added, "I'll bet that nigger is no 'count for nothin' else."

Luther seemed puzzled for a moment, then burst forth proudly: "He can butt."

The men roared with laughter. Buck gave him another of his bear slaps.

"That's all right," bridled the embarrassed boy, climbing into his wagon. "You jus' wait'll you see him butt sometime! He's *full* o' buttin' blood."

Cuddled together, wrapped and rewrapped in old quilts, the boys nested upon the soft tobacco in the space under the canvas top and soon droned themselves to sleep.

### III

Luther's wagon was second in the little train that crawled slowly into the Big Road next morning as the sun began lightening the shadows of Deep Run Hollow.

First was Buck Smith's big four-mule team: rugged, powerful animals that could, hour by hour, eat up the miles with four thousand pounds of sun-cured behind them in the scow-shaped wagon of hickory and white oak. The canvas top, in natural accord with the rising bow and stern of the body, was more sway-backed, more rakish than the others. Big bundles of fodder bulged under the rope on the rumble behind; buckets swung underneath; a smutty fry pan and coffee pot and a bright ax and lantern rested in their slots and hooks. Red, brass-mounted cow-tail tassels swayed and sparkled from the headstalls of the big mules, who, even under heavy strain, tossed their heads proudly. A small bronze bell tinkled comfortingly from the hames of each leader—leaders who by mere word of command, even mere inflection of tone, would steer the ponderous wagon as easily and surely as a fur-gloved horseman could guide his pair of trotters.

"Some kind er ol' team!" murmured Nubbin, over-powered by admiration.

Awaking sharp echoes from the woods and hollows, the little train rumbled down the Big Road. Gradually other wagons joined the file: one dawdling at a country store; another waiting at a crossroad; another, warned by the tinkling bells, hurrying in a trot down a deep-cut side road. Wagons of all shapes and sizes, carrying the tobacco down! Wagons mud-red from tire to top, from the limit of the sun-cured belt; others yellow with the mud from Green Spring country; one black-ened with the loam of Locust Creek—even a pariah of a produce wagon, with its butter and eggs. A giant serpent of wagons slowly winding its way down the road to Richmond.

And men! Black, and yellow, and white men! Old and young men, who yelled one to another above the rumble of the wagons. And a sprinkling of boys, a favored few, bound on a glorious sight-seeing orgy. Many would be the Munchausen tales carried back to their less fortunate brothers. Log schools, churchyards, and tobacco barns would be stirred to their amazed depths ere spring plowing began.

Luther's team held its place by dint of both boys walking. Sometimes, on the long steep hills, they be-came fearful as the gap widened between them and the big team; but Buck would wait at the top to blow his heavy mules.

Hours of plodding; then dinner by Great Stony

Creek! Coffee pots clattered and axes rung. A line of little fires soon puffed their smoke aloft, like signals. Luther and Nubbin toasted biscuits and sausage; absorbed tobacco talk; made friends with new boys who came up in diffident admiration to see these young paladins who could take the 'baca down. The boys were sorry when Buck called, "Hook up, men, I'm a-goin'!"

By midafternoon the men were fagged from miles of walking to ease their jaded teams. Luther would long ago have ridden but for his pride; Nubbin would have brazenly mounted, pride or no pride, but for Luther.

At one of his halts on a hilltop Buck called Luther. Nubbin followed closely as his partner joined the big man in front of the team. Pointing to a smoky haze in the east, Buck grinned delightedly: "Thar she is, boys! Richmond! We'll be in 'fore sundown."

The road grew smoother—Nubbin marveled at its smoothness. He marveled, too, at the sudden change in the men. Their plodding steps had become youthful; their seats in the saddle or on the wagon more jaunty; their voices brighter. Even the teams were infected with the change. Their step quickened. Occasionally they broke into a trot.

Soon the men mounted. Nubbin was relieved beyond words as he limped to the wagon. Luther resented his not entering into the spirit of their approach to Richmond, but perhaps he was just tired out.

Presently Nubbin asked, "Ain't hit tur'ble skeery,

wid all dat ol' smoke an' all dem ol' big houses, an' folks, an' things? What do hit look like—'xactly?"

Luther couldn't explain exactly what it was like; but it was powerful big, and everybody was hustling, and big policemen in funny hats watched you. Nubbin shuddered and, inching nearer the white boy, relapsed into silence.

At last the city! The first outlying saloon!—planted there to catch the wagon trade. Most of the train pulled to the side and stopped—a dram at Reiley's was almost a ritual. The wagons strung out like a fleet of rusty ships at anchor. The few people on the cinder sidewalks stared with interest. Tobacco was sure coming down!

"Is dis de great Richmon'?" inquired Nubbin, with a vague mixture of relief and disappointment.

Luther sniffed. Pshaw! The unpaved streets and sparse buildings of this outlying section were nothing! Just let Nubbin wait! The sights downtown would pop his eyes out. Why, they scared even Luther—at first.

Nubbin wished they were safely in Captain John's highwalled yard, of which he had heard so much—a yard full of wagons and men, but country wagons and country men.

The laughing drivers yelled or slapped one another good-bye, for here the train split into sections—some for Captain John Hundson's, some for Shockoe, some for Shelburn's—for any one of a half-dozen sales warehouses.

On the way downtown Nubbin made not a single

comment at the sights Luther pointed out, nor a single reply to his banter. He kept his head over the side of the wagon, occasionally catching his breath audibly. As they turned into Governor Street the electric lights went on. Nubbin flinched and looked at Luther questioningly. Why, the light was almost as bright as the sun—you couldn't look straight at it!

The wagons rolled in a clatter down the ancient cobbled hill of Governor Street, back of the Governor's Mansion, the men lolling jauntily in their saddles or sitting in the wagons with knees acock, hats turned back. The mules were almost in a gallop.

Buck Smith gave a loud whoop, and in his deep voice imitated a fox horn's *Toot-te-toot-to-to-o-ot!* A door slammed in a house on the corner, a window went up; women were on the porch, at the windows, waving. Luther heard a shrill voice cry, "O you 'bacca boys! T'-night!" He wondered why Buck acted so foolishly, made so much noise; why the women came out in the cold, half dressed.

With utter nonchalance Buck swung the four big mules and the heavy wagon downhill, around corners, through narrow streets, as calmly and with as little effort as a woman takes a stitch. Lounging in the saddle, he ordered his chariot by easy word or slight check of the leader line.

Luther was frightened. His arms were cramped, his teeth set. Nubbin huddled in the foot of the wagon, openly sobbing and praying. Spot, jolted off the seat, yelped in abject terror.

At last, with a swoop and a swing, Buck's long wagon rolled accurately through the big gate of Captain John Hundson's wagon yard. Luther, breathing relief, guided his team through after Buck.

Darkness came quickly down upon the night camp in the wagon yard. Red fires grew; vague forms, like misty giants, loomed and vanished again. Nubbin felt an eerie strangeness in it all. Even Luther was glad to join Buck Smith by his fire. But the cheerful champ of teams and laughter of men, the flash of bright tin cups and the aroma of boiling coffee and sizzling spareribs, soon lifted them and thrilled them with the all-pervasive, buoyant spirit of the occasion. Wasn't tomorrow the long-thought-of day of sight-seeing, of swaggering about the lower town with a pocketful of money, and of reunion, with toddies and gossip? Wasn't the 'bacca down?

After supper, with pipe smoke rising in the frosty night air, the *plunk-plunk* of a banjo came from the far side of the yard, where the Negro drivers had instinctively herded together. Buck Smith yelled over that there were three fingers of rye to swap for a song.

The banjo awoke, and quickened to a run of chords. Then a smooth black baritone began:

> "Road it mighty muddy,
> Way it mighty long,

But a-soon I'll git my toddy,
Fo' de mule he mighty strong.


"Wo'kin' all de summah,
Like niggah in de fiel',
Jes' to git some money
Fo' city folks to steal.


"Car' my 'ba-ac-ca down,
Car' my 'ba-ac-ca down,
Car'y it down Richmon' town,
Car' my 'bacca down."


## IV

Next morning, after their tobacco had been unloaded, the boys strolled through the warehouse. With shoulders bent and hands clasped behind them, with jaws working, they passed up and down the long aisles between the piled flat baskets; two of a long line of men, walking and acting one like another; pulling out bundles to bury their noses deep in the peachy smell; spreading open the mahogany and chocolate leaves to note their coloring and feel; pinching off a piece here and there to roll it on their tongues.

The Negro boy aped Luther's every action—even to pretending to taste samples. Both frequently spat brown licorice juice, like amber. Spot walked bow-leggedly behind, sniffing at the baskets and sneezing often.

Wandering into a storage wing, they were accosted

by a thick-chested hogshead roller, his pig eyes taking
in the small hound. "White boy," he said threateningly,
"ef you wants dat pocket-sized dog evah see home
ag'in, you bettah lock him in de Cap'n's safe."

Spot growled.

"Oh, you's a fighter, is you? You wait, I gi'e you
somep'n t' fight."

Laughing nastily, the big Negro slouched away.

"What de mattah wid him?" questioned Nubbin
apprehensively.

"I don' know," replied Luther, his face flushed, "but
he better not be tryin' to bully men around here. I'll—
I'll—I bet he'd be sorry if Cap'n John heard 'bout it."

Just then there was a flurry at the end of the warehouse—Captain John had come!

Captain John, red of face, debonair, military, the
idol of his customers, and their best friend!

His arm about Luther's proud shoulder, one of his
new dimes in Nubbin's pocket, he ambled beamingly
down the aisles, shaking friendly hands, slapping
friendly backs.

Luther's tobacco would be sold first! Yes, sir! The
son of the Captain's old friend should get his check
first and be free to enjoy the day. And the Captain
wanted the buyers to bid the limit on this boy's tobacco;
he'd brought it down, alone, with only a little nigger—
and there was no better tobacco grown in Virginia.

Captain John had a way with him, and when Luther's
tobacco had been sold the boys were jubilant. The top

price for sun-cured, the auctioneer had said! Wouldn't the home folks be tickled!

Did any fellers ever have such a trip—such a time! Chattering, whistling, they skipped arm in arm across the cobbled yard to feed the mules.

Luther must go over his mother's lists before the exploration of Main Street began. They perched themselves in the sun on the edge of a platform projecting from the far door in the wing of the warehouse, while Luther sedulously checked the items with a smudgy pencil stub. Nubbin was swinging his heels impatiently against the timbers. Spot was sniffing about in front, looking for stray bones.

Softly, very softly, unheard by the boys, the door behind them slid back. The small-eyed, ugly black face of the hogshead roller leered out for a moment, then furtively drew back. A peculiar sound, like animal claws, on a wood floor came from within. Spot suddenly froze, head cocked aside, one forefoot raised. Nubbin half whirled about and looked over his shoulder.

A huge brindle dog filled the open doorway. Slowly his powerful head swung, his vicious red eyes shifted from the boys to the poised figure of the little hound just beyond. A bullying growl issued from his throat.

With a terrified yell Nubbin rolled desperately over backward to the far corner of the platform. Spot squealed and darted for Luther's feet! The brindle snarled and charged!

Luther felt the heavy weight of the grotesque body as it struck him a slanting blow. Bowled over, he lay a moment confused and terrified. But the distressed muffled yelps of the little hound electrified him.

"Get a stick! Hit 'im, Nub—kill 'im!" he screamed. Running and dodging fruitlessly about the entangled dogs, he looked for a board, a stone, any weapon with which to drive off the bully, while he yelled boyish oaths and sobbed with fear and rage. He pawed at a protruding cobblestone which would not come free. Then a choking gurgle from Spot sent a shiver of fury through him.

Frenzied, he leaped at the brindle and swung his heavy-soled brogan into the dog's ribs. Once, twice, he kicked with all the power of his reckless fury, sobbing, mouthing: "Le' 'im go! Le' 'im go! You ol' heller! I'll kill you! I'll kick yo' ol' heart . . ."

The mongrel whirled from the little dog with a snarl and struck at Luther's leg. Before the boy could move, quick as a snake, the brute recovered and sprang for his throat.

Instinctively Luther stiffened and threw up a guarding arm, but he was staggered by the heavy dog's impact. Stumbling, borne backward, trying in vain to keep his feet, he screamed in terror as the beast's hot breath came in his face and he felt himself going down under those terrible fangs.

The little darky had been dancing up and down as if stung with hornets, his clenched fists beating the air. His lips stretched from his teeth in a tear-streaked grimace of horror, his shrill voice screamed:

"He'p! He'p! Run heah, somebody! Run heah! . . ."

When he saw the brindle bring down his partner he made a spring as if starting to his assistance. But the prospect of facing those savage fangs was too much for him. Holding up his ragged arms in supplication, he shrieked: "O Gawd! O Jesus! Have mercy! He killin' 'im. . . ."

A cry from Luther of "Help, Nub, hel-l-p!" reached a new spring in his consciousness. Fear, dreadful fear, had bound him; but the appeal in extremity from his friend, his own Luther, snapped the leash. The blood of the Congo, the spirit of lion-hunting forbears—and a butting grandsire—seethed within his little body, quickened within his soul. He went berserk.

With a sobbing snarl he threw his hat viciously to the floor, and sprang jumping, bouncing down the platform. Bleating an instinctive sharp "Baa!" his slim body left the edge of the platform, and, like a tattered arrow, shot through the ten feet of space—straight for the brindle's head. Against that head struck the crown of a Negro of buttin' blood—small, but of famous lineage; the grandson, indeed, of the buttin'es' niggah in de county.

## V

When Nubbin came up out of the blackness of long oblivion, he thought he must be in heaven. Before his tired eyelids could live, he seemed to hear a voice in the far distance say: "He's the'—buttin'es'—nigger—in—th'—world."

It must be heaven! On opening his eyes he was sure of it: a long-white-whiskered, white-haired old gentleman was pressing his head.

"Gabr'el!" he thought. "Rammin' home de golden crown!" But the crowning hurt terribly.

"Hit's too tight! Too tight!" he moaned, closing his eyes.

"Lie still, son! I'll soon be through."

He felt a sharp prick in his arm. Gabriel was trying to hurt him.

Dimly, amid much talk, he heard a tearful young voice, a voice that sounded like that of his beloved earthly partner. Luther was in heaven with him? That was good!

"Doctor, is he dyin'?"

"Dying nothing! When the hypodermic takes effect, I'll finish stitching his head and strap up that shoulder. . . ."

What funny talk for angels! But of course heaven *was* a funny place. Anyway, he could take a nap—Luther was there.

Later, when his eyes opened to full consciousness, they glanced about the walls. Big railroad calendars, a long black stovepipe, and an old buggy harness did not seem appropriate decorations for the walls of heaven. Trying to turn over, he cried out.

"Does it hurt so bad, Nub?" asked an entirely earthly voice.

"Who dat?" he questioned feebly.

"It's me—Luther."

The white boy leaned solicitously over the figure mummied in shoulder and head bandages. "You feelin' better?" he asked, stroking the black paw.

"You talks natchul," Nubbin remarked doubtingly.

"Why shouldn't I? That ol' dog jus' chewed my overcoat collar. He hardly scratched my throat. But if it hadn't been for you," his voice broke, "I reckon— I'd been—mos' killed."

Nubbin's eyes were drawn back to the old harness.

"Den dis heah ain'? . . ." he began, but his question was interrupted by a hot, black nose against his cheek. With an effort he looked into the face of what resembled a blear-eyed, disreputable old man with a soiled stock about his neck.

Smiling faintly, he asked, "He hu't much?"

No, Spot wasn't dangerously hurt, but there was a bad gash in his neck, which Luther had bandaged.

Captain John, Buck Smith, and a dozen others came admiringly into the room.

Buck Smith stood beside the boy's cot and, leaning

over, closed the slender black fingers about a narrow red-and-gold box from whose elaborate decorations stood out the words: "Full-Concert Harmonica."

Turning from the pinched face to crowd, he said:

"Men, thar lays the buttin'es' little nigger in the world."

Slowly Nubbin seemed to awaken to the reality of his own familiar world, to the actual significance of those precious words. His eyes opened wide; they rolled from Buck Smith to the nodding men, then back to Buck.

He moistened his lips; his hand squeezed tight on the new harp. Then, slowly, like sunrise, a beatific smile lighted his ashy face. He sighed, as if unloading a great burden, and, closing his eyes, murmured:

"Yas, suh, I got buttin' blood."

From *The Atlantic Monthly*. Reprinted in Prize Stories of 1929, O. Henry Award. (Doubleday Doran, N. Y.)

# MARISTAN CHAPMAN

The year that "The Happy Mountain" took the American reading public by surprise and by storm, another novel whose scene was laid in this section gave the seamy side of life there, as if through the eyes of a young woman from the outside world, married into a backward and narrow-minded community. Maristan Chapman's "Happy Mountain," however, from the title to the last paragraph, was sunshine all the way; it revealed a life hard but beautiful, language so rich in poetry and so generously appreciated by the author that she herself used it as well as her characters, to the adornment of her narrative and through that of our literature in general, and above all, a contentment cities well might envy, with good reasons given for being content.

Not everyone, however, can be always happy, even here. In the following story, taken from *The Atlantic Monthly*, the pressure of advancing civilization makes itself felt upon a spirit that can be broken but not bent. Such a tragedy has been so often enacted in America that though the tale rings true to its own environment, its truth is not confined to the Cumberlands. All along our early history and even in our later days there have been old people clinging like the old folks in Faust to little homes that block advancing progress, and this Faust-like spirit never pauses long for them. Leatherstocking in his old age knew what it was to be "crowded," and so did the pioneers and plainsmen moving westward as soon as they could see a neighbor's chimney-smoke. Something of their spirit yet lingers on our hillsides in defiant old women who will not be taken from their solitary cabins to the safe shelter of the poorhouse, or old men for whom, as in Dorothy Canfield's story, a road must be kept open on purpose. Last of the eccentrics, they are to be found only in lost corners of the country, and when they are all gone, a spicy tang will be gone out of the taste of American life.

# CROWDED

### By Maristan Chapman

THE heat of a late July afternoon made the leaves crinkle and creak, and the harsh snapping of twigs beneath the feet of the three mountain men cut into the droning air as they stepped up Cragg Hill and dropped aslant to Lowe's cabin.

It was Sunday, and the people were gathering into Glen Hazard for the second meeting, so the men— Virgil Howard, Rashe Lowe, and his son, Wait-Still-on-the-Lord—met many a neighbor facing toward them. The old people were striding smoothly, but the young ones, brightly dressed in new mail-order clothes, were prancing shamefully with the mischief of living.

"How you?" was the passing greeting of all; and Virgil Howard answered for the three, "Well as otherwise."

The three were bound for Bart's Deadening over beyond Lowe's cabin, for old John Bart lay stricken soul and body and they went to comfort him. For this reason their backs were turned to the church house. The sun was already westering, else they would have stayed for meeting first.

Directly Rashe spoke. "He's been bedfast these six weeks with scarcely the spirit to live, yet seems he can't let slip for the heavy matter that is resting upon him."

"He'd ought to make a struggle," said Howard. "It's not in reason for a man to lay down inviting death."

"So I told him," Rashe answered. "I said, 'Get up, John, and try to live. Don't you lie there like a dried apple and jes' wither.' And he made answer, 'What's to get up for?'"

"It's the crowding is on his mind," Waits broke in thoughtfully. "And he's right about we're getting powerful cluttered. Times have got so a man can't possess his soul with all the matters he's bound to do and own."

This was a thought large enough to fill their minds in silence as they went forward singly through the laurel scrub. They dropped beneath the shoulder of the hill and lost the last of that day's sun. A growl of thunder rolled around the back of the hills.

Presently Virgil Howard said : "Tell us how he came by his fear, Rashe. It will shorten the way."

So Rashe began and said:—

"When John and Luther were fifteen years old apiece they went to Mexico in the following of a Confederate officer to see the outside world and hunt a fortune. They set forth in homespun shirts and trousers and rawhide shoes, and fur caps they'd trapped the forerunning winter. They carried for weapons each a long knife, welded and beaten sharp upon their forge.

"Two years after that—about '68, it must 'a' been—John and Lute walked home again in the top ends of their trousers, and without cap or shoe between them. But they carried each an old army gun, and they wore each a store-boughten shirt. They came home covered with experiences and a dread of the outside world."

Waits interrupted: "Lute used to tell about that time, but John'd never let go of his tongue, though he made plenty free of it with every other thing."

"John was more afraid than Lute. He had longer sight, and he feared that talking about many things might bring them in train. Both had seen inventions and discoveries that looked to them to be ogres that fair et up men. Lute talked like a child talks about wild beasts to scare itself; but John was too scairt a'ready. It was Lute took in the twice-a-week paper that made them keep shet of all goings on.

"You recollect, Virge, how they'd never get things out of a mail-order house even when money was free with them. They'd say it would be letting in the outside to barter to and fro like that and they'd go on till a man would feel the outside was a contaminating disease."

" 'Tis," said Waits sorrowfully.

"You hush," said Rashe. "John and Lute fought roads and telephones and automobiles and moving pictures, each as they came, and all was too strong for them. So they backed up and backed up till they fair hid in their own place. They'd go down to mail-gathering to meet neighbors and get corn-credit at the store for meat, but every other way they lived lonely."

As the three went forward, storm clouds climbed heavily up the sky; the world turned copper-colored. A weariness came upon them, but they kept their way and Rashe held to his story.

"Come a time when John began to go a little mite strange. It wasn't so much the outside pressing in, as the much he made of it. First thing that told us he was not in his own senses was when he took a notion and stole and buried Mist' Carr's radio-box. The day before that night Mist' Carr edzacted it all out to him, how it brought voices and music in from outside without wires or anything—just fetched it, you might say, through the air. Mist' Carr, being half-outland, was proud of it, but John carried on a sight and said nothing less than the Devil could do such tricks. Mist' Carr said John had an obsession, which is the same as being fair et up with one notion till you've got no sense left for use; he claimed the notion of being crowded had et into John's mind, like.

"Well, sir, Lute's being took for killing Creed Morgan took up John's mind for a while, and the next thing was the airplane. It sent John right away from himself. You recollect the man that lit in the bottoms beyond Flat Rock Branch? Maybe you didn't come in that day, Virge, but the rest of us all stepped over to see an airplane close to."

"On the ground it's no better'n a mud wasp wrong way to," said Waits.

"You hush," Rashe went on. "Well, sir, we looked and saw; but nothing would do John but touch and feel. He took ahold of it by the wires and then stepped back to see all of it again and he swore the thing was trag. The driver saw John was very old and strange, and for his fun, like, he said would he fly off with him.

"Now I'm telling you, Virge, that while my mouth was yet hanging open John says 'Yes,' and we all looked like we'd been stuck in a maze forever. John says to the driver, 'It can carry me out as well as it carried you in,' and when he'd made the flyer promise to bring him home he got in."

A crack of thunder capped Rashe's words, and while it rolled off the three made their way over Lowe's snake fence and out to the stream side that led to Bart's Deadening.

"He told me next day," Rashe went on, unwinding his feet from the honeysuckle where it tangled him, "that trip was the end of him. After he got over feeling sick, he took notice, and what did he see but all his evil dreams come true. The outside was creeping up the mountains on both sides. He seen white lines that was hard roads linking across. He seen line wires from where the electric light company built their dam, and before long they went over where the dam itself was choking Green River. The driver took John so far as a big city, and it was terrible close against the edge of the hills. And, looking down on the hills, there was more town patches than a man could believe in.

"John was clean outside of himself all the next week, and before it was up he'd gone up to the Pen where Lute was and begged them to take him in with his brother so's the crowd couldn't get at him. Of course they couldn't put him in jail, but seeing he was touched a little, and Lute was failing from old age, they took John in as day visitor.

"After Lute died, John was turned away and had nearly escaped home when a mission house that took him in over a night held him. They was bound to keep him and do for him, but he got them to back a letter to me telling where he was and to go and loose him, so I went up and unloosed him. They said, "He'll die all alone in some awful backwoods cabin," and I told them that's where and how he wants to die and to leave him go; and they called us a pair of ungrateful old stubborns and we got free.

"John wouldn't have gotten home but that he was running all the time from the crowd. 'It's creeping up on me,' he kept on saying, 'and it makes a noise till you can't hear and it stinks till you can't breathe.' And soon's he got home he lay down on his pallet and says: 'Say a prayer, Rashe; I'm prayed out same as I'm crowded out.' Some words we'd learned when we were younglings came back to me: 'Give unto Thy servant the peace that the world cannot give, and defend us from our enemies so's we may pass our time in peace and quietness.' Maybe that's not the perfect of it, but it kind of eased him and he kept saying it over and over again."

And they had come at this time to the place of Bart's Deadening; and healthy corn stood green in the clearing among the ghosts of giant trees that had been deadened to keep them from drawing all the good from the earth. Storm and night closing in made a basin of heat and fear, and the gray tree trunks stood iron-strong in death.

"Corn in the clearing crowding in among the old trees makes a man think about John's being right," Waits said in a low voice. "Every year it's something new, and one day the trees'll fall and then it'll *all* be corn." His words fell slower, as if he were feeling for something that had gotten caught in the back of his mind. "The corn'll win because it keeps on being new—and the trees just get older and older—" His voice stopped thickly and he looked at his old companions to see if they took his meaning to mind.

"You hush," said his father. "A young-un hadn't ought to talk so. First thing you know you'll go strange like John. You mind me and hush."

The slanted log cabin stood over against them. It settled into the slope of the far hillside, trying to bury itself. It looked as if nobody lived there, but that a trickle of the blue smoke came from the crow-stick chimney and flattened in the storm-bound air. The yard before the house—unswept since Luther went away—was littered with tree scourings and trash of last winter, and upstart weeds grew in lusty bunches on the path. In the side yard a cow and a mule lay dead, nigh skeletoned for lack of food.

While they went forward to the cabin some hens, gone back half wild, gave a screeching from the tree where they roosted above the well roof.

"Wish I'd thought me to tote some feed for them brutes," Rashe said, "but I was took up with John, and they being strayed off till their last minute, they leapt my mind."

They shoved back the door of the cabin till it stuck against the earthen floor, and edging inside they found all dark save for a spark of fire. They gathered at the fire, judging old John to be sleeping on his pallet beyond. Their feet made no sound on the used-hard dirt floor.

Except the fire, there were only the hewn log table and stool and John's bed, homemade of slab siding. For all the hot night, a fire was a living thing to push back fear.

Presently a sharp thin voice came to them, commanding: "Rashe, come hyar!"

Rashe trod quietly to the bed; the other two crouched by the fire, not moving.

"Rashe," John whispered, "you reckon Heaven's got as crowd-filled as some folks say?"

Rashe looked down on the withered old man, who lay like a crumpled leaf the kind wind has thrown in a warm corner. John's eyes were alight, but the rest of him had been struck motionless forever.

"Judgmatically, I don't know, John; but not likely

it's altered much since you and me were to Sunday School down Mill Creek. 'Twas a good place then, and likely 't is now."

Old John Bart rested quietly. Then: "It's liable to be a heap crowded with all the folks' talk about going there—"

"Not all's going says they is."

"Maybe," said John, his eyes smiling, "maybe I'll go to the one of the Many Mansions kept for our kind of folks. And from what I seen of my kin and kind this eighty year they won't be a stifling lot."

"Take shame, John Bart, to talk that way of your neighbor-people with what any minute is liable to be your last breath!"

"Only my fun, like," John made answer. "They's several I'd be proud to meet. They's Lute—he'll be there, even if he did die out of the Pen. He done a good deed when he killed Creed Morgan, let law say what it will."

All rested silent, till directly John turned his eyes upon the two by the fire. A flicker of its light showed that he scowled.

"What is it, John?"

"Crowding," said John, "crowding my last breath away."

"You want we should all step out awhile?"

John's eyes agreed and all three moved through the door and across the yard to the woodpile, where they let themselves down restfully to wait.

Full dark had fallen. The heat lightning ran behind the ridge above them and the katydids argued in the near trees. Clouds thickened and lightened again for an hour and further. Then Waits spoke: "He's in no way aghast at dying. I trust the Lord I'll be as easy when my time comes."

"Some say his never talking about the outside kept his mind from getting air and light; but there's more light than comes from east or west," said Rashe.

They rested on the firewood through the night; the storm threatened and drew off, and when the dawn came it was neither raining nor letting it alone. Day came slowly, and it was silent of birds and beasts. The smoke had stopped from out the chimney and it was certain now that nobody lived there.

"I'll step in and see how he fares," said Rashe.

"And I—when you are come out," said Virge. " 'Twould be unseemly to crowd."

So they went in and came out singly, and Waits locked the cabin door and they turned again toward Glen Hazard to give the notice.

From *The Atlantic Monthly*, 1928.

# ALICE HEGAN RICE

More than one amateur psychologist has tried to resolve to
its elements the elusive and effective quality known as "Southern charm." All charm escapes definition, but this sort has been,
in northern minds at least, definitely localized; they believe
that it is found north of Mason and Dixon's line only when
brought there by someone from the Southward. Perhaps for
this reason it has become so closely identified with a Southern
accent that ladies living out of this district have sometimes gone
to the length of acquiring one—often at long range.

The effect of this attribute is above all pleasing; it comforts
and reassures the fortunate creature upon whom it is exercised,
inspiring in him a happiness whose result may be self-satisfaction,
but whose source may well be gratitude. No one, however,
seems to have pointed out that it is above all else kind, originat-
ing in a desire that the object should be happy—or at least
temporarily comfortable. At its best it does this by assuming
that his possibilities are already his traits. It praises him for being what he would like to be. Nothing is sweeter than such
praise, and no one bestowing it will be quite forgotten by the
recipient.

One thinks so often of "Southern charm" in connection with
youth, beauty, and romantic surroundings, not to speak of

wealth and the pride of race, that it may seem far-fetched to find it in fiction exercised by a little woman neither young nor beautiful, poor, of no family, and living on the edge of a dump. But when "Mrs. Wiggs of the Cabbage Patch" slipped into our fiction along in the nineties—soon to escape into our national consciousness—an analysis of her methods of meeting and improving life would have showed this gift at its brightest and best. She was called back by popular demand in "Lovey Mary," from which this chapter is taken. There is a certain wild reasonableness in all the doings of Mrs. Wiggs; her decision, when two bright but unrelated remnants have been bought for the construction of a pair of trousers, to make the front outen one piece and the back outen the other, as "nobody won't never know the difference, 'cause Tommy can't be goin' and comin' at the same time"; her pensive joy in having aimed at the cemetery and landed up at a first-class fire; her exit-speech, requiring Lovey Mary to bring back a bottle of Niagary water; for "I want to see how them falls look." This reasonableness gives force to her natural kindness in dealing with the embittered and self-distrustful girl whom chance brings beneath her wing. Frankly, she flatters Lovey Mary, with the golden flattery that praises what should be there—and would be with a fair chance. "I was awful mean when I come to the Cabbage Patch," Mary explains, "somehow you all just bluffed me into being better. I wasn't used to being bragged on, and it made me want to be good more than anything in the world."

Alice Caldwell Hegan married Cale Young Rice the poet; they live in Louisville, Kentucky, where Mrs. Rice was one of the founders of the Cabbage Patch Settlement. She has written other books, but none have eclipsed in popular favor those that tell the story of Mrs. Wiggs. However this homely philosopher looked for things that should be, she kept a cool practical eye on things as they were; she was no Pollyanna. Mrs. Wiggs might have lived almost anywhere, but she would have talked and acted as she did only in a part of the world where poverty and social graces could flourish naturally in the same environment.

# THE HAZY HOUSEHOLD

## By ALICE HEGAN RICE

MISS HAZY was the submerged tenth of the Cabbage Patch. The submersion was mainly one of dirt and disorder, but Miss Hazy was such a meek, inefficient little body that the Cabbage Patch withheld its blame and patiently tried to furnish a prop for the clinging vine. Miss Hazy, it is true, had Chris; but Chris was unstable, not only because he had lost one leg, but also because he was the wildest, noisiest, most thoughtless youngster that ever shied a rock at a lamp-post. Miss Hazy had "raised" Chris, and the neighbors had raised Miss Hazy.

When Lovey Mary stumbled over the Hazy threshold with the sleeping Tommy and the duck in her arms, Miss Hazy fluttered about in dismay. She pushed the flour-sifter farther over on the bed and made a place for Tommy, then she got a chair for the exhausted girl and hovered about her with little chirps of consternation.

"Dear sakes! You're done tuckered out, ain't you? You an' the baby got losted? Ain't that too bad! Must I make you some tea? Only there ain't no fire in the stove. Dear me! what ever will I do? Jes wait a minute; I'll have to go ast Mis' Wiggs."

In a few minutes Miss Hazy returned. With her was a bright-faced little woman whose smile seemed to thaw out the frozen places in Lovey Mary's heart and make her burst into tears on the motherly bosom.

"There now, there," said Mrs. Wiggs, hugging the girl up close and patting her on the back; "there ain't no hole so deep can't somebody pull you out. An' here's me an' Miss Hazy jes waitin' to give you a h'ist."

There was something so heartsome in her manner that Lovey Mary dried her eyes and attempted to explain. "I'm tryin' to get a place," she began, "but nobody wants to take Tommy too. I can't carry him any further, and I don't know where to go, and it's 'most night—" again the sobs choked her.

"Lawsee!" said Mrs. Wiggs, "don't you let that worry you! I can't take you home, 'cause Asia an' Australia an' Europeny are sleepin' in one bed as it is; but you kin git right in here with Miss Hazy, can't she, Miss Hazy?"

The hostess, to whom Mrs. Wiggs was an oracle, acquiesced heartily.

"All right: that's fixed. Now I'll go home an' send you all over some nice, hot supper by Billy, an' tomorrow mornin' will be time enough to think things out."

Lovey Mary, too exhausted to mind the dirt, ate her supper off a broken plate, then climbed over behind Tommy and the flour-sifter, and was soon fast asleep.

The business meeting next morning "to think things out" resulted satisfactorily. At first Mrs. Wiggs was inclined to ask questions and find out where the children came from, but when she saw Lovey Mary's evident distress and embarrassment, she accepted the statement that they were orphans and that the girl was seeking work in order to take care of herself and the boy. It had come to be an unwritten law in the Cabbage Patch that as few questions as possible should be asked of strangers. People had come there before who could not give clear accounts of themselves.

"Now I'll tell you what I think'll be best," said Mrs. Wiggs, who enjoyed untangling snarls. "Asia kin take Mary up to the fact'ry with her to-morrow, an' see if she kin git her a job. I 'spect she kin, 'cause she stands right in with the lady boss. Miss Hazy, me an' you kin keep a' eye on the baby between us. If Mary gits a place she kin pay you so much a week, an' that'll help us all out, 'cause then we won't have to send in so many outside victuals. If she could make three dollars an' Chris three, you all could git along right peart."

Lovey Mary stayed in the house most of the day. She was almost afraid to look out of the little window, for fear she should see Miss Bell or Kate Rider coming. She sat in the only chair that had a bottom and diligently worked buttonholes for Miss Hazy.

"Looks like there ain't never no time to clean up," said Miss Hazy, apologetically, as she shoved Chris's Sunday clothes and a can of coal-oil behind the door.

Lovey Mary looked about her and sighed deeply. The room was brimful and spilling over: trash, tin cans, and bottles overflowed the window-sills; a crippled rocking-chair, with a faded quilt over it, stood before the stove, in the open oven of which Chris's shoe was drying; an old sewing-machine stood in the middle of the floor, with Miss Hazy's sewing on one end of it and the uncleared dinner-dishes on the other. Mary could not see under the bed, but she knew from the day's experience that it was used as a combination storeroom and wardrobe. She thought of the home with its bare, clean rooms and its spotless floors. She rose abruptly and went out to the rear of the house, where Tommy was playing with Europena Wiggs. They were absorbed in trying to hitch the duck to a spool-box, and paid little attention to her.

"Tommy," she said, clutching his arm, "don't you want to go back?"

But Tommy had tasted freedom; he had had one blissful day unwashed, uncombed, and uncorrected.

"No," he declared stoutly; "I'm doin' to stay to this house and play wiv You're-a-peanut."

"Then," said Mary, with deep resignation, "the only thing for me to do is to try to clean things up."

When she went back into the house she untied her bundle and took out the remaining dollar.

"I'll be back soon," she said to Miss Hazy as she stepped over a basket of potatoes. "I'm just going over to Mrs. Wiggs's a minute."

She found her neighbor alone, getting supper. "Please, ma'am,"—she plunged into her subject at once,—"have any of your girls a dress for sale? I've got a dollar to buy it."

Mrs. Wiggs turned the girl around and surveyed her critically. "Well, I don't know as I blame you fer wantin' to git shut of that one. There ain't more'n room enough fer one leg in that skirt, let alone two. An' what was the sense in them big shiny buttons?"

"I don't know as it makes much difference," said Lovey Mary, disconsolately; "I'm so ugly, nothing could make me look nice."

Mrs. Wiggs shook her by the shoulders good-naturedly. "Now, here," she said, "don't you go an' git sorry fer yourself! That's one thing I can't stand in nobody. There's always lots of other folks you kin be sorry fer 'stid of yerself. Ain't you proud you ain't got a harelip? Why, that one thought is enough to keep me from ever gittin' sorry fer myself."

Mary laughed, and Mrs. Wiggs clapped her hands. "That's what yer face needs—smiles! I never see anything make such a difference. But now about the dress. Yes, indeed, Asia has got dresses to give 'way. She gits 'em from Mrs. Reddin'; her husband is Mr. Bob, Billy's boss. He's a newspaper editress an' rich as cream. Mrs. Reddin' is a fallen angel, if there ever was one on this earth. She sends all sorts of clothes to Asia, an' I warm 'em over an' boil 'em down till they're her size. Asia Minor!" she called to a girl who was coming in the door, "this here is Mary—Lovey Mary she calls herself, Miss Hazy's boarder. Have you got a dress you could give her?"

"I'm going to buy it," said Mary, immediately on the defensive. She did not want them to think for a moment that she was begging. She would show them that she had money, that she was just as good as they were.

"Well, maw," the other girl was saying in a drawling voice as she looked earnestly at Lovey Mary, "seems to me she'd look purtiest in my red dress. Her hair's so nice an' black an' her teeth so white, I 'low the red would look best."

Mrs. Wiggs gazed at her daughter with adoring eyes. "Ain't that the artis' stickin' out through her? Couldn't you tell she handles paints? Up at the fact'ry she's got a fine job, paints flowers an' wreaths on to bath-tubs. Yes, indeed, this here red one is what you must have. Keep your dollar, child; the dress never cost us a cent. Here's a nubia, too, that you kin have; it'll look better than that little hat you had on last night. That little hat worried me; it looked like the stopper was too little for the bottle. There now, take the things right home with you, an' to-morrow you an' Asia kin start off in style."

Lovey Mary, flushed with the intoxication of her first compliment, went back and tried on the dress. Miss Hazy got so interested that she forgot to get supper.

"You look so nice I never would 'a' knowed you in the world!" she declared. "You don't look picked, like you did in that other dress."

"That Wiggs girl said I looked nice in red," said Lovey Mary tentatively.

"You do, too," said Miss Hazy; "it keeps you from lookin' so corpsey. I wisht you'd do somethin' with yer hair, though; it puts me in mind of snakes in them long black plaits."

All Lovey Mary needed was encouragement. She puffed her hair at the top and sides and tucked it up in the latest fashion. Tommy, coming in at the door, did not recognize her. She laughed delightedly.

"Do I look so different?"

"I should say you do," said Miss Hazy, admiringly, as she spread a newspaper for a table-cloth. "I never seen no one answer to primpin' like you do."

When it was quite dark Lovey Mary rolled something in a bundle and crept out of the house. After glancing cautiously up and down the tracks she made her way to the pond on the commons and dropped her bundle into the shallow water.

Next day, when Mrs. Schultz's goat died of convulsions, nobody knew it was due to the china buttons on Lovey Mary's gingham dress.

From *Lovey Mary* by Alice Hegan Rice. (Century Company, 1902.)